D0734289

THE PASSIONS
OF FATHERHOOD

THE
PASSIONS
OF
FATHERHOOD

Samuel Osherson, Ph.D.

FAWCETT COLUMBINE • *New York*

A Fawcett Columbine Book
Published by Ballantine Books

Library of Congress Cataloging-in-Publication Data

Osherson, Samuel, 1945-
  The passions of fatherhood / Samuel Osherson.
    p. cm.
  Includes bibliographical references.
  ISBN 0-449-90778-3
  1. Fatherhood. 2. Parenting. 3. Father and child. 4. Marriage. I. Title.
HQ756.073 1995
306.874'2—dc20   94-25564
                     CIP

TEXT DESIGN BY DEBBY JAY

Manufactured in the United States of America
First Edition: June 1995
10 9 8 7 6 5 4 3 2 1

To Toby and Emily

CONTENTS

ACKNOWLEDGMENTS

A book is never the product of its author alone. Writers depend on family, friends, and colleagues for inspiration, support, and challenges to our preconceptions. This book is no exception. I count myself very fortunate in knowing so many generous, caring, and smart people willing to listen to my ideas and enter into a dialogue with me about them.

In particular I want to thank Anne Alonso, Irv Allen, Ray and Kathy Bollerud, Berry Brazelton, Olivia Bernard, Larry Parkes Daloz, Ted and Laura Englander, Chuck Erion, Dan Foley, Ron Giannetti, Peggy and Nick Kaufman, Justin Kaplan and Anne Bernays, Rabbi Barry Krieger, Jim Leone, Pat Light, Mark Lipman, Steve Krugman, Michael Morse, Robert Naseef, Eric Nichols, Daniel Osherson, Louis and Adele Osherson, Bill and LuAnne Polk, Len and Erica Radish-Fleischer, Nolan Penn, Bob Raines and Cindy Hirni, Lillian Rubin, Judith Schoenholrz-Read, Kjell Rudestam, Lisa Stuhlberg, Bordon and Ada Snow, Betsy Taylor, Barry and Karen Tolman, Rabbi Sheila Weinberg, Rob Wilson, and Jackie Zilbach.

My colleagues at the Fielding Institute have always been supportive and stimulating, willing to talk about ideas and enthusiasms over dinner, on e-mail, at faculty meetings, at the drop of a hat. Many thanks to you! And my gratitude also to the Harvard University Health Services, and Dr. Randolph Catlin, for encouragement and support.

I am very grateful to the many fathers and mothers who have been willing to talk with me over the years about their experiences of parenting. I have learned much from what they have told me and hope I have been able to convey that in this book.

My agent and friend, Jim Levine, has again been an invaluable help in the writing of this book, as have my editors at Ballantine, Ginny Faber and David Laskin. It was Ginny's initial suggestion that got me started on writing this book. Beth Bortz has functioned ably as an editorial assistant, always helpful and cheerful.

Finally, I am indebted to my family: my wife Julie and my children Toby and Emily, for their love for, and indulgences of, this husband and father who also writes.

PROLOGUE

There's a lot of writing these days about what fathers *should* be now that we've rediscovered daddy in our society. But many books are "son's books" or "daughter's books," exhorting fathers, blaming fathers, confronting fathers. Or they offer social prescriptions: fathers will restore authority to the family or help produce a generation of gentler, more loving children, depending on your political agenda. The very definition of what it means to be a good father has shifted from primarily provider/breadwinner to a more ambiguous role requiring emotional involvement and responsiveness.

Yet what really is a father's experience?

Fatherhood is one of the least understood and most mysterious relationships in our lives. It's a passionate endeavor that draws on our deepest yearnings to love and to be loved by our wife and children, as well as our most powerful wishes to get away from, even to harm or hurt those we love. Yet we fathers hardly have words for describing the intimate dilemmas of fatherhood, and even when we do find words, many of us choose to keep our passions private.

The essays that follow are my attempt to look at the father's experience from *the inside*. I've used my own parenting dilemmas—the father-daughter dance, cooperation and competition with my son, confronting my own childhood ghosts, finding my spirituality as a father—as a springboard into understanding what it's like to grow up as a boy who becomes a father.

My own life as a father is relatively unexceptional—no catastrophic illnesses, we're still an intact family, and there's no extreme abuse to confess to. My own parenting experience has been shaped by being white, middle-class, and raised within a Jewish religious experience. I grew up outside New York City in a suburb where rooting for the New York Yankees of Mickey Mantle and Whitey Ford meant rooting for all that was Good and True in the world. So why start with my own experience? Because I believe that there is a deeper rhythm of passion and hope that unites many parents. There's poetry in the ordinary, daily struggles of mothers and fathers, a High Drama of Overlooked Moments that I hope to capture in this book.

Throughout I try to attend to the passion and power of fathering, the intense feelings children arouse within men (as they do within women), and how we attempt to live well with these passions. My goal has been to penetrate the loneliness I often feel as a parent, a loneliness mothers may well understand, but perhaps all the deeper for fathers because it is surrounded by the ordinary silence that so many men take for granted in their lives.

AUTHOR'S NOTE: *An Invitation to the Reader*

Few experiences in life are more personal than parenting. When I set out to write about fatherhood, it inevitably became a very personal exploration. As I reflected on my own experience and those of the fathers I have met and interviewed, I became aware of the universality of the parenting experience. What parent doesn't wrestle with a profound love for his or her children, the anger children provoke, the way our hopes, dreams, and self-esteem are tethered to our children, the soporific boredom and intense satisfaction parenting brings with it?

I've struggled with the issue of personal disclosure in these essays: if I exclude myself and my family, then the narrative feels falsely distant, and yet if we're *too* present that feels personally uncomfortable and is perhaps limiting to the reader.

Like any parent, I want to respect the privacy of my family. Whose property are these family experiences—are they just mine to write about? In particular, how will my children feel about their appearance in these pages?

The way I've solved these questions in most of these essays is to adopt the voice of the second person, the voice of

"you," as in "You find yourself alone with your children . . ."
I find this voice creates some "play space"; it allows me to
look at myself and other fathers, to find some of the common threads between my own experience and that of other
parents.

This book is not just about me and my family. Over and
over I've heard mothers and fathers recount similar dilemmas in the courses on adulthood I've taught, the counseling I've done, the parenting workshops I've offered, as well
as in both hurried and relaxed conversations over lunch or
dinner with friends. We may live within the private bubble
of our own family drama, much of it unseen and unheard
by others, yet we have more in common than in difference
as parents. One of the greatest burdens of parenting is the
normal sense of isolation that may accompany it, of being
adrift in a swampy mix of feelings and experiences that
are yours alone. The second person, the "you," is an invitation to step inside, to join me in the experience. Particulars
of our lives may differ, but I hope that readers will recognize some of themselves in what follows.

THE PASSIONS
OF FATHERHOOD

CHAPTER 1

A FATHER'S ROOM

It's the first week in our rented country house in New Hampshire, one hundred miles and seemingly several centuries away from our city home in Cambridge, Massachusetts. We're away for a year to our favorite town in the country, where my wife, Julie, and I have spent most of the summers since before our children were born. The house looks out on a pond with no other houses in sight, although friends and acquaintances do dot the dirt roads of the village.

I'm to write a book about fatherhood in this old ramshackle wooden house while commuting into the city overnight once a week to maintain my practice and diminished teaching responsibilities this year. I've put a lot of my professional responsibilities on hold, hoping my colleagues will remember me when I return. Julie, a social worker, has had an easier time finding work in rural New Hampshire than in urban Massachusetts. Emily, our six-year-old daughter, and Toby, our nine-year-old son, will go to school in the three-teacher cooperative village school. Their city elementary school had 750 students; the country school has 52 kids total. We're all deep in culture shock.

Both in our late forties, my wife and I feel alternately too old to be making big changes in our life and also desperate: *If we don't do it now, we'll be living and working in the same three-block radius for the next twenty years.*

It's still the summer, though barely, with Labor Day close by, and the move hardly feels real. This early afternoon I'm standing by the living room window, looking out at the water, surrounded by mute, unopened packing boxes, preoccupied with a major question: *Where in our new house will I work?*

My wife and the kids have gone to town for ice cream, and they're due back in two hours. We're backed up on the unpacking, not sure where to put things, because we haven't decided where my study will be. I've been procrastinating about the decision. Julie and I have set a limit: Today's the day to *make up your mind.*

"Take the kids and let me think about this, and when you come back I'll have it worked out," I told her, trying to convey an air of confidence I didn't feel.

In the city my study was on a sunny third floor, overlooking a side street, but here in this old country home, all angles and jerry-rigged, it's not so simple. The topography of the house doesn't seem to cooperate.

There are two bedrooms and a third small room on the

second floor. The kids will each occupy the lovely bedrooms, looking out over woods and trees. The other small room is a good candidate, but it has already, miraculously, become the TV room for the kids. It's a cozy room, with nice carpeting, a fine place to worship TV. My wife likes the fact that the TV and video games are out of sight. It's a sort of clubhouse for them. I want to give them that room, to be a good dad, let them have space to really sprawl out after the confinement of our city apartment. I love the idea of their having a clubhouse, a gift to make up somehow for the disruption of the move.

But then where do I do my work?

There's an unheated room off the first floor living room. No way. Winters are serious business in New Hampshire; I don't fancy working on my computer wearing a parka and mittens.

"Use part of our bedroom," my helpful wife suggests. Our bedroom, also on the first floor, is big enough, with a view out to the pond. I could set up a writing desk along the wall of windows on the south-facing wall of the room. Tempting. But my "stuff" would spill all over. My desk is usually a disaster area: I file papers on the floor, I've never really mastered "neatness"—I've got it as a concept, but not a behavior—my study usually looks as if I earn my living raising wolves rather than working as a psychologist. I know what will happen in that bedroom—struggles about cleaning up, where papers go, keeping things in order. The normal detritus of my writing will be chock-a-block with our dressers and our clothes and our bed. All under the loving but demanding scrutiny of my wife. Who *has* mastered neatness.

I toy with the idea of buying a laptop and writing in the

living room during the day, cleaning up my work when the kids come home.

That's trouble! goes a warning sound. I'd be all entangled in the family—too entangled as I sometimes feel as a father.

The laptop would be staring at me in the living room, even when it was closed up tight. While I'm drawing on the floor with my kids, it would nudge me to *get back to work*. Portable computers scare me. My god, I could take it anywhere—even while having a catch with the kids in the meadow or while we're all sitting around reading on the porch. After all, I'm a responsible father, I want to be a good provider, so hearing my laptop's siren song—*Use me! Use me! Work! Work!*—would just intensify my constant, simmering feeling that I should do more: go write more of that article, keep your reputation alive, get the book done. That laptop would follow me around as if it had wheels of its own, an R2D2 from hell. A laptop would end up heightening one of the essential dilemmas of fatherhood: how to balance the wish to be camped on the outskirts of the family and the desire to be embraced in the middle of it.

I sit on a packing box and look around, imagining working in this lovely living room. The old wooden ceiling beams, a sunny picture window overlooking the pond. There's even a writing desk in the corner that looks generations old, handmade, built into the wall, the surface a thick, dark maple wood slab. The kind of desk on which the Founding Fathers signed the Declaration of Independence. I like that—the sense of tradition and history reassure me, as do the sturdy stone walls of New England, the timeless forests that surround our house. Sometimes it feels as if I'm constantly trying to invent my life, improvising as I go along. My life seems so different from that of my parents, less certain, without the security (and oppression) of clear definitions of what it means to be a father and mother.

Sitting in the room I find myself thinking about my own father, about growing up in the 1950s. *Where was my father's room in our house?* Some of my friends can identify their father's "room"—his tools in a basement shop or among the cars in the garage. Are these dads inside the home or out of it? Sometimes our dads almost seemed like appendages to the home. I'm not sure my father, who owned and operated a cluster of carpet stores in New York City, really had a room of his own in our house. The den, the TV room, was often where we'd find Dad in the evening. But in my memory he seemed more real in the store, more substantial outside the home than in it. Did he feel comfortable in any room in our house? My mom and dad have a good marriage, they're fine parents and superb grandparents, and I cherish the way they made our home seem safe and warm. Yet the stark truth hits me: *It was my mother's house.*

I want to make room for myself in this family, in this house. Suddenly I feel part of an ancient struggle, uniting fathers across the generations, to find our way into the home. In this old farmhouse living room, children and parents have for generations played and fought and laughed and cried. Not a bad place to write about the father's *internal struggle* to sort out competing impulses and desires: to be present and not present, to have our wives to ourselves and to share them with the children, to be similar to and different from our own fathers.

I look more closely at the corner writing desk, and I spot

Emily's "office," which she has already set up: several books from my shelves lean against one side of her desk, nestled up alongside a variety of writing supplies. Kneeling down to look closer I find my Scotch tape, a stapler, several pads of paper, and some pencils. Leaning against a side of the desk I find a large heart and some kisses drawn on the top page of my writing pad. A very large scissors is on the floor, and I remind myself that no matter how well you hide things in boxes, kids can find what they want.

My darling little six-year-old girl, my coconspirator in messiness.

Typical: my daughter's got her office set up before I have mine! Then I realize what I am seeing and my heart opens: my daughter is mastering this move, difficult and exciting for all of us, in part by snuggling up with me. Not snuggling up physically, although she does that, too, but emotionally—she's using my stuff to make this house feel her own. Familiar pieces of me—my tools, my writing paper.

Gazing at the large heart and kisses drawn across the top page of the writing pad, I find "I love you, Daddy" written in big letters across the top. I feel her passionate attachment, no, *our* passionate attachment to each other—father and daughter. It's a gift I treasure, yet I'm also caught by surprise at it, at times almost overwhelmed, left wanting to draw back. My kids' hunger for me can feel so intense, as if they want to eat me up entirely. Where are the boundaries?

Turning away from the desk I see that Toby's hockey mask lies on my reading chair, as does his copy of *Nintendo Power*, dropped where he had been reading it over the weekend. The young man in *his* office poring over *his* journal, studying reports of the latest products and game strategies. His nine-year-old's hunger for me, no, *our* hunger for each other, father and son, has a different quality than the father and daughter attachment. He rushed out the door on the way to town this morning and pushed away from me as I started to hug him, then he pulled me toward him awkwardly, unsure, displaying the traditional male struggle to get affection without seeming too "dependent." Whose struggle—his or mine? An off-balance embrace and then he's running toward the car with a part of me running alongside him. He and I are constantly playing with the boundaries of intimate communication, the limitations and deep resonance between sons and fathers.

As his mother and Emily got organized near the car this morning, Toby picked up a basketball in the driveway, then barked an order to me as I stood at the front door: "Dad, get over here!" He wanted me to play B-ball with him. My son is tall and thin; he looks like me. Did I sass my father with such élan as well? Toby sounded rude. I was tempted to reprimand him, but I'm learning the code: he wants me to admire him, to see his skill, *just to be with him*, and he's asking in a "tough-guy" fashion.

I walked over, and we enjoyed ourselves shooting a few hoops until his mother and sister were ready, then they went off to town.

Fatherhood is such a constant transformation, isn't it? At first as a father of young children I just wanted to know if I was doing things right, everything felt so new and like a crisis. Most early problems were solved by cuddling my children and being available to them. That's still important. Yet now here I am with my son on the lip of adolescence, watching him struggle with power, "coolness," tenderness, with the tug of boyhood and the allure of emerging manhood. He needs me to be "cool" in the deepest way—to be able to respond to his provocation and his search for independence while also letting him lean on me when he needs to. While he's transforming himself in the breathtaking process of preadolescence, I'm called upon to transform myself as well. *Whoa!* This fathering thing is a lot more complicated than just being the inspirational leader and guide! It's also about nurturing and nourishing and being nurtured and nourished by our children. Not so easy as a man when you're also trying to live up to traditional performance expectations, trying to be successful and powerful in the world outside your family.

Fatherhood is not just a role—provider, disciplinarian, friend—it's also a relationship, one that transforms us as much as our kids. Just the other night we were at a neighbor's house down the road for a barbeque party with some other families, wonderful people we've known (seasonally) for years. I found myself with a group of parents—one father runs a sawmill, another is a logger, another works in construction, a mother raises sheep with her husband. The aromatic smoke from the old brick grill drifted off lazily into the thick woods that surround the house. What was I going to be doing up here this year? several folks asked. When they heard I was writing a book about fatherhood the talk soon turned to our own fathers. These men, many of them raised in the North Country, talked about hunting trips they took with their dads when they became teenagers—a true rite of passage, bagging the first deer with Dad. I put down my tofu hotdog and listened carefully. What did these men treasure most about these times with Dad—that they learned how to shoot? That they brought home a four-point buck? That their fathers showed them how to be a "man"—a warrior/hunter who can find meat outside the supermarket, avoiding the long checkout lines? In part, yes—the men clearly expressed the joy of mastering hunting with their fathers, learning about guns, stalking deer, understanding how to read the trails. These are certainly among the wonders of mastery and competence communicated from father to son. Yet what really stood out as the men talked was the specialness of the time with Dad. It was the relationship with their fathers that the hunting trips brought to the surface—getting up together early in the morning, driving through the dark to a diner for breakfast, wandering through the woods, maybe talking, maybe not, sharing a pleasurable day with Dad. It was this moment of connection, feeling seen and heard and valued, that made these memories special. It was the feeling that their fathers wanted them there and valued them. That night I remembered the times in my boyhood when my father took me to his store in the Bronx on Saturdays, coming home in the well-lit train through snowstorms in the dark winter night, buying the Sunday paper early, the city edition, and the two of us sitting together reading it on the way home, his joy in having me there, wordless moments when I felt seen and heard and valued by my father.

This relationship with our children is the bedrock of fathering. It's true for daughters as well as sons. Teaching mastery is important, being able to discipline our kids is important, but our teaching and our discipline won't work unless we also communicate love and caring to our children, unless we really *see* our kids for who they are.

The relationship part of fathering can be very hard to "get" as fathers; it's all so different from what we expect. For many of us the image is that fathers are supposed to be in control, have answers, be good providers, defend and protect those who depend on them. The ideal image may be of Ward Cleaver, a father who lives in a house that just hums along through June's good efforts. Or maybe the ideal is Lord Chesterfield giving sage advice to a child who seems to want to hear it or even brave Odysseus reclaiming his wife, Penelope, and his son, Telemachus, after his heroic adventures abroad.

I lurch around the living room wondering: *What about the fathers who've inhabited this old farmhouse?* Farmers and woodsmen and businessmen. A chorus of North Country father-ghosts, all with dry New England accents, mocks me: *Well, young man, you can't even find a room of your own in this house—what kind of man, what kind of father are you?* I stare back in my mind's eye at these farmer-ghosts until they relent: *Well, truth be told, young man, we never really had a place in our homes either—we lived in the fields, on our plows and tractors, in our workshops and toolsheds. Maybe you can find a way in: Good luck to you!*

Then on some packing boxes I spot a pile of flyers for a workshop I led just the week before in Boston on "The Passions of Fatherhood." The flyer describes a typical daylong event I offer for men and women, complete with a nice bio about Dr. Osherson—Again I stretch myself across that chasm separating our public personae as men who are competent in the real world from the private selves who experience the agonies and struggles of being a father.

Memories of the people I met at that workshop come to

mind, reassuring me, reminding me that fathers of all ages try to find a satisfying "fathering self," a place within themselves that contains both their wish to be involved with their children and their yearning to be off on their own.

The group at the workshop, mostly men, ranged in age from their mid-thirties to close to sixty. Our children ran the gamut from newborns to young adults, or, as one veteran father said, "the stage when you realize you're still a father and no child ever completely grows up." The group included a fireman, filmmaker, several lawyers, a doctor, and a real estate developer. Several friends from a basketball league came together. I remember the shyness that pervaded the room at first—nervous conversation, men hunched over cups of coffee—the shyness of fathers who come to talk about fathering, the extraordinary vulnerability of fathers to the children they love so much. I was struck again by the way fathers feel judged by their wives and children. *Am I doing well enough? How do I talk about my uncertainties, my anger, my envy of my children without feeling that I'm a failure as a father? This whole parenting experience is so much more complicated than I imagined!*

Frank was a construction foreman, forty-five years old, with several teenage sons. An athletic, energetic man, he was the kind of guy you'd clearly want on your basketball team. And he obviously enjoyed fathering. But now he was worried about the recent battles going on between himself and his teenage children. "We've been doing some renovations on the house, and I can't get the kids to help—they say I'm always on their case, and I *do* feel impatient with them a lot; after all, I work all day, and here I am trying to cut costs to work on the basement playroom. They say

I'm a tyrant," Frank said with real feeling, "and I don't want to come across that way. In no time they're going to be off to college."

One of the other men in our circle, a buddy of Frank's, asked: "How come you're working on a playroom for the kids now?"

Frank stopped, as if he hadn't really considered that, then explained: "Well, I want the kids to have a place to play, to bring their dates, to hang out."

A friend across the circle observed: "Gee, my kids basically want to get out of the house now that they've hit their teens."

Frank reminisced then about how home projects were the only way to be around his father: "We did a lot of home construction. If you wanted to be around my father you had to get down on the floor and pound nails with him. That's what I did as a teenager when I was with my father." Feeling more relaxed, Frank went on: "I suppose this is my way of trying to keep the kids home. I mean, I don't want them to struggle with what I did—my eldest son says he already has the girlfriend of his dreams. I don't want him to marry as young as I did. All the kids are struggling with sex, the peer group, keeping up."

Next Frank's face lit up with a sudden insight: "I guess in some ways I don't want them to grow up!"

Hidden within "the playroom battle" was Frank's struggle to find himself as a father of teenagers. Their relationship was changing, and Frank wasn't sure he could change with it. Something new and different was being asked of him: he needed to be able to let the kids go more and yet continue to be available to them when they wanted to return. Did Frank fear losing a kind of intimacy he had come to depend on with his kids now that they were testing their wings? Was he lonely at facing the prospect of finding new relationships and adventure in his life?

Frank wanted his kids to grow up, but he also wanted them to stay children. A father now, he was reliving his own struggles as a son. Frank's teenage kids rekindled his old yearnings for something *more* from his own father.

We all want to do right by our kids. It's normal and natural, too, for parents to mix up their kids and themselves. The essence of doing right as a parent is getting clear about our own struggles and wishes and desires, sorting out what we feel as fathers so as to get clear what we want for our kids.

The father's search to find a satisfying "fathering self" is often hidden both from himself and his family. Many of us believe that fathering should "just come naturally," so the lingering sense of uncertainty we feel may be hard to acknowledge. Yet it is real and quite shared among dads. When I ask men where best to start in understanding fatherhood, right after words like "providing" and "protecting" comes: "unprepared."

At the group, a thirty-five-year-old father named Paul with a three-year-old daughter spoke of trying to find a place for himself in a new family dominated by the intensity of the mother-child bond. He said he feels like "a satellite orbiting mother earth, in contact but from a distance," and he wonders if there is a role for him beyond simply providing. Paul struggled to come down to earth, to mother earth. He wanted to make time to be with his daughter, he needed to feel he had something close and personal to offer his wife and child.

As he spoke, hungry for some connection with the other

fathers, Paul looked eagerly across the fatherhood circle to an older man named Alex, a father with children in their twenties. He said: "What's it like when fatherhood is over, when your kids are all grown up and you see how things have turned out?"

I admired Paul for asking that question. I felt the same curiosity about what other fathers experience, but I often stop before I ask the questions. My uncertainty feels too private, too personal. Maybe there's a fear, too. Once I told a friend of mine, quite successful as a father and in his career, how much I admired his commitment to his family. He replied, "Despite it all, my biggest fear is that I'm not doing it right as a father, that I'm letting my kids down." Here's a secret about fathers. What is our deepest fear? It's not that we might fail in our careers, or even have our marriages turn sour, although of course we worry about both those possibilities. The biggest fear is that we are failing our children. That fear leaves so many of us secretly ashamed and reluctant to really talk about what's happening for us as fathers. Perhaps fatherhood is such uncharted territory for many of us that we can't quite believe we're doing okay. If we are unsure of ourselves, if we are not perfect, we're convinced we have somehow failed.

Paul got his answer that afternoon. With a wry smile Alex, the older father, replied: "It's never over as a father!" And this sixty-five-year-old man spoke of how his kids come home to visit and they want him to have answers and solve problems for them, but not to take over, not to be *too* involved. "I've had to learn how to be wise and listen better without offering too much advice, too quickly," he added.

He concluded: "Sixty-five years old and I'm still a rookie!"

The evolution of our "fathering self" is not accomplished and finished once and for all, but continues as we and our children age.

All day at the father's group a young, recently married man named Arnie sat silently listening. He had asked during our introductions if he could just observe, since, he said, "I don't yet have children; my wife and I are just thinking about starting a family." Finally, later in the evening, Arnie spoke up: "Gee, after all I've heard from you all, I just want to ask—would you all still become fathers if you had to do it all over?" He went on to explain that he had never before heard fathers express the intensity of their feelings. This was the first time he understood that fatherhood normally and inevitably draws out the best and worst in men. Arnie was worried: Is it worth it to go through all this?

His question was a reminder of how little information boys and men get about the inner world of fathers, how much a mystery fatherhood can seem, and how all the competing passions that children call up in us can flood a father or father-to-be.

Fatherhood can feel like something added on to our identities, not a normal and natural part of being a man. How will we make a place for it? Boys don't usually rehearse parenthood, come to be familiar with it, in the same ways that many girls do.

The fathers responded to Arnie without hesitation: "Yes, yes, of course," talking of their deep love for their children, the treasure that children are for mothers and fathers alike. As Arnie listened to the fathers he seemed reassured, as if he finally could see positive images of men's "fathering selves."

Yet Arnie's question marked for me a deeper issue: Men are now coming into the family—the expectation is that we'll be more involved as fathers than in previous generations, and often we think we're supposed to love the experience, unambiguously. After growing up learning to be Good Warriors or Good Providers or just Good Boys, we may think that after marriage we'll become fathers, as our wives keep bringing up the question of *It's time to start a family, we should be thinking about it*, and we suppose it'll be all cuddly and hug-a-bear time with a cute baby. That hardly prepares us for the way parenthood raises the most troubling questions, leaving us wondering at times if the choice to have children is really worth it, wondering what we really get out of all the sacrifices parenthood demands of us, and facing that most painful task: managing mixed feelings toward those we love.

As fathers we often don't want to show too many feelings, so instead we put them into actions. We want to *show* people we love them, not have to say it. The same is true for our anger, shame, uncertainty. This isn't a moral flaw, a deliberate intent to withhold. Many times we may not know what we're feeling, or we lack a vocabulary for our most intimate feelings, or we feel that what we have to say is much less important than a paycheck or a stern and consistent approach to discipline.

Thinking about myself as a father, I know that I have a shadow side, a part of myself I hardly know, that I'm not sure I *want* to know: *Why do I turn away from fathering even as I'm drawn to it?* There's a tendency to avoid the hard work of fathering, to be the "nice guy," to avoid set-

ting limits, leaving those thorny issues to my wife. And, finally, perhaps most painful, there's my capacity for anger
toward my children: it's like an undercurrent, this gnawing, buzzing anger at the very creatures I so dearly love.

All of this is what I will write about during my year in
the country.

Except where will I do that? I glance at my watch and
see that it's two-thirty. And I'm still standing in the living
room.

A deep warning: You need a separate place to write
about fatherhood. *Don't lose yourself.* Internal voice: To really write about fatherhood you're going to have to be a
part of the family ánd separate from it at the same time.
Exactly like the experience of fathering.

I really want that upstairs TV room, but I feel a lot of
guilt asking for it, taking it. I imagine my wife and kids al-
lied against me: *They want me in that cold room.* It's easy
for them—they don't have to work there. I picture them
this very minute having a fine old time driving together
into town on the winding country roads, looking at the
cows and horses, laughing and joking, the happy family of
mother and children singing "Old MacDonald Had a Farm"
in delightful harmony—why, you'd never even notice Dad
is missing! In my imagination my wife turns away from
singing and driving and looks directly at me to scold: *You
selfish brute, taking the one room the children love away
from them!* Then she goes back to "Old MacDonald."

I feel a painful, burning anger at these very creatures I
love so much: *Is there truly even room for me in this house?*
I'm the major breadwinner, the primary provider, and I
can't even get comfortable here. A spiteful inner voice
counsels me: *Why, you should have your choice of rooms!*

Take the whole goddamn sunny bedroom as your study! Let the Siberian cold room be the bedroom. See how she likes that!

Easier to get angry at my wife than at the kids. Yet it's *their* upstairs TV room I really covet. Damnit! It's three o'clock and the kids will be home soon. *What to do? How to make this move mine?* This never would have been an issue before the kids were born. I could have had most any room in the house; I wouldn't have had to take into consideration other people's needs. There wouldn't be these kids who depend on me for so much, for whom I am so important. *This whole move would have been easier without the kids; I'd be free again!* The pond beckons, empty and serene. Damn the burden and yoke of commitment and responsibility! What a weight a family is!

Standing in the living room, my anger suddenly turns on me, as it often does when it has nowhere else to go. A good dad, I imagine, just provides for his kids—he doesn't demand a space for himself. I wouldn't be standing in this living room agonizing if I were a better father and husband!

The phone rings, snapping me out of my anxious reverie. I hurriedly search for it, tripping over the packing cases, my children's toys, the furniture. It's a friend from Los Angeles, calling to talk to me about a conference on parenting he's setting up. He wants to know if I'll be the keynote speaker. *Oh great, more commitments! More travel, time away from the family!* Part of me wants to paddle off onto the pond as we speak. Yet I'm also delighted by his offer. A parent of older children himself, he listens to my concerns. We talk about fathering and moving our families, and then my friend says: "The kids don't want you to be away, but remember that they can adjust if you're clear and available. If your kids know you really love them, these separations can be mastered. It'll be harder on you; you're the one who'll be away from home. Don't mix up your kids with yourself." As we talk I feel some of my loneliness drain away. The connection with another father, someone who has been through this, reassures me. United across three thousand miles by the phone lines, our national fiber-optic umbilical cord, we make plans. I tell my friend I'll see what I can do about my schedule, and then we say good-bye. Once the phone connection is broken, I'm back alone in my living room.

Don't mix up your kids with yourself. I wonder how often I see my own conflicts in them or assume I know what they're feeling when really I don't.

The phone call energizes me. Up the wooden stairs I go to the second floor. I'm back in love with my children, suddenly missing them. I want to see their rooms, their toys, get a whiff of them. Emily's Snaky, her stuffed animal, lies curled up on her bed, resting on Roundy, the pillow she's using to help her sleep at night in a new house. Across the hall, Toby's enormous stuffed toy gorilla, Tiny Kong, stands guard on his bed. With a fierce snarl on its face—teeth bared—it sits there, soft and cuddly and waiting for him.

I can still smell the warmth of my children in the unkempt beds, pressed into their very sheets.

Then I walk into the middle room that I covet—and I feel at home. The walls are unfinished pine, the studs exposed, the room is reminiscent of the bunk rooms of summer camp, of being a boy again. *Being a boy again.* There's a personal sorting out here. An intuition: *To really understand our fatherhood we need to return to our childhood.*

Sitting in this room, looking at the knotholes—I'd never noticed how each one differs from the others, like fingerprints—living again with echoes of my boyhood passions, I know I have to have this room.

There's my decision, now can I stick by it? The sound of the car tires crackling over the gravel drive interrupts my musing. *They're not going to like this!* Dad, with all his preoccupations, has to confront the Three Amigos, back from town. As I stand up and walk downstairs I feel a momentary urge to hide.

Yet then as my family comes spilling into the house I can't wait to see everybody.

"Dad, Dad, where are you?" asks Emily, heaving the screen door aside, no shyness or hesitation there. Her reddish hair is almost blond from the summer sun. She's found these amazing shoes that have little batteries and red lights in the heels that flash when you take a step. She prances in front of me, her feet twinkling. I pick her up and hug her and tell her how great her shoes are and that, well, she lights up a room even without batteries, and she smiles—"Oh, Daddy!"—and jumps out of my arms to go play.

Toby has some neat high-tops to show me; he holds them up wordlessly for me to see, a proud smile on his face. We high-five each other. "Awright!" I exclaim, "really neat."

A familiar groping for the current slang of his peers. Is it still "neat" or is it "gnarly" or "awesome?" Toby puts his arm around me, then bounds up the stairs to the TV room and his Nintendo games. As he goes, Julie and I look at each other: *Are we letting him watch too much TV, too many video games?* But this day we let him go.

My wife eyes the packing crates and asks the question: "So. Where'll it be?"

"I want the upstairs room."

She replies with an arched eyebrow, a signal that she doesn't like the answer she's heard. I want to draw back, but I hold my ground. How much of marriage and parenthood is doing things you're not sure of, holding your ground in the face of a wish to run away?

Julie replies:

"You sure? Why not the room off the living room?" *(Ach, not the cold room!)* And she starts to tell me again how it'll be okay; she's figured out some arrangement with portable heaters and all that that will make the room usable. It's not a bad arrangement; in fact, I'm impressed she was thinking about it even while driving into town. Her mind never seems to stop trying to make our home a better place. Does her very mastery, though, in some unintended way, undermine mine? For a moment I wonder if men will ever stop feeling under the control and scrutiny of women in the home. If our wives "own" the home emotionally, how do we fathers find our way toward authority and confidence as parents?

"Wait!" I say, putting up my hands. She stops, and I feel my anger rising. It's a fuel that gives energy to what I say:

"I *need* the upstairs room. Believe me—I have to write this book or we're going broke, I need that room to do it."

Julie gets quiet, her lovely green eyes looking at me while she mulls over what I've said. Then:

"All right . . . all right. You're right—you have work to do this year, you're not up here on vacation. I kind of forget that. You need a place for yourself to work in, and if it's the upstairs room you want, we can make that work, too." I love her even more then—for her faith in me, her willingness to listen when I am clear and direct.

Julie and I realize that the arrangement with portable heaters will work just fine to turn the cold room into the TV room for the kids, so they'll have a place for their clubhouse as well.

Upstairs I go to tell the kids while my wife begins unpacking.

"What, Dad, oh no! We like this room." They don't want any more changes in this season of changes. My son gets angry while my daughter implores me, *Please, please, Daddy*, hands together in an attitude reminiscent of prayer.

Their anger and disappointment washes over me. Facing my kids' anger at and disappointment in me is as hard as facing my own. I want to let them have their anger, but I also want to shut them up because I don't want them to be angry at me, I never want them to be disappointed in me.

Don't mix up your kids with yourself. I remember my friend's words. Children's anger is often much more fleeting than my own, they're more resilient than I am at times. Suddenly I realize that what they need to know is that there is indeed a place in the house, cozy and warm, for their clubhouse.

I get clear and concrete and explain about fixing up the downstairs room to be a great clubhouse.

"Let's go set it up, Daddy," says Emily, now excited. They both want to help me transform the downstairs room for them, it's going to be an adventure. We cart along the TV, the Nintendo system, games and toys. It all goes downstairs to the little room off the living room, as does our portable electric radiator, lots of blankets, and a large, thick, supercomfortable foam mat for the floor of the room. All of this transforms the cold room into a wonderful clubhouse and retreat for the kids.

Later that afternoon, Toby and I sit in that room and puzzle yet again over the instructions for attaching the Nintendo Entertainment System to the VCR and the TV. One cord goes here, another there—wires, controls, and attachments litter the floor. "You do it, Dad, you're good at this stuff," Toby says, and I want to rise to his faith in me even as I examine wiring diagrams that seem to come direct from the space shuttle program, with instructions written in Martian. I fit this plug to that socket, review the diagrams, make some attachments and turn on the system. Nothing happens. Blank screen. *Damn! This is father-stuff, I ought to be able to do this!* If only I had listened better to Mr. Wizard on TV as a kid. But he was always so boring and, worse, full of himself, a Wizard of the ordinary. Where's the Wizard now that I really need him? *Patience, patience*, I counsel myself. Reversing one cord and connecting it to another socket seems like a good idea. Then Toby remembers where the short cord that connects the game to the VCR goes. He reaches over gently to do it, and together we set up the rest of it.

"Watch me play 'The Legend of Zelda: A Link to the Past,'" Toby asks, already settling in with the game in which he is a single pilgrim intent on defeating an evil overlord through a spiraling series of adventures. He's been on this quest, charting his progress through various forbidding worlds, for weeks. Right in front of my eyes my son turns into a wizard: he uses complicated spells, charms, fighting stances in a game with pull-down menus and deepening layers and layers of strategy. I marvel yet again at the competence and mastery of this boy who sometimes can't find his shoes in an otherwise empty room. We sit up nestled together against pillows on the foam mat covering the floor. His arm rests on mine as he plays the game. "See Dad, here's Pegasus's shoes, I won these yesterday, I can leap over thousands of miles with them. And here, Dad, here's the Moon Pearl, now that I have it I can explore the Dark World without getting lost forever in it." *Hmmn*, I think, *I could use one of those.*

Then Emily comes in and sets down her crayons and huge pad of paper and wants me to watch her draw. "Wait, Dad, watch me!" instructs one sib. "No, Daddy, watch me," orders another. How can anyone doubt the crucial importance of fathers to children? They want to pull me in two different directions. *Oh, what the hell, you can never do it just right! Just do it.* I watch Toby and then I watch Emily and soon Julie comes in with a tray of tea and juice. We're all together now. She watches Emily, I watch Toby; I watch Emily, she watches Toby. My wife and I smile at each other across our tea, joined by and cut off by our kids.

As we sit together, enjoying each other's company, my family no longer feels like a weight. A circus, maybe . . . a three-ring circus, no, maybe four or five rings, and there's something going on in each ring all the time and you want to see everything going on in this magical and mysterious place under the big top but you can't, so instead you decide to just do the best you can and see as much as you can and be a part of it as best as you can. Sometimes you're the ringmaster, sometimes you're a spectacle in one of the rings, sometimes you're just in the audience, sometimes you're a lion in a cage going through hoops under someone else's control, trained to the domestic circus but deep down wanting to roar your way through the bars, to break free.

No, my family's not a weight. Sitting with my wife and children, I realize suddenly that I never could have made this move, taken this adventure, if I had been alone, if I hadn't become a father, if I hadn't married my dear wife. Life would have been too lonely, I would have been too thin emotionally, to have taken such a risk.

So as August turns to autumn I find myself writing in the mysterious small room on the second floor, a single window looking out on the pond, the fall sun and gathering wind often making the waves into crystals of light. A place to discover my passions again, this time as a man.

CHAPTER **2**

WAKING UP
SLEEPING CHILDREN

It's often my job on weekday mornings to wake the kids up and make sure they get downstairs for breakfast, while Julie gets out the orange juice and cereal and makes their sandwiches for lunch.

One cold Monday morning at 6:30 A.M. I walk up the stairway to our kids' bedrooms to wake them up for school. In a hurry, as usual, and none too pleased to be awake and facing a full day of work, I announce my impending arrival to my two somnolent children.

"Good morning, good morning," I call out with forced cheer through the gloom, sounding like a demented Santa

Claus. Ho, ho, ho, extolling the virtues of waking up in the pitch black to a chilly house.

I love to see my kids every morning. Even after almost nine years of parenting they still seem like a miracle to me, *My children, I'm a father—I did it!,* and each morning I feel a special anticipation at seeing those wondrous packages of life asleep in their beds. But on weekdays I sometimes feel a bit like a confidence man, selling my kids on how great it is to wake up when all they want to do is sleep. When *I'd* still like to be asleep.

Not to worry—neither child was having any of my sales pitch. Both kids had stayed up late the night before to watch a rental movie, *Kindergarten Cop*—it was a special treat on a school night, the occasion for which I've forgotten—and now they are exhausted and don't want to get up. In their own bedrooms, both children snore on, ignoring me.

When you strive to be an involved father, to be really *present* in your family, you learn first how clumsy you can be when confronted with the humble practical details of daily life. It's one thing to vow that you and your wife will share parenting, to divide up the morning chores so that the kids will be ready for school and you can both get to work. It's another thing to walk into your kids' bedrooms at 6:30 A.M. and bump full tilt into the world of childhood.

Your son's room in particular gets you this day. Your wonderful boy—he feels like the doorway back into your own childhood; he holds some key to a lock you're still trying to open. As you walk into his room you trip over his toys: Legos, action figures of X-Men, Batman, baseball cards overflowing their boxes, pictures of sports heroes, catalogued as to their value. You reflect on the fortune you passed up in your own childhood because you didn't save those baseball cards you and your friends used to flip endlessly. Your son recently told you that a 1956 Topps Mickey Mantle card sold for $2000. What fortunes did you hold in your hand when you were nine years old and let slip away?

As your son lolls, you look around his room. You say hello to the Michael Jordan poster, you look at the clothes on the floor jammed up against a Lego spaceship, all mashed together with comic books depicting one gory adventure after another. There's a disorganization to the room that feels so familiar to you: *His* bedroom looks a lot like *your* study. In fact, *his* bedroom looks a lot like *your* boyhood bedroom looked. The mahogany bed he's sleeping in seems a replica of the one you had as a kid; you'd never thought about that resonance before, or have you transformed your old bed in your memory?

You're momentarily lost in your own childhood, something seems very vital in that disorder of the child, of the boy. You remember how your imagination spilt all over your world, things that had little meaning for adults were sacred for you. You remember being thrilled by the story of Hannibal's wars against Rome, imagining the way his tents rustled in the Alpine breezes as he struggled to bring his warrior elephants down to the Italian plains, to crush Rome and avenge his father's defeat. You used to construct armies out of slips of paper, paper armies overran your room to your mother's dismay, when all the while you were likely trying to fathom the meaning of aggression and violence and perhaps make sense of your own father's victories and defeats. Now you look at your somnolent son and you're aware that part of you wants to go back, to be a kid again, to perch on his shoulders and revisit childhood.

Your son is less sure about the pleasures of childhood at this moment. He stirs as you sit down on his bed: "Owh, I don't want to get out of bed—go away."

You encourage him: "Hey, come on, guy, let's go, it's going to be time to go to school soon."

"I don't want to get up—I'm tired, school is boring, too much work, leave me alone."

There's something in his tone that angers you, the way he dismisses you, even as you admire his ability to challenge you. To order *you* around. You and he are on parallel tracks. He's going off to school, having to deal with teachers, assignments, friends, bullies. Living up, expectations, joy and excitement. You're going off to work: living up, expectations, joy and excitement all intermixed.

You're entering into a familiar murkiness here; the boundaries between you feel blurry. Are you the father or the son? You think of your own father—did he ever rouse you? Your memories are of your mother calling you, your father must have been getting up when you were, he was getting ready to go to work. You do some frantic reconstruction here: *Where was your father when you were getting up and getting dressed?*

This is one of those moments when you dip into your personal storehouse of how fathers act and you come up empty. How do fathers rouse their children? You've heard of fathers who rip sheets off their kids and of fathers who aren't there, but what's in between? How do you coax a kid into confidence in facing the morning? More simply: How do you just get him out of bed without tipping it over?

You remember your mother's cheeriness in the morning, how she'd have breakfast going, oatmeal or English muffins waiting when you arrived downstairs. Where was your father? Being depressed, girding himself up for the trials of the day? Owning a carpet store in the Bronx meant dealing with business associates who blocked him from making the big score—never living up to his own expectations for himself. "I was surrounded by naysayers," he'd complain. "Don't let that happen to you." Then you realize: *He was dealing with his own getting going in the morning, the weight of male performance.*

You don't want that weight to descend on your boy, and it already has! You wonder about some genetic strain of masculine angst in your family. Ah, but there's a mix here. Even as you worry, another part of you wants to make damned sure he is strong enough to bear the weight of male performance.

You pat him, rub him, exhort him, and threaten him— all to no avail. He lies there under the sheets. Wily negotiator that he is, he offers a deal, the words muffled through his bedcovers: Get his sister up first, then he'll get up. You're tempted to rip off the blankets in a gesture of parental power but can't bear the thought of becoming the impatient tyrannical father.

He ignores you as you stand there, and that seems the worst part of this experience: to be ignored. After all, you're the father: he's supposed to obey you, not vice versa. There's a familiar irritation: *you* don't have enough power, *you're* not big enough for this task.

You have to do something to demonstrate your power in this situation. Your departing salvo as you walk into your daughter's room is "Five minutes, buster." A threat he seems not even to have heard underneath his covers.

Ho, ho, ho. Inside you seethe at your own powerlessness. You have a whole day of work ahead of you, and you can't even control your own kids! Then you realize: *I'd like to stay in bed a little longer, too! Let's* face it, *I'm pissed at having to be up myself!*

So you walk into your daughter's room. She, too, is exhausted from watching the movie the night before; she had trouble getting to sleep because of the scenes with the madman father who's overinvested in his kids, so you had to sit with her and calm her, and now she's tired and protests that you always wake her up first. Go get her brother dressed, she suggests, then she'll get up. She pulls the pillows over her head and rolls over. Your wristwatch is still strapped to her wrist from last night. "I'll go to sleep if you give me your watch," she had said. She wanted a piece of you to hold on to. You thought it would just stay in her tight grasp all night, but you notice she must have put it on her wrist before she fell asleep. You look at the pictures above her bed, how many of them are drawings of you; her hunger for you feels almost palpable.

And yet now you can't get your loving daughter out of bed any more than you could your son.

You have to do something here, so you start pacing between the bedrooms, alternately mouthing threats and encouragement. You walk back into your son's room, and he's almost asleep. You return to your daughter's room. Poised between your children, you feel like a bull being taunted by two matadors. You want to do something to demonstrate your power, to get some control of this situation.

You yearn for a gong, a large metal gong that you can smash, that would make a shattering sound. No, that's not loud enough—you want a trumpet, Joshua's trumpet, that you could blast, play reveille, shock them up, let the noise of the trumpet lift them out of bed. Ah, the impotent fury of the father.

It's 6:40 A.M. and you hear your wife bustling efficiently downstairs making breakfast, putting their lunches into lunch boxes. *If she were here,* you imagine unfairly, *this wouldn't be so hard.* You imagine your wife would set firm limits, even as her soothing maternal voice lifted them gently awake. *No.* You know she struggles just as much as you with anger, love, embarrassment, with how to handle these power struggles. Still, you feel she'd do a better job at this—why not just leave it to her?

A friend of yours, a competent, involved father with kids almost off to college, once told you about being at a party where he and several other fathers had been talking about dealing with their teenagers. The men had a lot to say until their wives came over to join them. Then the fathers became progressively more quiet, subtly deferring to their wives in the conversation. Your friend wasn't being critical of the women, it was more about how he and the other men just seemed to *assume* that the mothers had more to say about parenting. He lamented how "My own voice as a father gets drowned out by the way I see my wife as a kind of Omniscient Mother."

Even as you consider going downstairs and saying, "It's your turn," you know that something important is at stake here for you—coming to terms with your desire to turn away from the nitty-gritty of parenting, to leave it to your wife.

But at what cost to yourself?

You go into your daughter's room and sit down and tell her firmly that it is time to get up and she needs to get dressed. You and she go to pick out her clothes, she having made it plain that the blue blouse the two of you picked out last night just won't do in the clear light of day. Together you and she wrestle with finding her red jumper outfit—undies, tights, turtleneck. Even after six years you can't remember where to find all your daughter's underthings and overthings. This is a source of both merriment and annoyance to your wife, who has a seemingly encyclopedic knowledge of where everything in the house is located. Desperately you search for the single pair of purple socks your daughter has decided she absolutely must have, dreading (even while secretly hoping) that your wife will come upstairs and help you with this task. Your daughter finds them first—"Oh, here they are, Daddy!"—and you wonder if there is a feminine gene for knowing where everything in the house is.

It's six-fifty and still no sound from your son. You look in the room, and he starts putting his pants on. Wordlessly you leave the room.

"Can I have a boost, Daddy?" asks your wonderful six-year-old girl. She means a piggyback ride downstairs—"the boost" you call it in your family. "Oh, I'm so tired, too tired to get to the kitchen. Can I ride on your back, Daddy?"

The boost is a special moment with your kids, one of the articles of faith of fathering for you—a moment of energy and connection and confidence from father to child. *I'm big and strong and can deal with what the world has in store for me!* There were moments growing up when confidence seemed in short supply in your family, and you want to make sure your kids don't hunger for it. Even still, on some dark mornings you search yourself for what Napoleon called "2:00 A.M. courage—the hardest to find," wondering who will give you the boost.

Your daughter hops on your back, presses your nose to launch the rocket (the rocket carefully shifting the angle of his head so that the nose is not broken by the launch signal), and you're off at supersonic speeds of one thousand steps an hour from the upstairs to the kitchen.

As you lift off the launch pad you hear behind you your son protesting from his bedroom: "Wait, Dad, wait for me!"

But you don't stop, you don't wait. Even as his pleas tug at your heart, the rocket flame burns hot: *You weren't ready, you didn't listen, and the rocket took off without you. Too bad!*

No, no, you're skimming over the depth of your anger here. At this moment, you're in the grip of a white-hot passion. You want to wipe your son out. It scares you, and you don't want to look at it. Running down the stairs is your way of crushing your son. It's enraged moments like this that make you cringe inside when people say, "You're such a patient father." Running down the stairs, with your daughter laughing on your back, you want to demonstrate your full power to your son. *You're an enormous rocket, he's just a grounded astronaut. No—he's a little ant too near the launching gantry, and he'd better watch out or he'll get burned.* At Cape Kennedy huge flames, stories high, roiling red like a burning ocean, pour out of the concrete blocks of the launch pad as the juggernaut booster rocket flings the space shuttle away from earth.

There is nothing worse than hurting those we love. You remember when he was born, *your first-born!* How perfect he seemed. You were going to protect him and defend him and be his pal and guide, and he would never be injured by life. One day when he was not yet a toddler you took him down in his stroller to a playground near your home; it was a city playground, lots of concrete surrounding all the play structures, and you took him out of the stroller on this lovely sunny day and sat down on the concrete with your legs out and sat him between your legs on the ground so he could play with his toys. You relaxed there, feeling pretty confident no hurt would befall him since you were like a fort that surrounded him, but you looked away for about a nanosecond and your beautiful, perfect son somehow fell face forward from the waist in that ungainly way only babies have. His mouth hit the concrete, and he opened up a little cut below his nose, his unblemished smooth skin ripped by the concrete. You saw he was bleeding and put him in the carriage to get him home and a mother saw all this happen—it was not a big cut, it really only required a bandage—and she smiled sympathetically at you as if to say, *It's amazing how they can hurt themselves, isn't it?* but for you the day changed from a warm sunny afternoon to a cold, bitter day in which your beloved child got his first (or so you imagined) wound from life. There's still a little mark on his face from where he fell, and almost nine years later only you notice it, but it is there, the mark that says that you should have protected him better.

It's taken a while for you to realize that not only can't you protect him from life's injuries, but you also can't completely protect him from being injured by *you*, by your anger.

Here's perhaps the hardest part about fathering, the unspeakable part—dealing with our normal and natural rage toward our children. Fathering puts us in situations in which we have little control, and we want it. We can want to hurt the very kid we are trying to comfort when he won't let us quiet and calm him; we can want to hurt the very child who reminds us of ourselves. Children disrupt our lives, they up the ante on our need to be responsible, they woo our wives away from us for a long time, and often they wind up reminding us of the most painful parts of ourselves.

Anger is often a father's way of responding to the powerlessness of parenting. Kids rarely do exactly what we want, when we want it. Thumbing noses at parents is a part of healthy growing up. After all, we did it, too. As boys we spend a lot of time in the male project of learning how to look big and strong and demonstrating our potency (even if we don't necessarily feel that way). It's a very valuable skill to have as a man, and then we become parents of children who become very skilled at demonstrating how *little* control we have over them. Our response to being made to feel small and powerless may be to get enraged, which is certainly easier than finding more creative solutions.

And, let's face it, fathering—like mothering—can also draw out our own sadism. In truth our kids are much smaller than we and quite vulnerable to us. Having so much power over another person may lead us, like the family cat who just loves to "play" with the mice she's caught, to toy with our power. One father related, with some shame, "There is a thrill to having your kids obey you; sometimes I just itch for my kids to confront me so I can blast them. I can become like a Marine sergeant, a tyrant, feeling like *you had this coming*."

For many fathers the underlying anger at their children leaves them feeling very ashamed and withdrawn.

Today we get so quickly into the "warm fuzzies" about

fathering—*Fathering opens you up to new parts of yourself!
Being a father is the best thing that ever happened to me! Be
a nurturing father—it's easy!*—that often men feel even
more ashamed of their anger. You sometimes see trendy
and New Age magazines with fathers testifying about how
they've found heavenly grace since they left their careers
behind to become full-time dads and you want to tear up
the magazine right there in the supermarket checkout line.

Once I was the "guest expert" cohost on a TV show
about fathering, and for the first half hour the host and I
and a group of committed fathers were talking about how
cute kids were and how nice it is to be with them, and I listened to all this until I couldn't stand it anymore and finally blurted out: *This is all very nice, but don't any of you
ever get really, really angry with your kids? I know I sure
do!* And I saw the producer behind the camera, a mother
herself, smile and shake her head with relief, saying, *yes,
yes!,* she understood, but here we were all these guys sitting around trying to act like "Hey, man, no problem." As
I spoke relief entered the group of fathers, too. One man
said, "Now I feel like we can really talk, I felt like we were
lost in the ozone until you mentioned anger." A father
talked about how awful it was to want to hit his screaming
child who wouldn't stop crying no matter how many hours
he walked him during the night. Another man spoke of
getting in such a rage during an argument with a teenage
son that he leapt onto the living room couch to be taller
than the boy, knocking him down into a closet in the process. Another man spoke of yelling so loudly in public at
his kids that they started to cry. Another told of hitting a
wall in frustration and scaring his children.

One of the first steps in dealing with child abuse is to

make it possible for fathers and mothers to talk about the wish to hurt their children so as to prevent acting it out. One of the hardest moments in life is to hate those we love, yet it is normal and natural to feel both.

Often, too, what angers us most about our children is something alive within ourselves. A father not too long ago was talking to me one day over lunch about his twenty-two-year-old son's chippy behavior and how clueless he was about what to do. The father spoke of how "disgusted" he was at his son's inability to get his life together. He felt so repulsed by the powerless anger the boy carried around that he didn't like to be around his son, and so father and son became more and more remote. Finally I blurted out, looking at the father, "Where is *your* anger and your own sense of helplessness in life?" Then the father exclaimed, "My son's just the way I was as a teenager, angry and unsure, just like I was," and that was the beginning of his understanding that he had to make time to be with his son again.

Dealing with our anger may be a matter of accepting and understanding it, acknowledging that it is there. One father of older children said, "I leave the room when I feel myself getting too angry at my kids. Rather than saying or doing something I regret, I try to get out of the situation and cool down."

Well, here in your own home you've left the room and made things worse.

Now your son is upstairs alone, crying, while you're downstairs with your wife and daughter. Good work, Dad! There are four place mats set, the food's ready, but no one has any appetite.

Expecting your wife to point out what a lousy job you've

just done, you're thinking what a performance it is to parent, how you can fall so short in front of this woman who is your partner and audience. How often we burn with shame at the way an eight- or three- or one-year-old or thirty-year-old child for that matter can leave us so turned around. You want to head off her comments, you want to say something like "Don't compliment me on how well I've handled this," and you feel a familiar sinking feeling: *you jerk*.

Your daughter smiles at you, shrugs her shoulders as if to say, *What can you do?* and you love her for her connection to you, but you almost don't want to be nice to her after having been so rotten to her brother. Wondering if she's enjoying being the good girl for her parents this time, you recall the words of a friend who exclaimed to you one day: "Having two children is a commitment to sibling rivalry!" You think about how rarely you can get them *both* to obey you at the same time, how if your son had just gotten dressed and come downstairs your daughter likely would be arguing with you about wearing the horse sweater or the bear one. How much of parenting is a thankless task of setting limits and having kids test them.

Part of you wants to just sit there in silence, to ignore your wife and daughter, tell your whole family to *get lost*, while you slink off to lick your wounds. Some days you do do that. Later, you all make up. But today you want something more from yourself. You think of your boy upset, alone upstairs. You don't want to just get angry or withdrawn. There's a dim stirring within you: *I am the father here, something more is demanded of me.*

Then your wife takes your hand from across the table, looks you in the eye: *You can handle this, maybe you better go back upstairs.* You think about your way of handling difficult situations: to sulk and withdraw. You learned early a crucial skill in being a man: *Act like you know what's going on.* Sometimes then you can figure it out, but often it just distances you emotionally. When you were growing up, you *trained* yourself to shut down emotionally in order to deal with difficult situations. It was a way of keeping cool when you felt on the spot, exposed, *too seen.* But now that you're a father, you need to open yourself up to what your kids are feeling, not shut down to it. You need to be creative here.

Your wife's words break you out of your funk. *Maybe you should go back upstairs to him?* With a start you realize that she's not sure either—you want her to know, to be an authority, but she's really not sure. Leave him alone upstairs until he comes down? Go back up? What to do?

You want to do the right thing in front of this woman, your wife. You want to be a father for her, a father as good as she is a mother, you want to meet her there. But you're riding around in your Lost Canyon of Inarticulateness. What should you do, what do you feel? Maybe that's the point, you have to be clumsy and unsure here. To get past the Omniscient Mother Syndrome means to take some risks, to be clumsy, to tell your wife that you need to be clumsy, maybe to let her confess that *she*, too, feels unsure of herself in family crises. Most of all it means finding within yourself the permission *to be a father even when you're not sure what to do.*

Your son is lost in the wilderness—Marshal Dillon, you have to saddle up your horse and go find him!

Up the stairs you go again without a clue as to what to do except that you're the father. There feels like something timeless in all this, the father going up the stairs to get his son, as if there is indeed something encoded in the genes. Still, you've got an angry, upset boy, and his upset is making you upset. When one of your kids loses his or her internal balance it sets *you* off balance: When kids lose it, it lets anger and despair out of the box, and then we can all indulge ourselves, yelling at each other and making a big stink out of everything. Parents have tantrums, too.

Still, it's seven o'clock, and even as you scoot up the stairs, Marshal Dillon without his horse, you are determined to blast your son, not to boost him, if he's not dressed when you get to his room. You can't leave this battle alone, you circle around it with your boy, you can't stop yourself. You're spoiling for a fight about his recalcitrance, wanting to punish what is alive in yourself. You think you're dealing with him, but aren't you really scratching your own itch, an itch that won't go away?

An unsettling question bubbles up inside as you bound up the stairs: *Did I have to grow up too fast, did I want to linger a little longer in my own childhood?*

A picture comes to mind of a gangly nine-year-old not wanting to go to school. It's you in the picture. Wanting a little more time to linger, to stay, to enjoy the moment. You were so adept at getting out of school. You can remember faking illness and having the whole glorious day to sit around the house watching TV, making lunch, organizing your baseball cards. Your "kid work" seemed infinitely more fascinating than your "school work." And your mother would go along with it, your father following her lead. You may have learned more from your reading and curiosity *out* of school than *in* school.

Ultimately what did you want as a kid? Someone to sit

with you and show you *how*—how to deal with all the imponderables: sadness, disappointment, not having confidence. Are you still looking for a father? Well, good luck—now you're the father!

You burst into your son's room, like the father intent on ripping the covers off—you can't stop yourself—and your son is still . . . languid is about the best word for it. Flat on his back in bed, his covers draped to the side, his legs frozen in midair, deep in thought. His pants remain draped over his upstretched legs, limply awaiting their orders. Is he having an out-of-body experience? Perhaps he is having breakfast on Pluto.

Your son looks at you, returning from Pluto.

Why not just blast him? You're just trying to get everyone to school, he's not helping, you've got a zillion things on *your* mind, and time's a-flying. Why not just yell: GET UP!!!

Sometimes you do do that, yet you're convinced that it is not really helpful, that what happens when you blast him is that your boy feels bad about himself and angry at you and he doesn't learn much about getting places on time or taking responsibility for himself. When you yell he gets discombobulated, falls more apart rather than getting himself together. Yelling about responsibility means he learns to yell, not to be responsible. Certainly there are times when you yell, a lot of times when you can't help it, but today you're on the edge of realizing a basic truth about fathering—that you have a nine-year-old boy in front of you who is simply a nine-year-old boy and you have a choice here between having a tantrum yourself or being a father. Sometimes you have the tantrum, sometimes you're the father.

Right now your tantrum and your fatherliness are locked in fiery combat.

You strive not to yell, but then you're so angry you do it, ridiculously—you pull the blankets off his bed. Momentarily giving in to your anger even at the price of your pride: He was no longer under the covers anyway, so you pull them off while he's sitting on the edge of the bed.

You have a *little* tantrum.

And then your wonderful nine-year-old boy stands his ground: "I wanted you to wait for me! I want a boost, too!"

Whoa. You're stopped in your tracks by the directness of his request. An awareness: *He wants you.* A few minutes with his father at the beginning of the day. *That's the boost.* That's what children want: their father. Time, response from Dad.

You think: He wants just what you wanted—a father, a father who can comfort and soothe him as well as help him grow and develop and "integrate" himself.

You think of your son's bravery in asking for what is rightfully his: you. You look at this boy of yours, growing so fast. He's nine years old, wanting some boundaries and control. He doesn't want to be ordered around and ordered around, he wants some control.

Most important, he wants a moment of soothing and comfort and energizing with his father. But not at the price of his pride. He's willing to grow up, of course, to get dressed and go to school and be on time (more or less) but not if it means being stripped of all sense of his power and control. And good for him!

Here is the "father hunger" of children—the child's wish to excite the gleam of love and interest in his father's eyes. How often do our kids obstruct our maniacal adult efficiency and orderliness as a way of getting us to hang back a little with them before we all rush off into the "real world" of school, of work, or adult preoccupations? "Daddy, I can't find my shoes, will you help me?" "No, Dad, I haven't gotten to my college application." Maybe at those moments there is a wish to linger longer, to get the boost from a parent.

As you stand there holding the blanket you've ripped off his bed, you find that taking *his* perspective in all this dilutes your anger at him. For a split second you realize that you need to be truly older than your son and to let him have a small victory in the interest of your connection. Sometimes as fathers we have to get off our high horse and go to our children. The father of an adolescent may need to leave the door open after his kid storms out of the house during a fight about limits rather than slam it in his kid's face as a demonstration of how big and strong he is, too. A father of a grown child may need to write that letter or make the first phone call, taking the first step to heal years of alienation. Sometimes we have to back off from them, not put them on the spot. Often we expect it to be the other way around, that our kids should come to us, bend to our will. It's easy to get pulled into a power play with our kids, especially our sons, who may excite the competitive gleam in their fathers' eyes. But at some point as a father you need to make a choice for the relationship rather than for your status.

Fine, except how to do that now, you wonder, first thing in the morning, before you've even had breakfast?

As you sit down on the side of his bed next to your son, you're proud of your boy for reminding you of what he needs, of asking for it, asking for you. Even as you're grateful, you are acutely aware that it's seven-o-five, and you feel rushed, wondering if you're ever going to get to breakfast. You're also aware of your wife and daughter waiting downstairs, and you're still not sure how you'll handle this. Maybe it's better that the women of the house are downstairs, you're rid of that awful sense of audience, of the women watching, seeing how well you're doing. Now it's just the men of the house upstairs. Free of watching eyes, you have some confidence you and your boy can work this out.

You know you want to say something to your son, you're not sure what, but you find the words: "Sorry, I didn't realize that you wanted me to wait. I do hurry sometimes. I'm here now, and I can wait while you get dressed."

There's something very important for you in being here with your child, in not rushing him too much, in responding directly to his feeling, in his knowing that you really see him. You recall one day long ago with your own father. You were a young adolescent dancing with your sadness, unable to get settled on what to do that day, go to the movies, play ball, see friends. Was it your neighborhood sweetheart spurning you? Not knowing how to woo a girl? Were you being picked on, or were you picking on yourself in that intense, nasty way that adolescents can get down on themselves?

You went into the living room, where your father was sitting, and he noticed you looked down.

"Hi, what's wrong?" he asked.

"Gee, Dad, I'm not sure."

Silence. Where we often got stuck. What do you say after "Hello"?

Your dad, generous man that he is, reached into his pocket and took out a wallet.

"Here, my boy, here's ten dollars; go buy some shirts for yourself."

To this day you don't know how he latched onto the shirts, and you feel both appreciative and disappointed as you recall the moment. You're grateful to him for trying to do something, but you can't help laughing at the incongruity: you wanted more of him, you suspect, not more of his wallet. It would have been nice just to sit and talk about loneliness, or handling girls, or your peer group. Maybe if he had said, "C'mon, my boy, let's you and me go buy some shirts." The two of you could have gone out shopping together.

As a father now you can guess some of what he might have been feeling when he offered you that ten dollars. Did he feel inadequate himself, that what he would have to say would be of little use or help since he himself didn't know what to do with discouragement and loneliness? Maybe you had discouraged him with your brief answers—your adolescent inability to understand that he was wrestling with how to get closer to you. Maybe he was offering some deeper wisdom with his suggestion of buying shirts, like "Change the outside [flashy shirts] and you'll feel better on the inside." Who knows? You went out and bought two of the newest tab-collar shirts at the extravagant price of five dollars each, and it really didn't do much for your loneliness.

Now, over thirty years later, a father yourself, you want to be more of a companion to your son and daughter, a source of solace, comfort, support. Also *mastery*—you want to urge them on, to set limits and expectations so that they will feel both inspired and pushed, but not at the cost of your respect for their feelings. We so quickly get into performance expectations with our sons, increasingly now, too, with our daughters, but you want your kids to know that you as a man can also be a source of caring.

Then you realize what's called for here with your boy: quiet encouragement of his mastery (getting dressed, getting up), soothing encouragement that yes, it's hard, but he can do it, combined with firm limits that he is *going* to do it. And some patience.

Sitting there on your son's bed, you take a different tack: "Gee, it's great you got your shirt on!"

There is some time, you remind him—and yourself. You talk together of an amazing contraption he has rigged up involving a Spider-Man superhero figure who hangs from the ceiling via some string he's found: "It's a trap I've set, so this guy [pointing to Spidey] can ambush whoever's after him."

Children have such wonderful protean energy. You think of how much goes on inside a child, how much the adults around them miss. Your son asks you what you think a good name for the family dog would be.

"We don't have a dog," you remind him, confused.

"Yeah, but say we did."

You offer him a string of names, to which he shakes his head playfully.

"Okay, what would *you* name him?"

Silence.

"That's it, that's what I'd name him."

You look at him puzzled: silence where there should be a name?

"Because, Dad," your son explains carefully, "whenever I called him I'd go 'Here. . . .' " and no one would know I was calling him."

You both chuckle together, and you give him a high-five, telling him what a wonderful, smart boy he is. You're speaking from the heart now to your beloved son. You reach over and put your arm around his shoulder and he snuggles up against you momentarily, then he pushes back converting the hug into a wrestling match, and as you roll around on the bed you're aware of how much a boy's aggression toward you is just a safe way of getting close while also demonstrating his manhood.

You realize more of what a child wants from a father: to feel really seen and heard and attended to. You're learning from both your children how important you are as their audience, how much they want to engage you and wrestle with you and feel you and have your confidence and pride and know that you are head over heels in love with them. You hope you'll be able to remember that as your children become teenagers and test you over and over. But for now it's enough to see your son's pleasure in your time together in his bedroom, time stolen from the morning rush, and to realize that *you don't have to do this father thing perfectly*, that you don't have to have all the answers, that being there doesn't mean endless hours of playing house or doing carpentry projects, that it has more to do with really looking at your kids and really listening, even if it's only a hurried bedroom conversation before school. When you think of how far children will go to forgive their fathers and vice versa, you know your son will forgive you over and over again for your mistakes.

Moments of real opportunity with our kids don't have to be major turning points in life, portentous slow-motion times of high drama. They can be moments as simple as getting your kids out of bed in the morning.

You think of your own father and how much you mattered to him without his being able to say so, of how much still may be hidden in those long silences on the phone or in moments when he hands the phone to your mother and suggests she talk to you. You resolve to try something different next time, like saying directly, *Dad, I'd like to talk to you, too, not only Mom.*

You and your son laugh together sitting on his bed, and in his laughter, his optimism, his energy, you feel some of your adult gloom begin to lift. *The optimism of children.* Suddenly the weight of your responsibilities seems lighter. And you realize: *Being with my children gives me the boost.*

You're drawn into the world of your children in a way you never expected. Confidence, optimism, there's a piece of you being reworked as your son finds those gifts with you this morning. Giving it to him means that you find it within yourself as well.

As you sit entwined with your child you're aware of the resonance you feel: it has to do with your own sense of how cold the world can be, how you can feel alone and scared and in need of courage. You thaw out as you remember: *Don't stay frozen and scared, have your dreams.* That is one of the hidden payoffs to parenting, one of the deepest mysteries: *Often you get back within yourself what you have given your children.* Your children become a source of nourishment for you. How do we miss this in fathers? We are nourished by our children, we share a need for each other. The term "father hunger" refers to the deep yearning in children for the presence of their fathers, but what of the "father's hunger" for his children?

This very hunger can drive fathers away from their children just as it draws them closer. We compartmentalize our lives so much as men that the pull of our kids back to the unfinished parts of our own childhoods may be too strong and too painful. Fathers often become angry at their children, envious of them, or authoritarian or withdrawn because they can't bear to enter again into the world of children or because they were never given permission when young to enter childhood at all. Maybe we hurry our kids out of their childhoods from our unacknowledged pain at what we had to let go of.

As you sit and talk to your son you think about what a marvel the world of childhood is, how easily we can miss it in our bubble of adult preoccupations, and you're suddenly determined not to let it all slip by you, not to be the father who, as his son is leaving for college, laments how little he has known his own children.

You want to say this to your boy, sitting side by side on his bed, you want to tell him to hold on to his imagination and his ability to play. You think what marvels your wonderful son and daughter are; you want to say all this to him, but you doubt he needs a lecture of Sage Fatherly Advice, so instead you exclaim: "What a wonderful boy you are! Have I told you today how much I love you?" and he says, "Well, no, you haven't told me, Dad, except now you just did, right?" and the two of you laugh again.

As you and your son sit on his bed you hear calls from downstairs: "Where are you both? What's going on?" *It's seven-ten,* you realize with a shock.

Your son's still not dressed. "I want a glass of water from the bathroom before I get dressed. Will you give me a boost?"

Up on your back he goes, and the rocket is launched

again, with its naked payload, this time in a speedy and precise trajectory to the bathroom sink across the hall. The explorer has a drink and then rockets back to his bedroom.

More inquiries and entreaties from the first floor.

"I'm going downstairs, join us when you're ready," you tell your son. This time he doesn't object.

As you go, having just set another limit, reminding your boy that yes he will be going to school, you grasp the poignancy of parenting: in becoming a father you lose your childhood, you really can't go back again, even as you regain it.

You rejoin your wife and daughter, happy to be there, feeling as nourished by your son and daughter as you are by the breakfast food in front of you. Your wife looks at you uncertainly, silently asking: *Where's the kid?*

"Wait a minute," you say, striving for a confident tone while also silently praying to the God of Time, *Please, please get my son down here forthwith!*

The three of you start to eat breakfast. It's seven-fifteen. Then seven-twenty. Your son's corn toasties look more and more forlorn. There's ten minutes to go. Footsteps on the stairs herald an arrival, and, with a wonderful smile, appropriately self-satisfied, your son arrives, fully dressed. He even has a turtleneck underneath his sweatshirt in deference to the chilly temperature outside. Nice touch.

He polishes off his corn toasties, and soon it's seven-thirty, time to leave for the school bus, down your driveway through the woods. Your daughter is frantic now, she wants to get a doll to bring to show-and-tell, while your son looks for his boots. Your daughter is yelling, "We'll be late, we'll be late for school." *God,* you wonder, *have they inherited that from me?,* but this time you keep your wits about you and tell your daughter to run upstairs and get her doll, you'll wait for her. Your son is momentarily confused about his shoes—Dad, will you tie them for me?— and you sit down next to him and tell him that you'll wait right here with him while he does it. You try to speak soothingly and calmly, and soon they're all together, shoes on, doll in backpack. Then out the door you all run toward the long driveway, and then you're walking with time to spare toward the dirt road where the bus will pick up the kids, so you crack your usual joke about leaving home, "A-w-right, m-o-v-e 'em o-u-t," as if the three of you are leading a wagon train or cattle herd (which is exactly what any family expedition feels like), and the kids laugh and you tell them again about the cowboy shows you loved as a boy, about "Rawhide" and "Maverick" and "Have Gun, Will Travel." As you all talk during the short walk about cowboys and what the Wild West was like and you remember to tell your daughter about Annie Oakley and they fill you in about what's on TV now, you feel a deep satisfaction.

You realize that you really can do this "father thing," that an age-old question is being answered when you're with your children: you have something to offer them, some love to give back, you're not just a mountain of rules and expectations and performance standards, but also a source of encouragement and hope and solace.

This day, your kids, your wife, have brought out the best in you.

CHAPTER **3**

FATHER AND DAUGHTER CLIMB A MOUNTAIN

One morning not too long ago I got the kids off to school and returned home, prepared to plunge into the day's business. Yet often the kids remain in my mind even after they've left. Sitting at the desk in my study I found myself contemplating two pictures my six-year-old daughter drew for me and taped to my wall: one of Mount Monadnock, a squiggly mound of blue ink with yellow crayon crescents denoting "all the boulders on the way up" and another of a girl with a big heart drawn on her, smiling, her arms thrown into the air in an expression of triumph.

A father once referred to himself as "the icing on the cake" for his daughter. Since his wife was so important to the girl, he felt that mothers transmit the core information about femininity, and he had a lot of trouble figuring out a way into the relationship. With a tone of mixed relief and regret he described himself as merely an extra. Yet I know that's not true, for him or for me.

We live in a time of changing sex roles, and fathers want to be there for their daughters, maybe *more* there than fathers in previous generations. Yet what is a father's role with his daughter? I'm not sure I have an easy answer to that question. But I know that one of the things my daughter has taught me about fathering is that fathers are as important to daughters as mothers are. Our daughters need us to affirm their mastery and to affirm their femininity. They need to know that the first man in their life is head over heels in love with them.

It's not a knock on the vital role of mothers to suggest that fathers are also vital to their daughters' well-being. Yet being the father of a daughter means struggling with difficult issues and allegiances about gender. A father needs to discover his daughter in a way different from discovering his son.

The picture of Mount Monadnock on my desk sums it all up for me. My daughter drew it after our trip there, just the two of us. If I had any doubts about our mutual needs for each other they were put to rest that day she and I climbed the mountain.

Several years before, I had started a summer ritual with my kids: our yearly hike on Mount Monadnock. My wife and I both enjoy hiking, so we tried to interest our kids by not pressuring them to get to the top, just to hike along the trails. My son at age eight, the previous summer, had made it to the top after several summers of meandering first one quarter, then halfway up before we turned around. This summer I organized a hike with my son and several of his friends, and we went up to the top on a sunny August day. The boys had about as much interest in hiking as in hog wrestling, but I got them engaged and they were great. We took our time and spent six hours, up and down.

It's not a torturous trip. "Mountain?!" a friend of mine from Colorado once exclaimed looking at Monadnock. "That's what we call hills out west." Yet it was big enough that I was proud of the boys and of our new ritual, "climbing the mountain."

Emily had displayed little interest in hiking, but even so I looked forward to future summers when she and I would do the same. So I was unprepared for her reaction when the boys and I returned to our house late that August afternoon to find Emily returning from her summer day camp.

"Where were you?" she asked.

"Oh, Toby and his friends and I climbed Mount Monadnock. Next year maybe you'll come, too," I added hastily, noticing a certain look in her eyes.

"You climbed the mountain?" she replied, hands on her hips, looking me directly in the eye.

"Yes . . ." I replied hesitantly.

"Well, then tomorrow you are going to take me."

And she walked inside to play with her toys.

The next morning I was up early getting ready our two

water bottles and various other supplies, wondering if she'd (1) remember and (2) still want to go.

Imagine: Your daughter wakes up that morning and jumps out of bed and finds you and says, "Let's go" and she's dressed in a flash and she makes clear that this is supposed to be just you and her, no need for Mom or her brother to come along. So while her brother sets off to a friend's house to play and her mom looks forward to a day of gardening, you find yourself preparing to climb Mount Monadnock for the second straight day. You wonder what the park rangers will make of your showing up so early after having left so late yesterday; *There's a man who really loves climbing the mountain!* You remember reading about a man who climbed Mount Monadnock every day for a year, through rain and snow, and you wonder how he did it.

As you drive through the early morning mist, the sun newly risen, your daughter is chatting away to you in the car, delighted to be alone with you, and even as you contemplate all *your* lost plans for the day (read a book? hike alone? have a date with your wife?) you also feel enormous gratitude to your feisty daughter for demanding her time with you, for asking clearly for it so you'd know that you really did have to make that time. You consider the fact that your son very much wanted to be with you yesterday but also made clear he wanted his friends to come along, too, while for your daughter it's enough just to be with you, her dad.

She tells you about how she's looking forward to school starting next month, going into first grade, a big step, and she's explaining how she's not scared anymore about having to learn to read next year in school, no, in fact, she's going to read every day to the whole class out loud, she says, she's going to read big books to the other kids, and you at first start to tell her not to worry about school and reading will be fine and she says, *Oh, she's not worried, really, Daddy,* and then you realize that the whole point of the monologue is to give you an opportunity to compliment her on how big she's getting and how great it is that she's going to the big school, to a new classroom, and you realize how much your wonderful, growing girl wants you to admire her.

You arrive at the park entrance and walk across the parking lot and find the trail head together and your daughter is bubbly and eager and you walk about a minute down the trail and she asks how far it is to the top and suggests you both stop and take a rest and you suspect this might be a shorter day than you had first thought. You open up the trail mix you've brought, having learned that kids need lots of snacks when they hike, and the two of you fish out the chocolate chips. Your daughter wants to eat only those, but you ask her to eat some peanuts, too, to give her a good sugar/carbo mix and then you continue along the trail.

Your daughter wants to stop again in a few minutes, and she shows you some bushes and leaves she's spotted on the side of the trail. You want to climb straight up the trail, you want to get your hiking rhythm, but her rhythm seems different, slower, and you remember the father whose daughter told him as he was rushing her to school one day when they were late: "Daddy, let's slow down so we'll get there on time." You laugh and decide to let her set the pace, actually it's kind of nice taking your time, and numerous hikers pass you by offering encouragement to the dad and his little six-year-old girl who are trying to climb the mountain. *Aren't they cute!* You feel a little too cute, and even as you love the attention you know that becoming a public "dad with his daughter" creates the danger of losing the special anonymity of your time together.

Your daughter wants to stop and play house in a little hut formed by the branches ("Let's pretend you're the daddy chipmunk and I'll be the mommy and these pine cones are our babies"), and you notice that you've only gone about five hundred feet in the first hour. But you realize that if you take a lot of rests your daughter is eager to go on; it's not as if she wants long rests, but more that she wants to know that she can control the flow of rests. Once you agree to stop, she sits briefly and quickly says, "Okay, let's go."

Control. *How many chocolate pieces? How many rest stops?* You become aware of a familiar feeling of resentment, that you're constantly skirting around a struggle with your daughter as to who decides what: how many chocolate chips are okay, when to stop, whose imagination is in charge of the games. A nasty part of you just wants to put your foot down: *A peanut with every chocolate chip, a rest stop once per hour! I won't be daddy chipmunk anymore today!* You wonder how come you feel so bossed around, whether this is the residue of feeling bossed around all your life by women, and then you realize that it's not women who come to mind. . . . it's your younger brother! It had been just the two of you growing up in your family, and there had been vicious struggles between you as to who was in charge, even though you were almost four years older. Younger sibs have tricks and an inborn stubbornness, probably crucial to their survival, that can drive a firstborn crazy. You remember

the time your parents left you in charge one weekend
night when you were in your early teens while they went
into New York City for dinner with friends at Lüchow's,
an enormous German restaurant. Big mistake. Heady
with your newfound power, you decided that it was vitally
important that younger brother go to sleep before you.
But when you inform him that it's time for him to go to
bed, he refuses to follow orders, refuses to submit to this
humiliation, so you mobilize the S.S. within you only to
encounter the S.S. within him. Next thing you know the
two of you are rolling on the den floor fighting about his
bedtime *(Vee haf ways of making you go to bed),* and despite your superior size and strength, despite all the
shaking and threatening you can muster, he will not give
in, the freedom fighter, weeping and scared, will not surrender, refusing to leave the den and the TV, and so realizing you can't kill him to make him go to bed, you call
your parents at Luchow's, have them paged, and they try
to sort it out over the phone, negotiating a fragile truce
until they get home later that night. It was back to baby-
sitters for a while. And despite your enormous love for
your brother, what do you most remember from such experiences? How unfair it was that he didn't follow your
orders, how he encroached on your authority, and if you
want to get right down to it: How come this sibling came
into a good family when it was just you and your parents
perfectly happy, and who really needed a new addition
anyway?

So as you walk along the trail, holding hands with your
daughter, happy to be there, she happy just to be with you,
part of you momentarily gets confused: *Are you her older
brother or her father?*

You feel your daughter's determined hand in your own, the strength with which she holds on to you, and you think of that determination: how she demanded this time with you, refused to cede you to her brother, the effort she's made to be here on this trail, to be a part of your world, and you love her for her stubbornness and refusal to surrender what is truly hers. That's one of the miracles of parenting: how we come to relive and even to love the very moments that caused us such pain growing up. You suddenly have a new insight into your brother and your own dethronement as a firstborn: *Maybe he just wanted what was rightly his. It wasn't a personal attack on you and your life. You didn't have to take it so personally!*

After a while you come to a spring, the only one on the trail, about one third of the way up, and that's good since it's a hot, hot day and both you and your daughter are starting to wilt. You wonder how much longer she'll want to keep going, this is already farther than she's ever come on the mountain, and you praise her, worrying whether you expect less from her because she's a girl. You don't want her to overstrain, don't want to demand too much from her, but on the other hand don't want to demand too *little*. So you praise her on how well she's doing, how far she's come, and the way her eyes get bright you know you've said the right thing. You reflect on how your praise, the moments when she feels really seen and heard and valued by you, so enliven your daughter, that such moments are like nourishment, a sort of food for our souls, as important perhaps as the three meals a day. You recall the lyrics from a Judy Collins song, "My Father," about a woman who grew up in Ohio remembering that her father always promised his daughters that he would take them to

France; he never did, but the light of their connection was so strong that the woman, a mom herself now, sails "my memories of home like boats across the Seine,/And watch the Paris sun set in my father's eyes again."

As you scoop water out of the spring, two women hikers arrive and refresh themselves and spot you and your daughter sitting there pouring water over each other's heads. It feels as if you're on a date, the two of you.

They encourage your daughter: "Wow, you've come far!" The women look to be in their mid-thirties. Your daughter leans over to whisper in your ear how pretty the bright purple bandanna looks on one of the women. She also confides in you that she likes the earrings on the other woman, and you wind up talking about their walking shoes. Is there a secret underground knowledge among females about such matters? Almost from birth your daughter has been fascinated with shoes; you wonder how much of this is genetically encoded, your son hardly cared about shoes or clothes, he was always interested in guns and cars while your daughter gravitated to dressing up dolls.

You reflect on how special it is to be the father of a daughter, how it's let you into a new world. You grew up in a household in which the only woman was your mother, no sisters, and here you now have this little girl showing you what it is like to grow up female, teaching you how to be the father of a daughter. Sons are such magnets for fathers. Being the father of a son feels more natural, you know what a son is up to, you were a son once, in fact, you still *are*. With sons and fathers there is a danger of overidentifying. The familiarity is reassuring, but it can also be a trap. With your daughter, however, you often feel in new territory.

You think momentarily about your own father, who grew up in a family with two older sisters and a very strong mother, then fathered two sons. You wonder if he felt more attuned to women. What was it like for him to have to mobilize his masculinity around those two rowdy sons when in fact he might have been more comfortable around women, maybe with daughters? Every child is a roll of the genetic dice; so many of our hopes and dreams and struggles as fathers are shaped by the fortuitous mix-up of prenatal chromosomes.

Of course we love our children regardless of their gender. We rarely think with regret of the child we might have had. Yet what happens to a father's yearning to show his sons how to throw a football in a perfect spiral, just as his father did for him, when he only has daughters at home? Clearly a father can find equal satisfaction in teaching his daughter how to throw a football, how to participate in Little League and other sports, if she'll let him. Yet a friend of mine, a successful university professor in his forties, tells me how relieved he is that his first child, now a year old, is a son because having a son gives him a chance to work out some early pain about his manhood. His father had been very sick all his life, and my friend had never really come to terms with a sense of "failed masculine lineage." Having a son reaffirmed his maleness, the potency of his manhood. Even as he spoke, though, my friend looked ahead a few years and worried about "the masculine clash" between father and son, the male's need to prove himself, the difficulty men have talking, the difficulty the father has in giving way before the son's power, the turbulent need for and fear of each other that fathers and sons may feel.

When a father has only daughters, is he in danger of remaining inside a charming, seductive, feminine circle in which he can be idealized? What does a father miss if he never confronts the challenge of dealing with the pressure of sons who may yearn for the paternal throne as well as for the comfort of father's lap?

Your reverie is interrupted by a question from the hikers. "Are you going to the top?" one of the women asks your daughter.

"Yup," she replies, blithely unaware that a mile and a half and two thousand feet of height remain ahead. They smile at your daughter and make brief eye contact with you while an uncomfortable thought oozes into your mind: *Is my daughter on loan to me today?* The women create some defensiveness in you. You feel as if she belongs to them, to the world of women, not to you, an ambassador from the world of men. You recall a poem by Adrienne Rich in which she gives voice to the lament of mothers through the generations when fathers declare: *My son is mine!* But do mothers also claim that same possession of their daughters?

You recall reading an article on fathers in the classroom in which the female principal of an elementary school was waxing poetic about how wonderful it is when fathers come into the classroom. She said that *the boys get so excited and want to play with the fathers*, and you were struck by the fact that she mentioned only boys because you know that the girls, too, respond to you when you come into your daughter's classroom. Several of them will run up to show you their newest art project, wanting you to respond, and you know that father hunger exists for daughters as well as sons.

And fathers, too, may hunger for affirmation from their daughters. A treasured memory recounted to you by a father comes to mind. His young daughter's name is Elizabeth and his wife calls her "Lizzie" while he calls her "Betsy," and one day to his delight they both called her to come out to the car to do some errands and she emerged from the house declaring, "I'm a Betsy!" The story reminds you of how much we fathers prize the direct expression of love from our daughters, even as it sometimes scares us.

Before you can blurt out *She's mine!* the two women smile again, this time to both of you, and bid you adieu, continuing on their journey to the top. Soon you do, too. The day is *really* hot, and you kick yourself for having agreed to try and climb the mountain on such a hot, dry day, and you look at your six-year-old and worry about how quickly water evaporates from such a young body. The two water bottles, now refilled with cool fresh spring water, reassure you; you pat them in your pockets—you've worn your trusty hiking shorts with the big pockets so that you don't have to carry a day pack, everything you need is crammed in your pockets—water bottles, trail mix, sandwiches, a space-age emergency blanket, Swiss army knife—you feel like a lopsided kangaroo in need of a chiropractic adjustment.

You take out a water bottle to show your daughter one of your favorite tricks—putting water into your hat and on your hair to keep yourself cool. First you douse your head, rubbing the water in, then you put water all along the sweatband of your hiking hat, finally repositioning the wet hat on your soaking head. Feels great on a hot day.

"Neat, Daddy!" And she looks up at you with those loving eyes as she douses her hat and hair. You think of how much she idealizes—and idolizes—you. Not too long ago, just before you left for a week of teaching across the country, your daughter was disconsolate and asked, actually tried to order, you not to go. "You can just cancel your classes and stay home," she pointed out quite reasonably. You mulled over that idea, not so excited about leaving your family behind either, then you pointed out in return that the students might be disappointed if you didn't show up, and even more to the point the dean wouldn't be amused. "What's a dean?" your daughter asked, and you replied, trying to keep it simple, that the dean was your boss and your daughter looked at you shocked, absolutely unbelieving. Clearly you'd just said something completely unimaginable, and she blurted out: "Oh, no, no, Daddy, you don't have a boss, other fathers have bosses, but *you* don't." And you remember how a few days later when you recounted this story to the dean, himself a father with older children, he sighed and said, "Just wait until she realizes that you do have feet of clay." And so as you reassured her that day that yes indeed you do have a boss, just like other fathers, part of you also wanted always to be her hero. What a great moment it was to be walking along this trail together, heads held high and wet.

After a few hundred more snack stops you notice you've begun to clear the tree line; the trail is lined with large rocks that your daughter has to scamper over. Some of the boulders are bigger than she, and at times you give her a hand or a boost over them. Finally you come to a spot where the scrub is so low you can see for miles, and you turn around to see the view, which stretches almost to Boston—lakes, forests, rivers, highways, it's a spectacular view. Your daughter is focused on her climbing, mostly looking down at the trail, she's nervous about slipping down or losing her balance. But once she gets her footing on top of a large boulder you tap her on the shoulder to get her to turn around and say, "Look," and she does and exclaims, "Wow!" and then says, "Thanks, Daddy, for bringing me up here!" and you both sit for a while. You continue on your way, but it is really getting hot. You've been hiking almost three hours, and now without the tree cover the sun beats directly down on you.

You worry about her and say how great it is that you've come so far and she agrees and you say that this is a new record for her and that it'd be fine to head back whenever she wants. You don't want to undercut her accomplishing her goals, but you don't want her prostrate either, and you wonder if people see you as an overdemanding father— *Look at that father trying to turn his daughter into a son!*— but on the other hand you want her to feel the equal of any boy, so what to do? The only thing to do is take your cues from her: she ignores your face-saving gestures, she wants to go on.

The two women hikers are taking a break up ahead, and they again offer encouragement as the two of you plod up to them. The three adults joke about the heat and the view and you reveal your nervousness about going on, saying quietly that you don't want to push your daughter too much and they smile at you and you see the friendliness in their eyes and they say, *It looks like you're both doing great, go for it!* and then they turn to your daughter, exclaiming what a great hiker she is. She seems perked up at their words, and suddenly you feel enormous gratitude to these women not only for their supportive words to your daughter, but for encouraging you to enjoy her.

The women move on. You and your daughter eat more trail mix before going on. She eats the chocolate chips, you eat the peanuts.

You're about three quarters of the way up and your daughter keeps going, but she is really pooped. Finally she suggests a rest and you see up ahead there's some shade so you continue on the trail around a set of big boulders that, together with some hardy scrub brush, offer a fair amount of shade. As you both slide down into the shady corner, you look up the trail and in the distance rises the baldheaded, rock-strewn top of Mount Monadnock, about a half hour away:

"There it is, darling! We can see the top!"

And she looks and smiles but seems out of energy. *I have pushed her too far!* you suddenly fear and think about helicopter rescues and going to get a ranger, but how could you leave her here while going to get help? The lazy stream of other hikers reassures you, but you don't want to have to make a scene, you don't want to *ask for help*.

Your daughter sits and looks for garnets, the reddish gems found throughout the granite at and near the summit of Mount Monadnock. So you sit in the shade prospecting together. Your daughter tells you that she wants to take some for presents to her friend Elena and maybe some for Molly, but Sally she's not so friendly with these days and certainly not Mary. As you pick up the lovely stones, you think about how relationship-building girls are, the intrigues of little girls as they reject and reform friendships again and again, and you marvel at how insightful girls are about people. How different your daughter's connections with girls feel from your connections with boys as a kid: in your experience boys weren't as brutal with each other as these girls seem. You recall a friend who was stunned when his daughter came home from fourth grade one day to report that she had been exiled by her female friends and how he wanted her to go right back to the girls and find out what was wrong and work it out. But then he went to his wife and she seemed to understand perfectly and suggested they let it alone, and, sure enough, in a few days the peer group had reorganized itself and his daughter was no longer on the outs. Sometimes fathers have to learn new strategies in dealing with their daughters.

Sometimes your daughter seems more insightful about people than you are; she seems to have her mother's internal gyroscope about love to guide her. It feels so easy to talk to your daughter about life, and as the two of you sit scraping through the dirt looking for garnets, you also consider how different the poetry of fathers to daughters is from that of fathers to sons. In his poem "A Kite for Michael and Christopher" the Irish poet Seamus Heaney writes of "strain" and tightness and weight, the burden of male grief and anger. Yet his poem "A Hazel Stick for Catherine Anne" shimmers with the softer imagery of "mother-of-pearl," of "the living cobalt of an afternoon dragonfly," the sight of "your first glow-worm."

The two of you start to walk on, and it feels so hot that your confidence flags. You realize you've been walking almost four hours just to get to the top. You finish off the rest of the first water bottle and are reassured by the weight of the other one in your pocket, untouched still. Your daughter hesitates on the trail, says she's really hot, and you bend down toward her.

"Honey, what do you want to do?"

She doesn't say anything at first. Then: "I want to get to the top."

But she seems so tired and sweaty.

"Well, we've almost done that—there it is, we can see it. It's about a half hour away. We could save the top for next time."

She points out that her brother *did* get to the top.

"Well, he's almost four years older than you."

"No! Three and a quarter!" your daughter reminds you testily.

"Right. Well, you almost did it, we can see it," you say.

She hesitates, then says wearily: "Okay, let's go back," and heads down the trail toward the bottom, looking pooped. You follow after her, so proud of her. Her blond-reddish hair bobs in the breeze as she walks.

Then she stops, turns around, and looks again at the summit: "No! I want to get to the top. Let's put some more water in our hats."

So you turn around again, energized yourself by her grit and determination. As your daughter finds her second, or third, or fourth wind, scrambling over the few remaining boulders, you hope that she will always be so strong, that she will be able to find such resources when she's climbing up the mountain called math, or science, or whatever she wants to learn. You want her to become a Supreme Court Justice or a world-class gymnast. Maybe even both.

Except then you remember also that you want her to have a family, to have children and marry a really nice guy. You think about how hard it seems to do both. You think about the female college students you teach who feel so much anxiety about giving themselves over to a man.

Many of them have mastered being competent, but they still haven't solved the question of how to be interdependent with a man. You wonder if women have to be strong and tough and powerful in isolation from men these days, and you hope that really isn't true. "The nineties are a lonely time for women," one student said to you, and you don't want your daughter to be more than normally lonely, you don't want her to miss how wonderful it is to be married and be a parent.

You wonder about the performance expectations placed on daughters in our hip, "liberated" age. One student, a thoughtful, hardworking science major, told you how crushed she felt after a recent talk with her father about her plans after graduating from a prestigious science-oriented university: "Everyone I know is going on to get their Ph.D.'s after graduation. Next year I just want to get a job. I went home over the holidays and wanted to talk to my father, and I told him about not wanting to study more, that chemical engineering was okay, but I didn't know what I wanted to do. I wanted some time, and he said that while I was figuring it out why not get a master's? That hurt, that he didn't understand."

So as your daughter runs up to the summit of Mount Monadnock, raising her arms high in a gesture of exultation (the same ecstatic pose that she captured in the drawing that hangs over your desk at home), both of you are thrilled at the way the entire world seems to spread out before you in all directions and you want to blurt out: "Always go for whatever you want . . . and remember to have a family!"

Instead, you catch up to her and she leaps into your arms and you whisper in her ear: "I am so proud of you!"

And she hugs you back, whispering in your ear how much she loves you.

After some time on the top prospecting for more garnets, you realize that it has taken you five hours to ascend and now you have to get back down.

So you start down, having saved that full water bottle for the trip back, except that about a half hour down from the summit you reach for the bottle and it's not there. The only one still in your pocket is the empty one you finished on the way up. You realize that you must have let it fall out of your pocket on the trail and now your daughter is thirsty and it's too far to go all the way back and you tell your daughter that you dropped one of the bottles and so there is no more water and she looks at you in that way that tells you she is learning sooner than you hoped that you have feet of clay and she says angrily, "Oh, Daddy! I'm thirsty" and you find again that there are few experiences in life as painful as disappointing your children. This feels serious: you have hours of hiking left and no water. Luckily some teenagers, two boys and two girls, come along heading up the mountain at this late hour; they're carrying bottles of seltzer and they give you enough to get you down if only your daughter drinks it. So now you're thinking about shortcuts, how it would be nice to get down a little quicker, before dark and before you have no water at all. So there's this trail you've never gone on, but it seems to link up the major trails and might save some time, so you suggest taking that trail. Your daughter is wary now that she realizes you can lose things, but she goes along. And as it gets darker you rush somewhat along this lonesome trail; now there are no longer any other hikers accompanying you and your daughter gets a little spooked in the gathering darkness and is clearly tired, so you try and go slow even as you are trying to rush, and she is grouchy, but after an hour you come out at the main trail, very near the spring, that wonderful spring where you can replenish your remaining bottle, and you know that you'll easily make it now to the bottom.

When you get to the spring you both take long drinks of the cool, almost sweet water. Your daughter lifts her head up from the spring and smiles right at you, saying, *We made it, Daddy!* and in her smile you see such forgiveness. You see that she will forgive so many of your imperfections. You remember a lovely woman who had felt rejected by and angry at her father most of her life, and then on his deathbed, when he was dying of emphysema, a tracheotomy rendering him voiceless, he made a simple gesture as she sat down next to him; he wrote her a note that said, "glad to see you, sorry can't talk." And the grown daughter, who had been unsure whether she should even have come to the hospital, found such healing in his comment, felt that he was apologizing for his whole life, their whole relationship, his lifelong inability to talk to her. You think about how much a daughter wants to forgive and love her father and how sad it is when either one makes that forgiveness impossible.

In a way fathers and daughters become lovers from the moment the girl is born. Not sexually of course, but there is a romance that need exist between the two. You think of the father who told you that the love between father and daughter is seductive, it's different, he said, from wife and husband, "Our daughters love us more unconditionally than our wives do," and how dangerous that love may feel to a father. We have to have a romance with our daughters without becoming too romantic. You recall a powerful short story you read once about an aging father whose wife is dying of cancer in a hospital and how he crashes his sailing boat up on the rocks one day in a fit of despair. He makes it to shore, but he is in a sense lost in his loneliness and grief. His daughter, who had been his sailing partner all her life, tries to comfort him, and alone in the house later that night the father and daughter, having finished off a bottle of wine, turn to each other for comfort, and then they are rolling and wrestling sexually on the floor, their passion for each other out of control. They push away from each other, realizing what they were doing, but both of them are caught in a prison of shame and guilt that will haunt them.

You think of the father's task of being passionate and tender and gentle with his daughters while also keeping the boundaries clear. How easy it would be to distance yourself from your daughter or to forget about your relationship with your wife while you fall in love with your daughter. You vow not to do either.

You think about how "fathers and sons" is such a hot topic these days, how we are flooded with books and films about father-son reunions, but what of fathers and daughters? Perhaps for many fathers the times with their daughters may be "less dramatic, more delicate" than with their sons as one father put it, but no less important. But for many daughters the feelings are not so delicate. You think of the psychological scars a daughter may carry through life from a father's neglect. You think of Muriel Rukeyser's poem "Waiting for Icarus," in which a daughter is frozen in life waiting for men, who seem to have the wings; she is unable to fly herself, having never learned that talent from her father.

Late afternoon shadows crisscross the parking lot as you

walk together toward your car. Your wonderful, tired, proud daughter gets in the car next to you and suggests you go and get some pizza since it's almost dinnertime— it's taken the two of you over nine hours up and down the mountain. Great idea. Over her momentary protest you suggest that her mother and brother come along on your date, and she agrees when she realizes the two of you have many stories to tell them from the day.

As you drive past the ranger station, you recognize the ranger who greeted you this morning. He's still on duty, and he waves good-bye, asking: "See you again tomorrow?"

CHAPTER 4

HARDBALLS

Raising a Tough and Sensitive Child

My involvement with Little League began over a year ago when the phone rang on a sunny Saturday morning in the spring as I was trying to pack up my son Toby, then eight years old, to get to soccer.

"Do you have your shin guards on?" I yelled above the sound of Ninja Turtles on the TV.

"What, Dad?" Toby yelled back dreamily, intent on squeezing out his last few minutes of the morning with Leonardo, Donatello, Michelangelo, and Raphael.

"C'mon, dude," I pleaded, sounding like an aging turtle. Toby lolled languidly on the couch while I negotiated with him as to when His Royal Highness would don his cleats.

Raphael did a neat flip on the screen, head over heels up

to the ceiling, avoiding a foot clan soldier and then catching a slice of pizza thrown by his buddy Michelangelo.

Toby laughed, while I stood there holding his shoes.

The phone interrupted my paternal vacillation between impotence and intimidation. It was a neighbor calling to let us know that the neighborhood Little League tryouts were beginning in fifteen minutes.

"Little League?" I replied distractedly. "We can't make it now, Toby'll be late for soccer."

Suddenly Toby jumped up. "Oh, Dad. I don't want to miss Little League!"

I almost dropped the phone. Little League beats the Ninja Turtles for his attention!

"Well, gosh, we don't want to miss soccer. Can't do both," I cautioned, sounding a little shrill.

"What difference does it make?" wondered my wife from across the kitchen, sounding quite reasonable.

I can hardly say *Because I don't want him to have to deal with hardballs, that's why!*

"Awesome pizza, dudes," observed Donatello from the TV. The turtle is holding the pizza while facing about six hundred evil-looking enemy Ninjas. The threat doesn't faze him. With amphibian savoir-faire he dispatched the pizza first, then his enemies.

"C'mon, Dad, I don't want to miss Little League. Why can't we go?" pleaded Toby, interrupting my own communion with the TV.

I couldn't think of an answer for my wife or son.

"Okay, let's go, get your glove and bat," I said in resignation.

While I went down the front steps toward the car, memories of Little League flooded me. The scene of some of my greatest triumphs and failures. Although I had some great moments—home runs to win games, a memorable stab at third base to corral an "uncatchable" liner screaming toward the hole at short—many of my memories were painful ones—striking out with the bases loaded, being terrified of the hardball, using my glove mostly as a shield to keep the ball away from me as it spun over the stony in-field. Once, around Toby's age, I cut my little finger going through a plate glass window at home, and I used those three stitches and a Band-Aid to put myself on the disabled list for numerous games.

Disappointment and fear and failure, the terror of the hardball, the embarrassment at being terrified. . . . You can't shield your kid from these, but what parent doesn't want to?

How do you hold on to your kid's sensitivity and inno-cence and caring while also helping him become tough enough to want to compete and win? Toughness and sensi-tivity: What parent doesn't want their child to possess both qualities, and what parent doesn't get twisted around try-ing to nurture them simultaneously?

To my surprise Toby's Little League experience helped teach me the key to raising a tough and sensitive child.

The key has to do with shame—helping your child man-age the embarrassment of being scared, of not succeeding, of looking foolish in public. Shame is the feeling that some-thing in you is defective, that you've failed to live up to an ideal. It's a normal and natural human experience—we all find ourselves not living up in some ways and resolve to do better.

Problems develop when shame is too great, too private, cuts too close to the core of our self-esteem. When we feel too exposed and alone, too vulnerable, we question our own self-worth and begin to feel that we're the problem, that something is wrong with us to the core. It's not that we just struck out and need to learn a better swing, but rather that we are an inept, incompetent "loser." When that happens boys and girls develop a hard outer core, a brittle toughness that drives out their sensitivity and innocence and capacity to empathize.

Sensitivity and toughness aren't just struggles for our children—they're not so settled in us either. In helping our children with these matters we have the chance to relearn them ourselves. It took my son a full year, with scores of practice sessions and emotional ups and downs, to make it onto a regular Little League team. As he ran out onto the Little League field—a player—my joy and pride accompanied him. My own loneliness as a father and my shame were present, too, running right alongside my pride in him. As a father you're tethered so tightly to your child, united with the child by your hopes and dreams that you participate intimately in his or her struggles with shame, hope, and vulnerability. You go right through it with them.

You discover, when you're a father, that it's one thing to have a catch on the front lawn with your son, but it's another thing entirely to have him stand in to bat in his first Little League game. It's his first real season, after a year of farm. The bases are loaded, his teammate Karen yells encouragement from first; she's just gotten an infield hit. No one has scored yet in this game.

Your boy takes his time, getting his bearings. He's got on the batting gloves he searched for at the sports store since making contact with the ball hurts his hands. You've practiced batting with him a thousand times. He's on his own out there, and you can't do it for him. As Bill Geist observed in a New York Times column entitled "Hardball": "I . . . just . . . wanted . . . my . . . son . . . *safely* on first base." He observed wryly: "That baseball term 'safe' suddenly took on a whole new depth of meaning."

The chain-link fence around the field is an unyielding reminder of your separateness. "No parents allowed on the field," the coach of a rival team had rebuked you several weeks ago when you had wandered onto the sacred space to show your son something.

The parents mill around the bleacher area or stand near the fence, cut off from their kids, no longer able to do it for them, wondering what their role is now. You and your wife stand with another father, a man you've met at the field on Sunday afternoons when you've gone to practice with your son. He was there with his son. He's talking now about how much pressure had been put on him as a kid. He was a good athlete, went to college on a baseball scholarship. Now his son reminds him of himself:

"My son didn't expect to pitch the last game, yet the coaches asked him to. He got shelled and took it very hard. I told my son about all the games I lost as a kid and all the times I struck out. Of course it didn't do any good—he still felt awful. Maybe there's too much pressure on him here." He goes on to talk about his brother, who used to step out of the box when batting and who got teased unmercifully for it by his father and the other kids. Just the other day this brother, at age forty-five, brought up his Little League trauma of three decades ago: "Of course I was so scared. It turned out I needed glasses—I could hardly see the ball."

You return to your own son's struggles to see the ball. The pitcher, an older kid who's been in Little League several years, smokes a couple in there. You remember that your son is part of a new, younger team playing the league champs from last year. His nine-year-old opponents are already veterans.

It's two balls and one strike when the pitch comes in, and it's inside, fist-high. Your boy stands his ground . . . and you hear a dull thudding sound as the ball hits him and bounces feebly toward the first base coach.

Your boy looks stunned and drops his bat, grabbing his right hand. You wince as if hit in the stomach. Should you jump the fence, go to him? You want to help, you want him to know how precious he is to you, but you don't want to overwhelm him. How much support is enough?

You search within for models: How comforting were men in your own life? You find that you don't have lots of images of men putting their arms around you, comforting you. You try to recover the images and instead you bump into mental newsreels of sluggers doing home run trots, enormous fullbacks barreling through the line, football linemen blocking and tackling, basketball players doing slam dunks. You get desperate: *Where's an image, heartfelt and real within my own experience, of a man being tender and kind to a little child?*

And face it: you don't want to have to trot out there in public and be the only father consoling his son. *Why couldn't some other kid get hurt? Damnit!* Then you realize what you're thinking. You may have a sudden insight into courage: there's as much or more of it in a man being kind and tender as in his being tough and demanding.

Before you can move, though, the coach is out there, along with the assistant coach and the umpire. The coach is smart, and he accentuates the positive as he runs over to the batter's box: "Hit by the pitch, drives in a run!" The assembled adults survey the damage while the other kids watch speechless.

An evil-looking blood blister has formed on the right side of your son's palm, where the ball pinched his finger against the bat when it hit. He shows it to the coach, who puts your son's hand in his own. Your son also holds his battered hand, and you can see he's trying not to cry. Nothing is broken, though.

"Ow! That must sting," says the coach, who is a caring man. He starts walking with your son down to first base, congratulating him on driving in a run. The sight of the older man, the coach, a corporate lawyer in real life, a tough guy, walking down toward first base with his arm around your son, kindles a feeling, a wish that someone would do that for you. You puzzle for a moment: *Are you the boy or the father here?*

You stand there frozen, unsure of whether to cross the chain-link fence, as you watch another man comfort your son.

The blister on your son's hand looks as big as a silver dollar and as dark as a piece of coal. You can see his struggle to hold on to his composure, and you feel proud of his gumption. As he trots to first base, you worry about blood infections, pus, and blood clots. *Why isn't there a medical team standing by?* an irrational part of you demands. *Where's the ambulance by the side of the field?*

You can see that your son just wants to *do it right*. He struggles to keep control and not cry. You and he are united in an age-old male understanding: *Don't break down in public. Don't show too much vulnerability on the playground, the Little League field, the office, or the boardroom.*

People applaud your son, the wounded warrior.

Then the umpire, walking back to the mound, suddenly stops and raises his arms, yelling something to the coaches.

Since your boy was hit on the hand, the ump is saying, and "since the hand is part of the bat in major-league rules," he was not technically hit by the pitch. In fact, that was a foul ball and thus strike two. Everyone looks aghast and groans; the coach eyes the ump, who apologizes and says them's the rules, pointing out that the blood blister on the hand is proof of where the ball hit.

The ump gestures to your son, who is standing on first base holding his hand, his eyes still wide with pain. The boy is supposed to go back to the batter's box.

The ump puts on his chest protector and yells: "Play ball. The count is now two and two."

Then your son starts to cry. All the pain floods in, and now he has to go back into the batter's box and stare at that rock covered with cloth as it darts toward him.

He can't do it. The coach starts walking your son to the first-aid shack across the field to get ice for the now swollen hand.

"Should I go to him?" you wonder aloud as you watch your son walking along looking so forlorn and defeated. You yearn to hold him, you don't want him to be so alone. *You* don't want to be alone—an invisible thread pulls you toward him. Should you? You don't want to be an overprotective father.

"No . . ." your wife starts to say, sharply. You look at her, and she stops. There seems a sudden tension in the air between you. She's not sure what you should do. Suddenly you don't want to look like a wimp in front of your wife, and you recognize that this is just one more skirmish in a long struggle between you about raising a son: How much comfort do you offer, how much regression do you permit?

She wants him to be able to master this pain on his own, not for you to hover around him and sissify him. But is some fantasy of hers also punctured by the sight of her weeping boy at Little League? Savvy mothers know they have to be careful about their wishes for an "ideal" masculine son—a male who is better and stronger than their husbands perhaps, the perfect male to love and reflect their own grandiose yearnings. Sometimes it's mothers, not fathers, who are unable to tolerate their son's vulnerabilities, their deviation from "manliness," and sometimes fathers need to be able to stand by their children in the face of their wives' momentary abandonment.

So, standing by the fence, you realize that mothers, too, have a vested interest in toughening their sons up, and sometimes they may do so unreasonably, caught in their own worries and fantasies. One father who attended a Little League game with his wife realized that *she* was the one who actually wanted to "kill the umpire" while their son batted. She reminded him of "a mother bear in the woods with her cubs."

So you feel a special kind of gratitude when the other father standing next to you, the sports hero, says without hesitation, "Yes, go to him." His affirmation gives you permission—you feel freed by the fact that another father agrees that you need to go and comfort your son. His affirmation makes you feel less alone. You carry it along with you as you go over to the other side of the field to be with your wounded son.

And your wife seems freed up by him as well. You can

tell she's thinking, "Well, okay, the fathers agree that this is not coddling your son."

There is, of course, a difference between coddling and comfort, between toughness and brutality. Fathers and mothers have to explore that line. When a kid has given it his or her all, it does not undermine toughness to provide comfort as well.

You hurry over to your son near the first-aid shack, and he shows you his blister. It feels weird to be the only parent comforting his child. You worry about your own male lineage: *How tough am I? Who comforts me?* And you envy the rest of the parents back in the stands who can all root happily for their gladiator-children.

The coach hands you several ice packs and then, giving your son a friendly tousling of his hair, trots off back to manage his team.

The ice packs are the chemical kind in which one set of crystals has to be brought in contact with the other in order to create the "icy" cold effect. That means you have to smash together the contents of the bag. You wrestle with the bag, punching and prodding it, but to no effect. You feel increasingly perturbed by this ineffectuality, and you redouble your wrestling efforts, suddenly feeling that it's extremely important that you force this bag to work. Suddenly you have an enormous need to prove your manhood and your competency and ability to get things done. You want to force this bag to submit by the force of your bare hands. The bag, unaware of this paternal drama, remains unmoved, the contents unsmashed.

Your son gets interested. "Here, let me try it," he offers, forgetting about his blood blister—a dark purple, swollen splotch protruding from the base of his ring finger.

Putting the bag on the ground, your boy gives it a powerful stamp with his foot, producing a loud pop, as the chemicals mix together. You walk back to the bench with the ice pack draped over your son's right hand, your arm around his shoulder. His team is now on the field, the bench empty.

"You stay, please," he instructs. You avoid your wife's eyes as you walk into the now empty dugout area, convinced that every parent there thinks you're too enmeshed with your child, and you sit down next to your boy on the wooden bench, looking out at the two teams on the field. The coaches are shouting instructions near the batting area. Sliding down next to your son, a baseball cap on your head, you look like a Little Leaguer on steroids.

Your son leans up against you, holding his bruised hand close to his chest. You want to have a heart-to-heart talk with him, you want to *do something paternal* to justify your sitting in the dugout, the off-limits area for parents. You start to say something but notice that your kid is watching the game. You want to impart some wisdom, like "Gee, hardballs hurt!" or something about "life's knocks," but it seems he already knows all that.

Then you find yourself thinking about your boy and how hard he's worked at this Little League thing—how he's practiced hitting and catching, how he tries to stand in there against the very new and scary reality of hardballs. You recall that when the coaches asked him if he'd like to try catching (since he's one of the biggest kids on the team, making a good target), he put on the chest protector and mask and shin guards and caught the hardballs coming right at him, even as he, a chip off the old block, tried to use the glove more as a shield than as a target. And you realize your son's courage and grit and drive and determination, and you say to him: "You know, I'm really proud of you!"

He doesn't say anything, still looking out at his team, and you wonder if he's really heard you, but then you feel him snuggle up closer to you, and you know you've said the right thing.

Sitting there with your feet tracing circles in the dugout dirt, your son's head on your shoulder, you contemplate what kids need from their fathers. Often it's not grand words or deeds—they just need their fathers to *be there*, to witness them, to provide a steady male presence.

And you also acknowledge that just "being there" as a father is not so simple. How often fathers and coaches lose sight of their children's needs. How easy it is for a father to step out of the batter's box himself, to back away from being there for a kid, to be shy of *that* hardball.

You think about the fact that it's been a year since your son first went to the Little League tryouts, that day he left the Ninja Turtles behind. You remember all that's happened to him, and to you, in making it to Little League. He went to the tryouts and was put on a powerhouse team. The coach back then didn't want your boy on his team, this new unskilled rookie, since the team was a "monster team" favored yet again to win the championship. As the practice sessions went by, it became clear that the coach wanted your boy to go back a level, to farm league. This was not a bad idea in itself except the coach would not talk to your son about it, and you could feel your son's hurt pride and his desire to stay on this team even if it was above his head. Here was the age-old boy's struggle to come to terms with his disappointment and his wish to keep up with his peer group.

Then comes the practice day when team uniforms arrive and all the kids are joking and playing together, including your son, except you realize that there is no uniform for your son, it seems that they're "short" one, and oh gosh the coach hems and haws and says well the kid can stay but he doesn't want him to get hurt playing and you realize that the coach won't confront your son about this, maybe he doesn't know how, maybe he's just ignorant, maybe his dad was a deaf mute, who knows, but you know that someone has to *deal with this*, that the last thing you want is for your boy to be left alone with a sense of failure and sorrow. You want him to learn a key lesson that sports teaches us, that not winning can be mastered, that losing is also a part of life. You don't want him to feel shame at not making the team, but rather to look at what he needs to do, to learn how to hit, field, and throw and feel okay about himself. But how?

The coach, Casey Stengel in his own mind, starts to walk away, and you spot your son now sitting alone in the bleachers beginning to get the picture. You have to act fast. But what can you do? You remember the father who went in screaming to the Y the day after his kid was cut from swim team and demanded, yes, demanded, pounding on the table, that they take his kid back on the swim team and yes sir they did except that the boy dropped out anyway within a month. That doesn't seem like the right strategy, but what else is there to do besides walking away and saying, okay, fine, go to farm and screw these dorks, but that doesn't seem right either. So you do what every father has to do, which is *to do something even though you don't know what to do*. You go up to the coach and say, "Look, do you want this kid on the team or not? Because if you don't want him, then I don't want him on this team." The coach looks down, his foot pawing the infield sand; you're in danger of becoming two moose kicking up sand at each other. But then he says, remarkably: "Well, I don't want to hurt a kid, and I don't want him to get hurt" and you realize who else needs to be part of this conversation, so you go get your son from the bleachers. He's shy about coming over, but you put your hand on his back and whisper in his ear that we'll do this together, it's important for him to hear what the coach has to say. So the three of you stand near home plate and the coach finds the words, God bless him:

"Listen, son, how would you have felt if you had to bat against that big kid today?"

"Scared."

"How about if a hard grounder was hit to you at third base?"

You love your boy more than ever as he replies: "Sad . . . and scared."

Then the coach seems to get the point, to see the light: "Listen, in farm," he says reassuringly, "you'll learn how to handle those grounders and how to stand in the box against bigger pitchers."

"Farm!" Your boys looks as if he's going to cry.

The coach keeps going, a note of tenderness entering the man-to-man talk: "If you go to farm this year, I'll come visit you twice during the year, now I don't say that often, but I will come visit you and watch you and find out from your coach how you're doing and next year there's a very good chance you'll be in Little League, too."

Your son brightens and agrees: "Okay, I'll go."

And you realize that being there for your son forced you to do some growing up yourself.

Of course every parent wants his boy and girl to be tough enough, to be able to stand up for themselves, to bear the pain necessary to get ahead. However, toughness alone, toughness without the awareness of our own vulnerability, without the ability to grieve for our failures and admit our needs, is no gift to give our kids.

Your reverie about the past year is interrupted by the end of the inning, and your son's team returns to the dugout, inundating you with Little League kids. You sit there like Gulliver among the Lilliputians. It's the seventh inning, and the kids are starving for their snacks. The coaches and other parents produce juice and crackers and cookies.

As you sit with the team, you're surprised at the compassion of these nine- and ten- and eleven-year-olds. The other kids are kind and supportive of your son: "Hey, are you okay?" one asks. "Want some gum?" suggests another. This is not just the competitive peer group you remember from your own childhood. "The same thing happened to me once," offers another kid, and your boy and his team talk about wounds and hard knocks, and they joke about getting hit on the funny bone. They want to laugh even as they cry. They're doing a lot of restorative work themselves. Even as they struggle for the Gatorade and snacks between innings, pushing each other and jostling, even as they razz their opponents, these kids still have the capacity to rally around the injured one. They recognize need, and they know how to care for each other.

As you sit there you realize that you love your son even more for his ability to depend on you and to show you what he needs. You value the way he can push aside that proud male determination to get on with things no matter what the personal cost. You say a prayer: *Maybe he'll be easier on himself than I am on myself.*

Then you wonder: *Did I struggle like that when I was so terrorized by the hardballs in Little League?* Were my friends as forgiving as my son and his friends and I didn't even see it?

Suddenly the idea of forgiveness for failure seeps into your head. Was I less forgiving of myself for all those Little League failures than everyone else had been? Watching your son master his fear and express his need heals an old wound within yourself.

And then sitting in the dugout, you begin to notice the gentleness and kindness of many of the fathers there. Many of them are encouraging and understanding of hesitation, failure, and uncertainty, as well as of success. When a kid strikes out, another boy's father goes up to him as he drags his bat back from the batter's box and says, "It's okay, you missed it, but your swing was good, here's what you do next time . . ." and the man shows the boy some trick that may have worked for him forty years ago and then pats the kid on the back: "Soon, son, you'll be hitting it a mile." There are the fathers and mothers who are truly soothing and encouraging of mastery: "It's okay, Jeffrey, you can do it." Kids are named, adults know who they are and care what they do. "Okay, okay, you got the glove in front of it, that's good."

Another father brings pockets full of bubble gum to the game, and he walks up to the dugout fence, asking innocently, "Anyone here want some gum?" Over the innings every kid winds up with a mouthful of the stuff. How wonderful that fathers can dispense sweetness, too!

Your son's Little League feels different from your boyhood memories, different from your expectations. It's supposed to be a very competitive place, and we all know about the crudeness of kids and the "toughening up" that goes on in little boys and girls who are desperately trying to live up. Maybe, though, we overlook the compassionate and caring expressions of both children and fathers.

Sitting in the stands one day a father tells me about how he deals with all the violence his kid is exposed to, and our talk turns to the Ninja Turtles. His son yells with pleasure every time a turtle foot lands in some evil person's anatomy. The father talks to his son about the turtles, saying that yes, yes, they like to fight and kick and be violent, and that's fun, but what else do they like to do? They like to eat pizza, dance, be with the girls, and so on.

That's an interesting and useful approach, but isn't there also a playful side to the violence and the aggression that we need to appreciate? A friend of your son's comes to bat for the other team. Saul, a charming kid, one you really like, a boy who burns with humor and spunkiness. He stands there with his helmet balanced precariously on his head, while your pitcher gets ready to deliver the pitch. Saul looks determinedly at the pitcher, who stares back. Barry Bonds facing Nolan Ryan wouldn't show more concentration and purpose, except Saul is straining to keep the oversized helmet from falling over his eyes, while the pitcher drops the hardball and can't find it.

Your son yells, "Strike out, Saul!" and you find yourself joining in. You all root for your son's best friend to strike out. You're aghast until you realize, *This is only a game.* What a fun place Little League is! Saul does strike out, and as he walks back to his dugout a father yells, "Good try, Saul, good try—you'll get it next time."

Maybe as a father what you can do is witness this struggle, be a part of it—the aggression, the compassion, the wish to be the best, the exaggerated performance expectations the kids place on themselves. You can make it all part of the dialogue between father, mother, and child. Yes, we want to win, but we also want to love; we want to be on top and be tough, yet we also want to be able to express our vulnerability.

If ever you doubted that the mere presence of fathers is precious to children, those doubts are erased forever as you sit on the bench and watch one of your son's teammates go to bat. He's a good player, a big kid who's been practicing his swing. He stands in, and the pitch comes and he wallops the ball over the head of the outfielder, who tracks it down all the way at the fence, and the boy takes off and is passing third as the throw comes in, and he crosses the plate safely, driving in several runs and giving your son's team the lead against this powerhouse team. Everyone swarms around to congratulate the boy, who finally comes over to the bench and sits next to you and looks agonizingly over his shoulder at the stands and exclaims, "Oh, where's my father!" and you remember that the father had been here a few minutes ago and left to go to work, the night shift, and you think of the responsibility on fathers, of how kids want them there so much. You think of all the times you've tiptoed away from your own kids and now wonder what you've missed. The hunger of kids can seem overwhelming to fathers. But how many fathers sneak away for a cup of coffee and then find that they've missed out on something special?

That hunger for a father's response and affirmation may be something we put away in cold storage growing up. When we become fathers ourselves, we may have an impulse to turn away from our kids' need for us or punish them for it or get angry at them for being too demanding or feel sorry for ourselves for being too burdened. Or we can let our own needs thaw out and be a guide to what our children hunger for. You smile at the slugger and tell him what an amazing shot he just hit and he should be sure to tell his father about it when he sees him later and the boy smiles back at you.

We're all fathers to children, we cover for each other. There's an extraordinary innocence and trust and responsibility that men, fathers or not, have with children, given the power we have. We become a sort of mirror for their self-esteem, reflecting back what is best in them. It's amazing how much they care about our love and responsiveness to them.

The whole spectacle takes your breath away: how hard your boy's worked to make it into Little League, how much it matters. Maybe it matters too much. You know as a father how seriously kids take their performance, especially the boys, for whom it feels like a test of their manhood. The girls on the field seem still protected by their femaleness, as if our expectations are not as high for them. They have a sort of "feminine immunity" like puppy immunity.

You think of your daughter and how she'll be of Little League age in several years, and you want her to have the same chance—to be able to test herself and really struggle alongside other kids. A lovely, intelligent, athletic female student I taught once lamented, "I loved baseball as much as my brother, yet my father could not see that because I was a girl. It hurt a lot that he'd take such little interest in my athletics." You don't want your daughter to feel that way.

You recall reading that fathers often have too high expectations for their sons and too low expectations for their daughters. Thinking of your own girl, you realize that there is something very important in Little League, where boys and girls play together and root for and help each other. The neighboring town has separated girls' Little League from boys' Little League, and you wonder if something very vital—the chance for the sexes to be teammates together, admired on the same field by their parents—is lost in this arrangement.

Maybe the key to raising tough and gentle children belongs to fathers in a special way. Maybe the key comes from the father's determination to be closely involved with both sons and daughters as they struggle to master shame, failure, and success. We need to stand near and with our children as they come to grasp the balance between asking for help and demanding too much of themselves and as they learn to come to terms with their own failures and successes.

Being there for your kid does not involve a heavy agenda; it doesn't mean endless heart-to-heart talks about "your shame and mine." You don't have to get in your kid's face. Your reassuring presence, eye contact, pat on the back, spending some time together—this is what's involved.

And so is paying attention to your tendency to back away from kids, your own and others, who need you as a father.

As your son's team goes back onto the field after their at-bat, still leading the league champs, he throws down the ice pack covering his hand and suggests, "Dad, why don't you borrow the coach's glove, he doesn't need it right now, so we can practice batting and catching?" You pick up the old glove, it feels familiar to you, just like the one you used to wear in Little League yourself. You laugh as you see it's a Gil McDougald model, it just *feels right* on your hand, and to your astonishment and delight and gratitude you and your son walk over to the practice area near third base to work on dealing with hardballs.

CHAPTER 5

SEX TALK

When I was about fifteen years old my father and I had our first and last sex talk. My friend Gary and I had just come indoors from playing football in the neighborhood when my father appeared in the living room.

"Boys, come with me," he intoned, and beckoned toward the den. He looked the way men do when carrying out some distasteful manly duty; frontier fathers probably wore the same tight-jawed gaze when going to shoot the infirm, beloved family dog.

Gary and I must have picked up the scent because we were skittish as young colts. Without looking at us, my father walked quickly into the den; we remained in the living room.

"Uh, say, Dad, we're busy," I yelled into the den, unwilling to approach the room and unable to think of what Gary and I were busy with.

Deep down we knew: This was the Talk About Sex. Dread. Gary's father had died a few years earlier; my friend didn't have anyone to give him the sex talk. My mother and father had been whispering conspiratorially in the kitchen moments before, and she probably told him that this was the time for him to have a talk with his son. And why not include Gary, too? Now the three men (or the man and two boys) were playing hide-and-seek around the house.

"Sam and Gary, come in here, I want to talk to you." Sigh. Feeling at once anxious and protective of my father, I trooped with Gary into the den.

I hopped onto the large TV set in front of one wall, sitting on top of it, while my friend sat on the couch on the opposite side of the room. My poor father, thus double-teamed, couldn't face both of us at the same time. Dad spun around and around trying to get our attention; he didn't seem really sure, though, of what he'd do once he got it.

Then things got serious.

"Do you know what a screw is?" he asked.

My father, inspired, sounded like a shop teacher trying to teach by the Socratic method. Radiating authority and omniscience along with equal parts of confusion and uncertainty, he both embarrassed and intimidated me at the same time, which is probably how my father felt about the two giggling adolescents surrounding him.

The possibilities for nervous joking were endless.

"Oh, Dad, next thing you'll ask about is nails!" Giddy laughter from the young captives.

"Sure we know, Mr. O! Want us to explain it to you?" Gary and I tossed our anxiety around the room in this way for what seemed like an eternity. A dictionary appeared at one point as we digressed into an intense conversation about the origins and meanings of the word "screw."

The entire lesson ended in chaos as my father finally gave up and surrendered with a plea to "let me know if you have any questions." The three of us fled the room in evident relief.

Perhaps our kids' sexuality more than any other area forces fathers to confront their loneliness and unpreparedness along with an anxious feeling of *having to do something*. We live in the age of AIDS and teen pregnancies. We also live in a time of greater openness between the genders; maybe our children don't have to struggle with as much sexual shame and secrecy as we did. Yet our relative sexual looseness does not really make it any easier to deal with the intimate, personal questions that sexuality raises for us and for our children.

Doing the right thing by our children means getting away from the belief that we have to have the Big Answer. It means communicating to our children a basic confidence in their ability to make choices and to listen to their bodies, helping them to understand that asking the right questions is more important than having the answers when it comes to sexuality. Information about "the plumbing" is important, but more important is validating the mystery and uncertainty we feel all our lives about sex.

For me, dealing with my children's sexuality has really been a continuation of my own sexual education.

It takes but a brief immersion in parenthood to realize kids are constantly trying to understand their bodies. Your six-year-old daughter feels her front tooth coming out and can hardly wait for the tooth fairy to visit, but then as she sits in bed wiggling the tooth late one night, trying to make it come out quicker, she feels some blood on her tongue and starts to cry, suddenly becoming very upset as she turns to you, her father, and wails, "There's blood there, I feel blood! Daddy, I'm bleeding." She pleads that the tooth fairy won't want the tooth if there's blood on it, and she wants to know if she'll bleed when she sleeps and then you get it: she's asking a basic question about how bodies function—is it okay for there to be blood in my mouth when a tooth comes out? *Is there something wrong with my body? Is it doing what it's supposed to?*

And so as you comfort her, reassuring her that blood usually comes out along with a loose tooth and that the tooth fairy will love her tooth nonetheless, you may also realize that you're having a talk about sexuality, about how bodies work. In some dim corner of your mind, you may even think about how in a few short years you'll all be grappling with her experience of bleeding in a different part of her body.

On the way downstairs you consider what a mystery sexuality is. How much we live within our bodies as kids and how much as adults we live in our heads, that bubble of adult preoccupations. And yet neither kids nor grown-ups have the words to ask directly what they want to know.

"Gee, Dad, you know when I rub my penis it really feels good," a five-year-old boy whispers to his father conspiratorially as they stand together in the shower. My friend recounts this comment to me over lunch with a tinge of anxiety. "I wasn't sure what to say. Then I just laughed in a friendly way and said, 'Yup, it does.'" In the shower the son then advised his father: "No, no, Dad, it *really*, *really* feels good!"

Who's giving who the sex talk here?

My friend went on: "I smiled and said, 'Yup, it *really*, *really* does!'"

Fidgeting with his wineglass, my friend asks, "Do you think I said the right thing?"

There are many different ways to say the right thing. In his brief, matter-of-fact, reassuring response the father is telling his son that yes, he can talk to his father about his body without being shamed or rejected and that those good feelings are nothing to be frightened about.

In a way parents want their kids to know everything about sexuality and to know nothing at the same time. Who wants to think of his kid as a sweaty sexual being?

Having a sex talk with your children *is* a bit like shooting the family dog—it means the death of illusions about your children, the illusion that they will stay young and innocent forever. "I just want them to stay kids," protested one father whose wife urged him to go for a drive with their teenage sons and "have a talk with them."

You think about your own son and his willingness still at age nine to come to you with questions about how his body works. You wonder whether he'll still be able to come to you for information when he's an adolescent. It may be very hard for a teenage boy to admit that he doesn't know. How often fathers and sons struggle with a masculine clumsiness about intimacy—each trying to demonstrate that they know it all, *Hey, man, it's easy for me!*

It's not so easy even with an eight- or nine-year-old. The

other night you and the kids were playing together quietly in the living room doing a puppet show with their stuffed animals and in the midst of the laughter you suddenly found your older child making his two stuffed bears engage in sex play, all the while watching you to see your reaction. Clearly he and his older friends from school had been talking, and you wondered aloud to him if he wanted to know more about sex and your younger daughter said eagerly, "Yes, yes" while your older boy said, "No, no." Did he want to remain a child longer, perhaps intuiting that there was a whole new world out there that he wasn't entirely ready to hear about? You wanted to clarify sex with your son without having your little daughter hear all about what your son thought he was doing. There never seems a right time to do this and, besides, where was your wife, wouldn't you know that this would all be happening on a night when she worked late?

So you're very grateful the next morning when you report to your wife "the latest news from the sexual front" (as the two of you have taken to calling it) and your wife suggests that when you're all gathered at dinner that evening you casually raise the question. "So, who knows where babies come from?"

Which you determinedly do during a pause in the conversational free-for-all that passes for dinner at your home and suddenly neither kid seems interested. They both get very quiet, and then one says, "B-o-r-i-n-g!" and the other says, "G-r-o-s-s!" and even as both you and your wife attest to what an interesting subject it is, both kids seem suddenly extremely fascinated with their peas and carrots, a remarkable transformation in itself, and you are left hoping that they will indeed ask when they are ready.

You're left thinking about your own sexual education. You remember how as a boy *lust* and *love* often got mixed up and how as a young man you thought you wanted sex when what you needed was intimacy. The penis has such power it can seem to rule your life. Like "old flat top" of the Beatles' song, "Come Together," "he just do what he please." How grateful you felt to the four lads from Liverpool when you realized they were singing about the penis.

You think about the mystery of all this: the blue flame of passion and the softer glow of intimacy and connection. How wonderful and mysterious it was to take off a girl's shirt, her bra, to feel a girl's breasts for the first time, how wonderful making love feels.

You think about how much you wanted to score as a kid, to prove your manhood, but also how often you were at bottom just lonely, how much sex was a way to get close to women, to provide some comfort and not feel so alone in your male body. Even when you become a man, rushing through sex and sexuality still seemed intertwined, and you recall ethics professor Jim Nelson's point in *The Intimate Connection* that for many men there is a "genitalization of sexuality," by which he means that men ignore their bodies and focus on intercourse as the sole and only goal of sex. Nelson points out that men confuse sensuality and sexualty, and you wonder if maybe there is a sexualization of comfort and intimacy as well. Isn't it true that the only way many men can be close and comforted and feel the reassurance of bodily contact is to have intercourse with a woman? We want to be held and touched and comforted, but we have to score to get those "goodies" from the women in our life.

You realize that you hardly even discovered that women had clitorises until you were in your thirties. You were truly a believer in the myth of the vaginal orgasm. That little clitoris seemed a useless appendage, which actually meant that you didn't really *know* how women had orgasms for the first decade and a half you were "doing it." That was a distinct disadvantage. You recall that a friend of yours, age forty and married, was *still* unsure exactly where his wife's clitoris was located. You hope that doesn't happen to your son—you want him to know all he needs to know to feel confident and have fun and be responsible sexually. Or to your daughter—you want her to know where her clitoris is, indeed, you're proud that she has already found it. You hope she doesn't forget it.

Sexual information for you as a kid was something hushed and dirty, as if it had to be disguised in a plain brown wrapper, like a girlie magazine delivered to a suburban home. How did you even learn about condoms? That's lost in the murkiness of your memory, but you do remember the first time you went to buy a condom, you were in college and knowing—or hoping—you'd need one later that night on your Big Date, you walked into a pharmacy in downtown Philadelphia in the mid-1960s. No condoms were displayed within easy reach, no, they were all kept back behind the counter like a controlled substance. Did you need written permission from an authority to purchase one? You waited until no one else was near the counter and then asked the pharmacist for a package. He did not call the police or laugh uproariously *(You! You want a condom—for what!),* but still there was the nick of shame surrounding the moment. Taking that package filled with mystery, you felt like a real man, but then the young pharmacist said with disdain: "Using a condom is like taking a bath with your socks on."

But, boy, were you lucky a few years later when you

were traveling in Sweden in the 1960s! You were staying that summer at a university and there was a lovely Swedish girl who thought you were really something and yes she wanted to go to bed and you hardly knew what to do except you knew this was not an opportunity to miss and she even knew the English word for condoms and you said, "No problem," you'd get one, even though you had not the slightest idea of where to find a condom at midnight in a small suburb of Stockholm. You went down to the dorm counselor, who thankfully was still awake, and screwing up your courage and risking all for this heaven-sent moment, said, "I need a condom." Thank god he didn't mock you or betray you; instead, hardly looking up from the magazine, he replied matter-of-factly: "Well, sure, there's a condom machine in the girls' and boys' bathrooms," as if we were talking about where to buy the daily newspaper, and you hurried into the men's room to find that yes indeed there was a condom machine and to your relief you even saw it was fully supplied and you bought several and took them upstairs in your search for the Holy Grail, which you and the Swedish girl found that night even though you hadn't yet discovered what a girl's clitoris was for.

Most of all you remember the need to live up, the intense hunger to show you were "with it," in the know, how impossible it felt as a young man to admit ignorance. At college you became involved with an older woman, Lillian, who wondered when she first met you if you really were sexually experienced and you remember with a nostalgic twist in your stomach that time on the way back to her home after a Charles Aznavour concert telling her that oh yes, you had indeed slept with numerous women and boy you wouldn't let her down. You were acting like wow could you perform, when in reality she was the first woman you would sleep with. The pressure to perform felt like a part of sexuality—you're *supposed* to worry and worry about delaying your orgasm and act like you know it all even when you wish you had a map of the female body that you could refer to in bed. In retrospect you feel great gratitude for Lillian's caring ability to help you relax sexually, for taking it all so much less seriously than you did.

Is it your sexual exploits you most remember about lovely Lillian? Thunderous orgasms and exotic positions? No—what you recall most about your time with Lillian was sitting in her downtown apartment in the city so far from your own childhood home and how wonderful it felt to be part of her life. Her kitchen and TV and the hominess of her apartment helped wipe out the starkness of your college life, the loneliness of letting go of your parents and your childhood home. And you realize that actually you were less interested in sex than comfort and companionship and that, yes, you very much wanted to sleep with her but you also wanted her to be your friend and companion who would reassure you and help you feel okay about yourself.

Love and lust: how to combine them? Often boys and men get so focused on the latter we miss our needs for the former. "Here come old flat top, he come grooving up slowly." You think about how Lillian was right ultimately, she *was* too old for you and the relationship ended with great pain. How vulnerable you were to loss even as you tried (often successfully) to play the role of the sophisticated, urbane, man around town who could become the lover of a thirty-five-year-old woman.

You think about how finally you needed to take your

time with the woman you ultimately married, not to rush sexually, to really find out about each other. How you needed to talk, get to know the woman, not feel such pressure to perform.

Do we ever sort it out as men? Do we really learn that sex is about taking your time and not feeling rushed? The truth of the matter is that for most men you know the answer is no.

When you talk to men, grown men, healthy men, men who have fathered children, often in happy marriages, a secret comes out: we have lots of questions and uncertainties about sexuality. Slowly, slowly, after we get through the anxiety of not looking like a real man, of being laughed at by our peers, we may begin to talk about orgasms and pressure to perform—coming too fast, coming too slow, about fantasies about other women, other men ("Do you ever feel like just leaning on another man, feeling what it's like to be held and comforted, to be passive and receptive, not always in charge?"), about how to be present and available with a woman as opposed to just wanting to get her into bed.

When we talk openly in this way we're providing each other with the sex talk we wish we had had with our fathers. And then it turns out that even as fathers and grown men we're still learning about love and relationships, learning that there is more to sexuality than plumbing and performance.

One night talking with a group of men friends one father revealed that he pressured and pressured his wife to go to bed with him just the past weekend and then he realized that he was not horny but lonely—that what he wished for was comfort and connection and release from feeling so under the gun at work and unnoticed at home, but he kept putting it in sexual terms. How wonderful it felt that evening to be able to talk about our human needs to touch and be touched, to be valued, to feel less lonely. To realize that these needs are as much a part of our sexuality as how many seconds it took to reach orgasm and how to delay that ("Think about Grand Central Station and all the people walking around there").

Part of you believes that every other father *did* have a great sex talk with his father, that there was this thunderclap from the gods in which each other man got the right stuff that helps him deal with women. You still worry that your ignorance and uncertainty are signs of your own shame. Then you think about how hard it is for men of any age to get information about sexuality and their bodies. Your seventy-four-year-old father comes to mind, how you saw his nakedness one day as he was casually changing clothes while you were talking in his bedroom during a visit and how you wondered about the aging of the male body, what will happen to you as you age. Do you still have sex when you are seventy-four? Eighty-four? Ninety-four? What is it like to make love with a woman in her seventies? Part of you is a boy-man who *still* needs to go to his father for answers and support. The lament of another man, a minister, echoes in your ears: "I'm forty-five years old, have raised two sons, and I'm *still* waiting to have the sex talk with my father."

No wonder it can be hard for us to know what to say to our kids about sexuality. Their sexual curiosity and questioning opens up our own sexual struggles. In trying to be there for a kid we relive our own sexual history and insecurities. A sixteen-year-old son asks his dad one day as they're driving along together alone: "Say, Dad, when did you first have sex?" and the father may wonder: Was it early enough? How well did I perform? How good did I do? Did you score?

One father had to field that persistent question from his teenage son: Who was the first woman you slept with? He told his son that the first woman he slept with was his wife, the boy's mother, at age twenty-three.

The boy replied: "Oh, Dad, how could you be such a nerd!"

The father found himself close to tears at being reminded by his own son how "behind" other men he's always felt with women. Our kids can intimidate us. And in our panic to be a good-enough father, we may tell our children more than they want to know.

Above all we may be unable to find a way into our kids' experience of sexuality. No one talked to *us*, so how do we talk to them?

The fifty-three-year-old father of an adolescent daughter, a man who had grown up in a household with four brothers, once lamented, "In an Irish family I never even knew my mother had underwear," much less how to deal with female sexuality.

"My wife tells me to talk to our kids about sex," another father says. "They're in their teens now, but where do you start with a kid—Hey, do you know about getting laid?" Imagine the pressure on a father and son who only begin talking in adolescence, starting with sex.

We still sit around confronting sexuality as a matter of nuts and screws and "where to stick it." Here we are, highly educated, hip, with-it fathers, all veterans of the 1960s and the supposed sexual revolution, and we sound like shop teachers when we try to explore with our kids one of the most delicate and mysterious of human experiences: sexual passion and love.

We fathers get bogged down because we focus on matters of plumbing and overlook matters of the heart. That's what many of us missed ourselves: the opportunity to talk about what we feel, what it means, how we make choices to "be sexual" or not.

Boys' questions about sex often carry the same anxieties about relationships that we experienced but were unable to voice. For example, a boy will say, "What about this AIDS thing? It's got me worried." What he means is that he's thinking about becoming sexually active or he has a girlfriend. AIDS is easier to talk about than his own sexual yearnings. Or maybe he'll bring up a friend, like the boy who said his buddy has gotten a girlfriend pregnant and that it's ruined his life when he himself is on the lip of becoming involved with a girl. What this boy is scared about is women and relationships—it's not just a question about birth control and contraception, it's about going too far too fast, it's about whether girls entrap men, it's about what you have to do to prove you're a man.

"How do I know if I've gone too far with a girl?" asks a seventeen-year-old student on a term paper in a psychology class I co-teach. I've asked them to write about relationships in their own lives.

Whoa! I'm stunned by the question. Gee: how *do* you know? I take a trip to the familiar Lost Canyon of Inarticulateness: I'm not sure. In the margin of the paper I find an answer from my female coteacher: *Ask her.*

Ask your partner about what you don't know? *Oh yeah. How great.* You *can* do that. Yet a part of me remains unsure whether it is okay for lovers to talk about what they're feeling, what they want for themselves sexually. Can a man really express uncertainty to the woman he's involved with?

So I wrote on the student's paper: *Yes, ask her,* and, also, *How great it is that you're asking the kind of questions that I couldn't ask in college!*

After class, the papers returned, the student came up to thank me for my comments, and I could see that my praise of his willingness to ask a tough question was worth as much as the practical advice to "ask her."

Then I understood what a kid wants—validation for asking about the relationship stuff that troubles him or her—power, dominance, going too fast, and getting hurt.

Maybe kids don't expect us to be the Answer Man. They want to know if we're there for them, if we can tolerate their asking. In this way fathers can create the groundwork for a dialogue about our bodies and the pleasure we derive from them, which is really what "sex" is about, and by adolescence that dialogue may expand to encompass the parts that intimacy and love play in sexuality.

It was only after I left class that day that I wondered about the deeper unasked question neither of us had spotted: *How do I know if a girl has gone too far with me?*

So many young men experience things going too fast with too much pressure to perform sexually. Yet we grit it out and stoically act like all's just great to all the world, while old flat top runs amuck in ways that may cause us great shame and loneliness.

As fathers we remember that vulnerability and want to deny it at the same time. A father will fulminate about his son getting "too involved, too fast" with a girl and, then, remember that he was seventeen—the same age as his son, who is now engaged—when he got married to the boy's mother.

Maybe here's the bottom line for fathers: We see too much of ourselves in our kids, in our boys in particular, and we want to protect them from being hurt. We want to shield them from the incredible vulnerability that we ourselves felt. Maybe that's why it's so hard for fathers to admit uncertainty about sexuality, why they shy away from dialogues about values, choice, desire, and love. We imagine we'll protect our kids with information, with hard and fast rules, as if sexuality could be tamed so easily.

What will truly protect our kids? Perhaps our confidence in and availability to them. To communicate however we need to—clumsily, smoothly, in whatever style suits us—that this stuff *can* be talked about. That, yes, you can ask, and, yes, there are many questions, some that will go on through your life.

After all, who are the people who have been the most help in our lives? Usually the ones who have said they have faith in us. A forty-five-year-old son remembers his father telling him one day thirty years ago: "My father said, 'Sex is fun, just remember to use a condom.' I found his nonchalance and confidence in me very freeing."

Just remember to use a condom. Fathers need to say this to their sons and to their daughters. Now it's no longer just about birth control, it's also about your child's health, perhaps survival. You were stunned by the comment of a teenage daughter of a friend, a hip, savvy girl in a privileged Midwestern suburb, a lovely person whose parents are involved in her life and who know about her decision to become sexually active. One day she and her father were talking about AIDS and he spoke of the importance of protecting yourself sexually these days, trying to remind his daughter to use a condom, and she blithely replied, "Oh, we don't have to use condoms; my boyfriend checked and no one he's slept with has AIDS." Her quick dismissal of the threat of AIDS, her belief that one can be so certain of a partner's sexual history, brings to mind how much adolescents want to deny mortality, *to deny reality* at times. The vulnerability of adolescents: Was she responding to pressure from her boyfriend not to use a condom? From pressure within herself not to have to ask her boyfriend to use a condom? And the vulnerability of the father and mother who suddenly become aware of how risky the world of sexuality is for their children. Thinking about how close to the edge our children live these days can make any parent want to go lie down and put cold compresses on his or her head.

Yet the key is to keep talking. The father of this lovely girl insisted to his daughter: "It's not that simple!" and they talked about why you *do* need to use a condom. As your friend told you about this, he admitted that part of him wanted to lock his daughter in a closet so she couldn't date, to set 10:00 P.M. curfews, to forbid her to date this boy, as if he could command the tide to roll back. But finally he confessed: "The most important thing is to keep our relationship, our communication, open and alive, all of us—me, her, and her mother. If I get up on too much of a high horse I know she'll just shut down."

Confidence in your kids, an openness to questions, keeping your relationship alive. But there's more. How about the daughter's or the son's wish to be admired by, to impress, their father with their sexual vitality and potency?

Every child wants to preen in front of his or her father, not just have a dialogue.

Here's where a lot of us freeze up as fathers, particularly with our daughters. We shut down just at the point where our children need us the most—to admire their developing sexual potency and attractiveness, that crucial part of any person's self-esteem.

Over lunch a forty-year-old female friend, herself now married with a young daughter, tells you her wonderful adolescent memory of being taught how to flirt as a fourteen-year-old not by her father, for whom the subject was too hot, but by a neighbor. She walked into the living room of her house and the neighbor was sitting there talking with her father. The neighbor complimented her on how good she looked, encouraged her to preen a bit, and taught her about flirting in that way. Her father, she remembers, stood up to look at some books in the middle of the conversation, clearly uncomfortable yet also seemingly grateful to the neighbor for doing what he himself could not do—helping his daughter feel attractive to men.

Fathers can see themselves so quickly in their sons, but what of our daughters? What of the importance and depth of the daughter's need to feel sexually admired by her father?

One father found himself speechless and emotionally "shut down" when his fifteen-year-old daughter paraded through the living room in a flimsy dress during a small dinner party he and his wife were hosting for friends. He was baffled and tongue-tied, but knew he needed to respond. After the girl drifted out of the room, the parents and their friends talked about how "hot" things felt with their adolescents, and the father confessed how at sea he felt with his daughter's sexuality. He had grown up with two brothers and was more used to the "male locker-room" approach. But then one of the other mothers said, "All you have to do is tell her how beautiful she looks, what a lovely young woman she's becoming." She knew from experience how vital a father's affirmation is to a teenage daughter. The father did take his friend's advice, telling his daughter after the party what a beautiful woman she was becoming. That stopped the provocative behavior, as the daughter evidently got what she wanted from her father. The father's talk with his group of friends, male and female, helped to "detoxify" this struggle and to clarify the best response. Maybe the love between a father and daughter is too hot to be left to fathers alone. We need our wives and friends.

What an opportunity having a daughter is for a father's sexual education. You're in the bathroom with your 6-year-old daughter who's taking a leisurely bath half lying on her back, playing in the warm water with the innocence and provocativeness of all young girls, and you get to talking about the birth of her new cousin and she talks of herself having a baby one day while you imagine yourself a grandfather. As your daughter talks about her "eggs," you recall how your wife explained over dinner not too long ago that she has all the eggs she's ever going to have in her body, that's something you never realized before, that all the possible children she may ever have are waiting now in her body, and looking at your daughter you think how wonderful the female body is, how extraordinary it is that this little girl carries your hopes of immortality forward in all those eggs, those unborn children, your grandchildren, waiting to happen. How appreciative you felt of your wife when she explained about the eggs, something you had kind of known and hadn't known at the same time.

You may even think of what a different perspective your daughter provides you on the female body, a source of such mystery all your life, and here you are looking at it, indeed you've seen the vagina more often since your daughter was born than you had in the first forty-one years of your life. And you reflect on what a beautiful organ it is, just like all those flowery, enveloping Georgia O'Keeffe prints, and how mysterious female anatomy has been for you all your life. And then you hear your daughter start to tell you how babies are born, that the egg just grows bigger and bigger and that makes a baby, and she's wondering what makes the egg start to grow, and could it just start like that, and you realize that a piece of information is missing, about penises and sperms and *how* eggs start to grow. So you say that, well, actually there are sperm and those make the eggs grow and she stops playing in the bath water and looks up at you with the confused expression of a child confronting something she never thought of. And you are also confused about what to say next; you don't want her to think that eggs just grow out of nowhere for fear she'll have nightmares about strange things happening in her body, but on the other hand you don't want to interest her too much in this penis-and-sperm thing, worrying that tomorrow at school recess she'll want to put a penis into her vagina, to find out what her daddy has been talking about. Are you being a sexually overstimulating dad to have brought this up in the first place? Are you in some unknown way being provocative here? Then you rebuke yourself, recalling how important it is for your daughter to feel admired by her dad and not to feel that he has abandoned her while she comes to terms with her sexuality.

And while you're wrestling with your thoughts about all this, she asks: "But where does the sperm come from?"

And you look at her and you remember that you and your wife have agreed that the kids will let you know what they want to know and you want to answer directly, and so you plunge ahead and say: "From the husband, the sperm comes out of the man's penis."

So then she wants to know, "But how do the sperm and the eggs get together?" and you want to tell her and don't want to tell her. You feel a sadness in telling her that the penis goes into the vagina and deposits sperm near the egg, it feels like a betrayal, maybe because the reality of intercourse signals the day when she will no longer be just your little daughter, that it foreshadows some fundamental change in your relationship, when her passion for you will belong partly to someone else. But you know, too, that you want to be there for her and to explain what she needs to know, particularly because you see her smart mind working and the thoughtful look in her eyes, and so you go ahead and explain about penises and vaginas and the uterus and how sperms meet the egg, all this in simple and direct language, and she listens and laughs and at first thinks you're joking, but you assure her you're not, and then she gets serious and quiet and obviously is thinking about what she's just heard as she splashes around in the water, and you look at your exquisite six-year-old girl, perfect just as she is, and you wish you could hold back time even as you are so proud of her. Another feeling begins to emerge inside you, a joy and relief, some great pleasure in talking to your daughter about sex, in watching her body, in being her father, and you strive to put it into words—it has to do with feeling that having a daughter has demystified the female body for you, that in explaining to her about sex, watching her listen, seeing her love for you, you have helped heal an old wound about women. You remember how as a kid girls seemed constantly to have so much power, the power to ridicule you and to make you feel like such a fool, that even as you loved your girlfriends in elementary and high school, wishing you could be even more like them, another part of you saw them as critics, judges, as *the other*; they always seemed to know so much more about sex (even if that wasn't true), they seemed in control of what was happening while you thrashed around with old flat top. And here is your daughter teaching you about female vulnerability and need, and suddenly now you feel very grateful to your daughter for this chance to talk about bodies, and men and women, and you realize how we all, men and women, are dependent on each other in this sexual thing.

You think, too, about what it will be like when she is fifteen and comes downstairs in a flimsy dress and how you'll respond. You think about what daughters want from their fathers, and you realize how vital it is that fathers be able to respond to their daughter's developing sexuality in a trustworthy fashion. The vulnerability of the daughter and of the father hits you. The father needs to be able to go, *Wow! What a woman you are becoming!* without being seductive. Now you realize how easy it is for fathers either just to shut down or to become overly flirtatious and how painful either alternative is for both the daughter and the father. The daughter is left feeling abandoned by her father just when she is opening sexually to the world, and the father, though he may love his daughter dearly, ends up imprisoned inside walls built of his own inhibitions, impulses, and fears.

You're struck by how possessive of your daughter you

feel, how much you want to hold on to her and keep her your little girl. How scary a daughter's sexuality can feel to the father because, let's face it, fathers and daughters are lovers, not sexually, but fathers and daughters need to fall head over heels in love with each other, they need to woo and flirt with each other. If the first man in a girl's life doesn't feel she is smashing and beautiful, what will it truly matter to her what the men after him feel?

Then you may realize that a father has to be confident within himself in order to communicate his confidence and faith in his daughter, confident he can let go of his daughter, confident that his daughter has not replaced his wife, that he's not overstepping bounds. He needs confidence to be able to acknowledge her and tell her what a beautiful and exciting woman she is, even as he keeps romance alive with his wife.

And as you pass your son's bedroom later, glancing in at him as he sleeps, you may wonder what kind of affirmation a boy seeks from his father. You think about how boys want to impress fathers and be impressed by them, how often boys don't want to know that their fathers don't know or aren't sure because, after all, your father is your male lineage and every son wants his dad to be a Superman even as he wants him to be just a human being. How difficult it is for fathers to be Men of Steel and just plain flesh-and-blood men for their sons at the same time.

You hope that you'll always be smart enough to look past the swears and provocations to his deeper, unaskable questions, even as you know you won't always be that smart. You hope you can always help him remember that it is okay for him not to know, for him to take his time sorting out what he feels about his body, about those he loves, about what he needs sexually, in the widest sense, that it is okay for him to ask about what he isn't sure of, to ask for what he needs.

And as you walk into the living room and see your lovely wife sitting there, you realize that you wish for yourself those same treasures you just wished for your kids.

As I write, my own father comes to mind. And suddenly I feel enormous gratitude toward him. He must have done something right because I did call on him when I really needed him, years after that day of the adolescent Talk About Sex. It was a moment when the loneliness and anxiety of dealing with sexuality as a young man became overwhelming.

In the fall of my senior year of high school, I flew alone on a weekend from New York City to Washington, D.C., for a college interview. Although I was only away from home a few days, I felt lonely that Saturday afternoon. The prospect of college looming ahead was alive in my mind and the knowledge that in not too long I'd really have to leave home. Sitting in a drugstore having lunch in the seedy area of downtown near the university, I was watching a college football game on the TV above the grill. An older man sat down next to me and started to talk to me and within a few minutes asked me if I'd like to come back to his apartment and watch the football game there.

Something in the man's tone scared me, scared me sexually, although I couldn't have said that then: What would really happen in that room? Even then I wanted to ask: Why don't we just watch the game right here in the drugstore? Who knows, maybe he was just lonely and wanted to fill the emptiness of the apartment. Maybe he just wanted to share his love of football in private. Maybe my loneliness that day confused me, led me to hear something he didn't intend.

I was unnerved enough that I excused myself. I left the drugstore in a rush and went back to my hotel room to watch the football game, alone and scared. What did his invitation mean? What did it say about me?

So picking up the bedside phone in the hotel, I called my father, who was working in his carpet store that Saturday afternoon.

"Hi, Sam, how are you?" His questioning tone reflected how unusual it was for me to call him at work.

"Oh, fine, Dad, just wanted to talk to you."

"What about?"

"Oh, nothing, just here I am in Washington watching a football game."

So we talked about Washington, my college visit, football, and how his business was going that day.

What amazes me now is that we didn't talk about the drugstore incident. I didn't mention it, I didn't want to. All I wanted was to hear my father's voice—to be reminded that I was okay, that home was not so far away, that I was still Sam, his son, no matter what. It's hard now as a father not to think of all those adolescents gripped by anxieties about sexuality or their sexual identity who can't or won't call their fathers. How lonely and afraid an adolescent can feel underneath the bravado.

So I know what I most want to say to my kids: *Call me. I'm here for you no matter what the questions.*

CHAPTER **6**

Growing Past
Our Bounds

Letting Go of Our Children

As I watched the little school bus come down the country road toward our house on the first day of our children's new school year, I was struck by how very different it was from the urban school buses we were used to: stubbier and shorter, it could hold only twenty kids, fully loaded. Emily was starting first grade and Toby fourth grade in our year in New Hampshire.

The driver is a neighbor who lives down the dirt road from us; sometimes he brought his two-year-old along on the route.

This first day of school in September, the bus still felt

imposing to me and daunting to my daughter. Back in the city either Julie or I had always dropped the kids off at school. We lived near enough to the elementary school to walk there on warm mornings. Each morning parents would congregate in front of the school, before or after dropping off their kids. Often it would feel like a rush before work, but dropping your kids off at school is a wonderful, brief entree into their classrooms. You get to see the teachers, meet the kids your child hangs around with, see their work: "Dad, just stay a minute and let me show you the model I'm building." Even when our eight-year-old felt shy about having his dad hang around too long, another third-grader would come up and want to show you something *he's* working on. Now, this year in the country, the little school bus picks our kids up right in front of our house and takes them to the village school, four miles away. *Too far! From our home in Cambridge four miles would take you right into Boston.*

We want our children to be independent, of course, but not *too* independent. We think of letting go of our kids as something that happens in adolescence, and we imagine it as a poignant time for fathers and mothers. Yet, in fact, the separation process is one that starts from the earliest days of parenthood. Often parents learn from children how to master letting go. Sometimes, with the best intentions, we undercut our children's attempts at mastering separation. One thing I've learned from my kids: The best way to help our children deal with the process of holding on *and* letting go of their family is to deal with what it stirs up in *us*.

Separation is an odd feeling, it has an internal gravity of its own. Even in Cambridge, with the school so close, I'd often be aware of a strong pull as the door of the school closed behind them: I'd want to go with them, to be with them, to suddenly suggest, "Let's take this day off and go have some fun together." Often I was relieved to get the kids to school, as I was looking forward to getting to work, seeing a friend, or going to exercise; some days I'd pray, *Oh, please, God, don't let the kids be sick,* and then all of a sudden I'd feel a sudden yearning to linger a while longer with them.

School opened yesterday in a neighboring town. Our local paper had a picture of a youngster weeping as his mother dropped him off at school; standing alone, the child was literally balanced between his teacher waiting at the door and his mother walking toward her car. The mother looked stricken. I wondered: *Where's his father?* Probably at work. Typical—the dad's out of the picture. *What does he feel?* I wondered. *What's appropriate for a father to feel, to do when separating from his children?*

Despite our protestations of confidence and our urgings, Emily had been crying and crying the day before: "I'm scared of school, I don't know anybody."

We were in the car driving home from town after buying some school clothes. We had done a string of errands, all by car—we were learning that in the country people *live* in their cars. The kids had done well with the errands. As we turned toward home, Julie was driving, I was sitting next to Emily in the backseat.

Then Emily started to weep: "I want Daddy to come with me the first day, I want Mommy to come with me!"

White clouds moved across the hills outside the car windows, dark shadows lumbering toward us. It had been a cold and wet summer, some said the result of a volcanic eruption in the Philippines. As Emily cried I felt an empty, lonely feeling in my stomach.

I had assumed we'd go with the kids on the first day. I was as much caught in the memory of our city routine as Emily was. The week before at the PTA dinner, though, Julie had asked the other mothers how they handled the first day of school with their children.

The consensus advice: *Don't take them, let them take the school bus. Be clear with them that they're going on the bus and you'll meet them at the bus stop when they get home.*

"I cried when they left on the bus," testified one mother, "but the kids were so proud of themselves when they got off the bus at the end of the day. They had done it themselves, and they were proud of themselves." *Mastery.* The kids learned to cope with a new experience and felt better about themselves for it. This is what we want to teach, but at what cost? I wondered. And there was the deeper, more painful truth I felt: *I'm too old to be trying to master separations myself!* But we decided, Julie and I, that we would send them alone on the bus the first day.

On the way home in the car, my six-year-old daughter was clear about what she felt: she wept hysterically, explaining that *she can't read, so how can she go to first grade*, and all the reassurance in the world that no one expects her to read after kindergarten, that she's going to learn how to read *in* first grade, didn't help. *But I don't know anybody in the school*, she wails. We remind her that she has several friends in the school, that she has visited the school several times, met the teachers, and that her brother, too, is going to the same school. (Toby seems to take the change more calmly—it's the same bus he took to camp, he knows the driver, and several of the kids in school are his friends.)

When Sartre explained, *"L'enfer, c'est les Autres,"* Hell *is other people,* he may have been thinking of riding in a car with a hysterical child whom you are unable to comfort. The walls of the car seem to press in on me at those moments. It's very tempting to blame someone for this torture: *If Julie wasn't driving she'd reach out to comfort her, what right does she have to be driving!* Or: *Stop that shrieking, you're acting like a six-year-old!* Then I remember that my daughter *is* six years old. But still, unfairly: *What right does she have to be scared of school at her age!*

When a kid falls apart with fear and despair or anger, it shakes up our internal world. The wailing hopelessness rattles me. I suppose a child's panic and terror brings forth my own loneliness. I think about the transition *I'm* going through, that my wife is going through this year—the kids going off to school so early means longer mornings during which I'm alone in the old farmhouse we're living in. My wife is going to work after a year at home with the kids, I'm commuting down to the city two days a week and will be away more than I'd like. All this is the price we're paying for our "year away."

I put my arm around Emily, who is exhausted and just crying softly, my brave girl, she's close to falling asleep, and as we drive along I explore my own fears and emptiness. *Will I be able to complete this book, the writing commitment that I have undertaken for this year? How lonely will it be in an old farmhouse with not a neighbor in sight? How* cold *will it be? Are three cords of wood really enough?*

Then from the front seat I hear someone (my wife? my

son?) ask Emily what clothes she plans to wear to school the next day.

"Oh!" she perks up, suddenly thoughtful. "My black leggings and the sweatshirt with flowers on it and a pair of black shorts." Her voice has a decisive tone to it; the crying has stopped.

With a start I realize that Emily has been able to shift to a new subject quicker than I can—I'm still brooding about loss and separation and loneliness.

The next morning both kids are eager to see what this new adventure holds for them. They get dressed in the cold morning in their new house. I contemplate the optimism and courage of children as I sit on the floor of their room, encouraging them.

Then there's a glitch. Emily's treasured leggings, the kind that hook under the foot, have a rip in the elastic band. I hold my breath, expecting the worst.

"Oh, no problem," Emily observes, holding the ripped elastic leg band. "Mommy can sew it tonight." She looks purposefully through her drawer and pulls out another pair of pants: "I'll wear this one today," she decides.

As she pulls them on, while her brother gets dressed near his bed, Emily bends close to me and confides: "I'm scared today, but I won't be tomorrow or the next day." I tell her how proud I am of her, give her a big hug.

Then I realize: *My children teach me about mastering separations.*

This fall the morning mist on the pond—wonderful, wispy clouds of vapor dancing in the breeze—was invoking the spirit of friends from the city not with us this year. We began to speak of the spirals of dancing mist as the "lake gods," a family term invented to refer to friends and family encouraging us in our year of change.

Over breakfast Toby looks out the window and sees the mist on the pond this chilly fall morning. "Look, it's the lake gods dancing for us."

"Yes," says Julie, "they've come to wish you a good day at school." She's drawn the lesson too sharply, too full of good cheer.

"Oh, Mom," advises Toby, now pragmatic, "just stow it." But he looks longer at the lake gods dancing on the mist and seems to like the thought.

Through the forested dawn, the little bus comes down the road. With its headlights on, all bright and cheerful, the bus is reminiscent of the Little Engine That Could. "I think I can—I think I can."

The kids are sitting on the front step of our walk as it pulls up, and we're out there with them—Mom with a camera, me with a cup of tea, the four of us sitting there savoring the beauty of the lake, the lake gods pirouetting through the mist, reminding us of why we had made this change, this year away.

As the bus approaches, I can feel my internal gravity resisting this separation. Astronauts off in their lunar module. *I copy you, home base.* I don't want to launch them, and I do want to. My eyes start to itch, there's a puffiness, and I remember that I picked up Emily's conjunctivitis. *Conjunctivitis?* That's a kid's eye infection. How embarrassing: total merger with my children.

The bus comes to a stop. The driver gives us all a cheerful, if sleepy, hello. I want to give my kids something before they go. I look at my son, and he seems so brave, so organized, regardless of how rattled he may feel inside. I have an urge to bend on one knee, so we're eye to eye, and wish him "Godspeed," my hands on his shoulders, as a king might say to his trusted explorer about to set to sea.

My son would likely find that a little much.

For days, though, I've been trying to find some advice, some magic words that would ward off loneliness and fear. But nothing very profound comes to mind. Where's the fatherly bon mot to see them through, the treasure of insight that will make the kids turn to me in gratitude and reply: "Thanks, Dad"?

Instead of the magic solution, the charmed protection against their human share of terror, aloneness, curiosity, and joy, all I have is the comfort I can provide, the arm on the shoulder, the soft words of encouragement, the reminder that "I love you" and that they are great, wonderful, blessed children.

And that comfort is no small gift for me to give to them. Yet how much comfort to provide? What about *mastery*? I remind myself. I want them to cope with this and not to cling too much. Where's the balance? Yet let's be honest here: I'm not sure even who's doing the clinging, them to me or me to them.

My son in his jeans jacket with the attached sweatshirt hood and my daughter in her flowered sweatshirt climb aboard the bus. Julie wants to take a picture of the kids getting on the bus. Toby rolls his eyes—"Oh, Mom!"—and then both kids smile for the camera. A friendly word to the driver from us and they're off. As the bus pulls away I notice that Toby and Emily go to separate seats.

To my surprise I find myself crying as their bus leaves. Julie does a double take, asks am I really crying, and I joke: "No, my conjunctivitis is just acting up."

Alone now, unfamiliar with our marital solitude after the summer soup of unstructured time with the kids, we sit on the stoop with our cups of tea.

"Don't you just want to go and observe?" Julie asks. "It's not like I want to merge with them—just want to go and watch. Be a fly on the wall. I want to see what they're doing, *how* they're doing."

My wife as usual is on target, except I *do* want to merge and go off with them!

I'm not sure why I imagine them as lonely or vulnerable during these transitions. For me the school bus was a fun place. We got picked up at the end of the dead end street I lived on, and the five-minute walk to the bus stop was always mixed with the fear and wish of missing the school bus. The bus was a portal into a new world, a world away from my family and all the preoccupations of our house. It was a social world. We relived the TV shows of the night before, Maverick's exploits or Paladin or Steve Allen or Ed Sullivan. On Mondays we used to divide into two groups, depending on whether we preferred Steve Allen's irreverent humor to the traditionalism of Solemn Sullivan, as we called him. There were neighborhoods on the bus—the younger kids learned to stay out of the back of the bus where the bigger boys used to sit and practice swearing, concoct evil plots, and comment on the opposite sex, while the younger kids sat up front, nearer to the bus driver.

When I was quite young the school bus driver and I had the same first name, so I was convinced for days that we were related.

We go off on the school bus all our lives, and parents and children have to negotiate that. The school bus soon turned into an airplane for me. Every summer during my college and graduate school years I went to Europe and the Middle East, usually to work, once as a busboy in a restaurant, another time at a university, always finding time to hitchike around and have adventures I wouldn't write home about.

One summer I got a job through a contact as a research assistant for a psychology professor at the University of Paris. I was reading articles in American journals and summarizing them in English for him. Sounded simple and safe enough, particularly to my parents. There was a tone of pride in their voices as they spoke of their son spending his summer "working at the University of Paris." Except this was 1968—the summer of the riots in Paris. Mai soixante-huit, May '68, in the simple phrase the French use to refer to the student riots that created national turmoil and brought down the De Gaulle government.

My pleasure in having a cozy room in the professor's home in a Parisian suburb gave way to a fascination with the goings-on in the student quarter, on the Left Bank of Paris. I began finding places to sleep there. I quickly learned the French word for tear gas, *lacrymogène*. You had to watch your step walking down the main street, the Boulevard St.-Michel, since the students had ripped up the ancient paving stones and hurled them at the police. Oh, the glory of it, sharing my baguette with French students in the sunny courtyard of a liberated building.

One night on a side street near the Boul Mich, a group of students came running past, telling me to run, *vite, vite*, and I looked further down the street and there was a wave of the dreaded French Riot Police, the CRS, clad in their helmets and uniforms, looking like Darth Vader before there even was Darth Vader, in hot pursuit of them, of us. Here was terror. The day before a young French girl had been blinded when a French cop, by accident or intent, had fired a tear gas grenade point-blank into her face.

But what feels wired into my memory, into my being? The exhilaration of the run down the street, of fleeing into a chemistry laboratory and barring the door by putting a broken bench through the door handles and standing there listening to the CRS troopers pounding on the door but unable to get in.

Did they have a battering ram? When my compatriots learned I was American, what fun we had! How my pride surged. What do the Americans make of what's going on in France? Will Nixon be reelected? Tell us about the Doors!

Mastery.

No, there was no battering ram, we all slept in the building, about thirty of us, and the next day after a triumphant breakfast I walked one of the female students home down a battered street past a phalanx of angry, watchful French police, hoping that the American passport in my inside coat pocket still retained its magical ability to stop tear gas grenades or truncheon blows.

When my mother called and asked how I was, I told her, "I'm working at the University of Paris." I left out the other parts.

You leave out the scary parts when talking to your parents. Yet the danger and excitement and stupidity of it, thumbing my youthful, seemingly immortal nose at the gods, seemed to be exactly the point. There must be a god who protects parents from knowing the risks their children are taking. And each generation imagines the world is surely more dangerous for its kids.

Now here I was on an early fall day in New Hampshire, twenty-three years after my Parisian exploits with French girls and rampaging police, watching my children drive away on a little yellow school bus, off on their own adventure. How will it go? Will they tell me when they return, or will it be that they're "working at the University of Paris"?

I can't work all that morning. My concentration is off, and even though there is a lot for me to do, I don't get down to it. Julie and I sit around together, drain several cups of tea, and realize that we're waiting for them to come home. I'm not going to be able to concentrate until I know how this first day went for them.

We consider a joke: "Wouldn't it be funny if we were standing on the stoop at three-thirty when they return, just as we were when they left—Mom with the camera, Dad with his cup of tea, as if we had been frozen in exactly the same position all day, just waiting for them."

They probably wouldn't get it. You have to be a parent.

About midday, I decide to make calls, a good way to get something done when you can't concentrate. I call up my friend John in Boston to talk about a writing project we're doing together. There's an odd tone in his voice, he sounds distracted, and finally he confesses: "Actually I'm kind of disoriented."

John explains that he's just helped his daughter get settled over the weekend at her first apartment in Boston and he spent part of the past week in the Midwest dropping his son off at college and staying for the freshman orientation.

"Geez, it must feel weird to have them scattered all over the country like that," I suggested.

"It's not a question of scattered, it's the loss I feel. Our home just does not feel the same." John tells me about shopping earlier in the week at the supermarket. "Going to buy soda pop and fruit, then realizing that we hardly needed them anymore. Our son is the big consumer of soda, he's the one who loves fruit."

We reserve the word *loss* for traumatic, big events like the death of a loved one. Yet loss also means the breaking of familiar routines, trusted assumptions about the world, reassuring habits of the heart.

"I cried last week at the college orientation; my wife was more composed then, and now *she's* crying," John explained.

One child settled, now the other. "My daughter is in a loft with three other women," he continued. "These lofts are so strange—there's more people in that part of Boston than in the downtown at night. At least she's relatively safe—it's above a section of jewelry stores, lots of police patrols."

How safe are any of us? The daughter of a friend of mine was murdered in New York two years after her college graduation. In *Captain Newman, M.D.* Leo Rosten reminds us how capricious our lives are: "how can one deny that all our lives hang by threads of nothing more than luck? A vagrant microbe or an oil slick on the road, an open door, the leak in a gas line, a madman encountered by chance—against these what matter all our painful accumulations of virtue, knowledge, nobility, sacrifice?"

It's one thing to acknowledge the thread of luck and hope that keeps our lives together, it's another to think of our children's lives balanced so precariously.

My friend John's pain seems deeper than mine. I'm waiting for my kids to come home that afternoon; he's not sure when his daughter will come home to visit: "Sam, she's no longer in her bedroom when I go to check."

The circle of his daughter's orbit away from him is on my friend's mind. He wonders whether she'll move away from the East Coast entirely, perhaps out west as she has mentioned: "She's been off at college, but there's a rhythm to that. We know when to expect her home. Now she's got her own job, she's become an independent decision maker; she can go wherever she wants." If a child's departure for college creates anticipatory grief for many fathers, the first job can begin true mourning.

When my brother and I both moved out of the New York City area after college, my father hit the roof, and I remember thinking how like a Neanderthal he seemed when he protested, "But the grandchildren will be raised in New England!" as if you needed a visa to visit here. His objections seemed so silly that it was easy to dismiss his pain, but now I can feel what he must have felt—the sense of not being able to breathe, of having to let go of what you value so much and to adapt and rearrange your life.

There's a vulnerability that parents are prey to in the connection to their kids. We live so much of our lives within them. Fathers may construct their family lives in part to protect themselves from this fact, keeping busy at work, being competent around the house, always having some home project to do, making sure their kids are all right, and then the kids leave and they confront their aloneness and reliance on their kids. When will they call? When will I see them? Are they okay? A father of teenagers recently told me, as he prepared for their departure from home over the coming years: "I am nowhere as vulnerable as in the place where I connect with my children. The thought of their being hurt or worse is staggering. Part of me is convinced that if one were to die I simply could not go on living."

And yet our kids' departures from home do not bring down unrelieved gloom. A year after his daughter moved across town to her own apartment, my friend Tom called me for one of our periodic talks. An involved father, he had really missed his daughter. We hadn't spoken in several months, and now something had changed. Tom sounded quite cheery, and he was "happy to report that my wife and I are having a great time—we're getting past the depression." He went on to say that his fear was that his children were going to disappear completely, and that was not the case. His daughter calls quite often, she comes over for dinner. He's also noticed that the quality of their contact has changed: "Now that she really is more off on her own, my daughter will call spontaneously, she initiates it, not like the perfunctory Sunday phone call from the kids when they were in college."

Often a couple's sex life improves after the kids leave home. "It's not so easy to have sex with your wife when your home is inhabited by teenagers, struggling with their hormones," another father, fifty years old, told me. "Now that the kids have their own places, it feels like my wife and I are back in our early twenties; we make love when we want to, and it's easier to stop seeing your wife as a parent, it feels more like we're dating again, like before we even had kids." As he spoke of their "dates"—going off on long bike rides together, talking and laughing over leisurely dinners—it's clear that their relationship, not just their sex life, had become fun again, and enriching.

Yet for many parents the wells of sorrow run deep, too deep to fathom. They carry a sense of finally, irrevocably having missed out on something now that the children are no longer there; they worked so hard all those years when no one really saw what they sacrificed in providing for the children. And then the children leave. I hardly had time to say thank you to my parents as I beat it out the door to adulthood. It just didn't seem important then. Now that I'm a father Yeats's observation that no man has ever had enough "of children's gratitude or woman's love" sounds different to me. Less like an indictment of fathers and more like a lament.

In his poem "Hearing My Son Play," Alvaro Cardona-Hine describes a father entering his teenage son's bedroom to listen to his boy play Bach and Brahms on the violin. There's first a soupy, swampy merging of his son and himself: "handsomely into his instrument his door he/you hear him enter you sense/this antecedent of sorrow/a quiet an almost invisible presence." The father and son are joined: "you and I my son we two are rivers."

The father's awed appreciation of his son's accomplishments becomes filled with a sense of growth too wonderful to oppose yet also frightening: "I remember your smallness in your mother's arms/it was the smallness of an instrument/that would grow out of bounds."

The speed with which our children grow, catching us unawares, is captured in William Kloefkorn's poem "Out-and-Down Pattern." A young son pushes a football into his father's stomach and tells him he's doing "an out-and-down pattern." The boy is "halfway across the front lawn" before the father can position the ball in his hands, and finally he gets ready and he throws the ball in a high arc to "the figure/that has now crossed the street,/that is now all the way to Leighton Avenue." As the ball begins to drift down "weightless/atop the streetlights and the trees, becoming at last that first bright star in the west," the father sees that "My son is gone."

Maybe it's the recognition of missed opportunity that fuels our sorrow, but maybe also when our kids move we have a sharper sense of being stuck in our own lives. Perhaps we envy the easy, fluid intimacy our children have, so unlike the fixed, predictable loneliness that pervades our lives. Maybe the loneliness comes from not having our sorrow recognized and validated, by others or by ourselves.

The kids leave the house, wives become occupied with other projects, and a man has to confront his own internal sense of emptiness at age forty or fifty. That may be the first time he's had to do so, the busyness of work and family life having masked it until then.

One father, seeing his adolescent daughter play the piano at a school recital, put his jealousy into words: "I looked at her playing Mozart, and my admiration was tempered by resentment. Here she knew—she knew about music and passion, things I've struggled all my life with." It may be hard for a father to imagine filling the void that departing children have left in his life. Where does he find the freedom and passion to seize new opportunities?

One of the hidden secrets of fatherhood is how much and how early your kid begins to separate from you. Wallowing in the stressful early years of fatherhood, you think that this will just go on forever, that your kids will take over your life and never give you a moment of privacy. Yet the separations begin to come so quickly—going to school is such a big one, then sleepovers and weekends at friends' houses, then the adolescent who connects to the peer group, and then the transition and "launching" of kids into adulthood. We talk about them as if they were missiles, but our hearts go with them, as well as our envy.

And there is also our sense of mortality: the aging of our children marks our own aging. A father of a daughter, now twenty-two, is clearly proud of her ability to finish school and get herself a fine job. But then he quotes Gerard Manley Hopkins's poem about Margaret grieving "Over Goldengrove unleaving." There is a definite element of sadness in my friend's voice. He explains the Hopkins poem: each burst of growth also marks the passage of time, brings with it the reality of death. He's reminded of his own growing older, "of my own mortality."

Where are the poems about fathers letting go of daughters? It's easy to find father-son poems about letting go, harder to find father-daughter poems on this theme. Perhaps the letting go is different. It may be that the rupture between fathers and daughters is less sharp than that between fathers and sons. Maybe daughters don't go off in quite the same way as sons do. In a way daughters don't go as far, many of them remain as "the family ambassador," staying connected. Or is it harder for fathers to speak of the letting go of daughters because it taps some deeper loss for them? Our daughters may become like our "second wife," and the reality of letting go of a daughter may leave a father sunk in a gloom for which he can't really find words.

Fathers may get tripped up as well by the lousy educations we receive as boys about mastering separation and loss. There's so much emphasis on performance and living up, on controlling your feelings. We look at the men around us for models, and what do we see? For me my father comes to mind. When I went off to college in 1963, to the University of Vermont, there was no interstate direct from Westchester County to Burlington, Vermont. It was almost a day's drive, and my parents packed all my stuff in the trunk of our car and drove me up. That evening we met my college roommate, unloaded the car, and then we all—my parents, my new roommate, and I—went out to dinner. The next morning my parents and I stood in the dormitory parking lot and tried to say good-bye. I stood there eager for them to leave, yearning for them to stay, teetering between wanting to get on with "my life on my own" and wanting to run back into their car and drive back to New York with them. My mother was very clear about her feelings, even as she tried to hide them: she wore dark glasses on this most cloudy of days, and she clearly had been crying her eyes out. My father seemed much more opaque, hard to read. I can't get him into focus. I remember him standing by the car as we all said good-bye. He worried about having the right maps for the drive home, he said he and my mother really ought to get started, they had to make sure to beat the Sunday afternoon traffic home to New York. There was a handshake from my father, an eye-to-eye look between us, a hug from my mother, and then they were gone. Did he cry on the way home?

But when my kids left for school on that school bus on a September morn twenty-nine years later, I finally knew what my father had felt that day in the UVM parking lot and had been unable to say or even show. How much fathers feel that they can't express. The memory of my father that day now filled me with a warm feeling: *He felt sad to see me go! Behind his opaqueness lived passionate feelings of love and relief and regret and pride!*

We go through this together, fathers as well as mothers, in words unspoken. Suddenly the father, absent from the newspaper picture on his child's first day of school, comes into focus, and I feel less lonely waiting for my children to come home, less like a freak with my mix of sadness and relief and confusion.

Months later a friend of mine, Ben, calls to suggest we meet for coffee. He says he's struggling with some career decisions and wants to talk. Sitting in Friendly's coffee shop early in the morning I'm baffled at his talk about wanting to close down his law practice because he's really quite successful, but he tells me how bored and tired of his work he is, and then he mentions that his kids are near to graduating high school and they spend so much time outside the home in sports and he's enjoyed the time coaching them in hockey so much and a certain desperate tone enters his voice as he tells me that, well, the truth be told he's thinking of opening a camp for adolescents and he realizes how much he enjoys his kids and wishes he could have more of them just when they're soon going off to college. We talk about our love for our kids, and he laughs and says, well, maybe he won't leave his lucrative law practice, maybe he could simply spend more time with his own kids or if they won't do that since they are now determined to prove their independence, then maybe he'll master this change and loss with other kids. He'll keep on coaching hockey in his spare time, he'll find other ways of coping rather than changing careers, and he'll look forward to his children's visits home from college. As we talk together over the hot coffee we both feel good recognizing the truth: Our children are going, they're growing up. My friend sighs and says, "I'll miss them" and stares at me in silence.

Then he says, "So enjoy yours!"

"But mine feel halfway out the door already!" I protest.

"Have another one."

"Come on, Ben, that's not realistic—they all grow up."

My friend's sense of loss touches my own: "We fall in love with them, give them so much, and then they leave us," I blurt out, somewhat morosely.

My friend looks at me without saying anything, then looks down at his coffee. A few moments pass, then we start talking about who's got the check for breakfast. There was a time when I might have thought: *Oh, just another dumb, inarticulate man, leaving me out on a limb here, I have all these feelings and he doesn't.* And yet I don't think this now. I felt a deeper connection with my friend, the silence between us holding so much hope, loss, and love. Some of that loneliness of being a man melted away: his silence felt warming and not cold, a big change for me, not to feel angry at men's silence but warmed by it. Maybe it came from watching my children go off to school, from thinking of my father looking at me with love unspoken as he drove away from that UVM parking lot. And so, instead of being disappointed, I felt, *Ben knows, he understands.* A father may feel there's more than you can put into words, more than you can say, so why try?

Maybe we make too much of the separation part and not enough of the connection. Just as we leave, we also return. As grown sons and daughters we are constantly returning to our fathers and mothers for emotional refueling, just as they return to us. After a divorce, for instance, a son may spend some time with his father just wanting to make sure that his father still loves him, that he is still his father's son. A daughter goes to her father when she's having difficulty at work "just to talk"—she wants less for him to solve the problem than to feel his presence, to be refueled by his love and attention. This year I anticipate Thanksgiving in our house, look forward to making up a snazzy menu, printing it off on my computer, sending it to my parents and the friends who are coming. I talk with the kids about the visit of their grandparents and suddenly I realize: *I want to see my mother and father*. And when my parents arrive and I've coaxed them into staying several days, making it clear that they're not imposing on us, I see how they are nourished by their time with us. Now I understand, as I never could have at age twenty-five, the amusement of my friend Ted, who tells me as Christmas nears that his aged father called asking him to bring his son over. His dad wanted to give him a model railroad set, it's the set he had as a boy, and his father now wants to give it to his grandson. When Ted tells his father that his grandson is away on a school trip that weekend, the old man replies, "That's okay, why don't you come alone?" And so Ted goes home and they search through the attic, through the detritus of years, to find the old Lionel locomotive and the track, and then his father suggests they put the tracks together, and he and his father set up the whole set and spend the afternoon playing with the trains, just like in the old days. Later, as he tells this story, Ted says to me: "I think my father really wanted just for the two of us to play with that old train set; the gift to my son was just a pretext."

We truly do a dance of separation and connectedness, parents and children, all our lives. One moment we're the daddy, then the son, in search of mom, in search of dad, then we're the daddy again, as our kids search for, reject, and refind us.

This cold fall morning, the first day of school, talking on the phone with John while I wait for my kids, I want to find something to say, to connect directly with my friend. So I speak the truth: "John, it's good to talk to you. When are we going to see each other?"

"Yeah, it'll be good to see you; I want to hear more about your year away in New Hampshire. How is that going? There are a lot of changes in your life, too, aren't there?"

So I start to tell him about how great it is to be here and how scary. We look forward together to seeing our kids, mine in a few hours, his when they find time to come home. I know suddenly as we talk that my kids will do fine, they'll muddle through just as I did. In a few hours I'll be able to see that look of mastery and accomplishment on their faces, their satisfied expressions telegraphing that *we did it, we made it to the new school and back on our own!*

And then I realize how I learn about mastering separation and change and loss: from my kids, from my wife, from my parents, and from my friends.

John and I joke, scheme, make plans together.

Off we go in the yellow school bus, the energy of our schemes and jokes lighting the way through new territory.

CHAPTER 7

SPIRITUAL PASSIONS

"**D**addy, which part of me is Jewish and which part of me is Christian?" asks your daughter as you drive home through the lovely New England countryside, the trees just showing a hint of the foliage season soon to begin.

It's the day before Rosh Hashanah—the Jewish New Year, which falls in late September this year—and you've been talking with both your kids in the car about going to temple the next day. Since your wife is Protestant and you're Jewish, the kids have gotten a quilted version of religion, combining all possible holidays. Easter, Passover, Christmas, Hanukkah, about the only one you haven't brought into your house is a Shinto Day of Worship. That'll be next. You seem to have all religions in your home, but do you have any?

It seems sensible that the Jewish New Year is celebrated in the fall rather than on January 1. You like the idea of beginning the new year in a time of endings and beginnings: harvest, the passing of summer, the reopening of school. As you and the kids get into a confused dialogue about calendars, you realize this is the year 5753 on the Jewish calendar. For over three thousand five hundred years the Jews have been doing their thing, subtracting a few years for the Creation and prehistory. You point out this long lineage to your children with some pride.

"But there's only 1992 years in the world," replies your son, a child of the Western calendar.

"No, no—that's only since the birth of Christ."

You try to explain that Jewish history goes way back, before the birth of Christ. You don't want to sound possessive about this, as if Judaism is *better* than Christianity or anything, but you do want to interest your kids in this part of their religious heritage.

"Well, Daddy, do you mean the Jews lived when there were cavemen and dinosaurs and everything?" your thoughtful son responds.

Sometimes you wonder which part of *you* is Jewish. You were raised a conservative Jew, but somewhere along the line, almost without realizing it, you drifted away from organized religion. Something happened: the 1960s. You were so busy questioning authority, rebelling, protesting the injustice all around you—and Judaism seemed so insular, so smug. You remember the undercurrent of materialism in the suburban Jewish community of your childhood, the self-congratulatory way that families would parade their cars and possessions—"the chosen people," chosen perhaps to shop? Your bar mitzvah was a painful experience that you struggled through awkwardly, never really feeling welcomed as a young man into the religious community. Much of the ritual and tradition of Judaism has felt pretty empty to you over the years.

Yet you protest too much. Clearly Judaism did give you something, for you *feel* Jewish. You remember the last time you went by yourself, just for yourself, to temple—thirty years ago, in the fall of your freshman year in college, a time when you were very lonely. The University of Vermont in the early sixties was a very un-Jewish place, far from home, where you were filled with the sadness and emptiness called "homesickness." You went that fall to the High Holy Day services at a synagogue in Burlington and felt very soothed and restored by the service itself, the language, the singing, the chanting. That freshman year visit to the synagogue gave you a sense of belonging, a sense of coming from somewhere and being part of something. It reminded you of home in the deepest sense when you felt internally homeless. That's a gift you want to give your children—a sense of belonging in the world, a feeling of rootedness.

So here you are, not particularly devout yourself, wanting to provide your children a framework of spiritual values and belief that roots them in the world.

You wonder: *Does the ecumenism of your family allow you to sidestep basic questions about faith?* A more nagging question: *Where is the spiritual part of you?*

Having a child raises anew unanswered questions about spirituality, faith, and how we make meaning of our existence on this planet—questions that some of us put aside when we were young. It's hard to give our children a sense of meaning unless we ourselves are clear about our views on what C. S. Lewis called "the deeper magic before the beginning of time."

All parents, whether in same-faith or interfaith marriages, struggle with basic questions of faith, belief, meaning-making. It's pretty hard to raise a child with *any* kind of spirituality in America today. How do we incorporate spiritual values into our child rearing when we live most of our lives in a nonspiritual world? Thinking about our children's religious education necessitates a continuation of our own.

Fathers confront a basic dilemma about spirituality: To really educate our children morally we have to enter the mystery of belief and faith with them, yet we ourselves may not be comfortable with our own vulnerability and uncertainty about faith. We may not feel all that comfortable with "organized religion" or the "values thing." Or we may not have given much thought to the values and beliefs we want to hand down to our children. Fathers can play a crucial role in vitalizing ritual and belief for their children. Yet to do that means to explore our own vulnerability, our joy and shame about belief.

Religion and being spiritual are two different matters. Spirituality means nurturing your "spirit," the sense of joy and wonder in the world; religion refers to established practices and rituals for worship and prayer. For some people they come together, but for you that hasn't so far happened.

There's a bit of the pagan in you—at times you feel there's more spirituality in the pond outside your home than in all the synagogues of your youth. You want your children to know of mystery and wonder—Jewish, Christian, Hindu, Native American, and whatever else lives around you.

Just the other day you read a passage by C. S. Lewis that moved you very much: "Say your prayers in the garden early, ignoring steadfastly the dew, the birds and the flowers, and you will come away overwhelmed by its freshness and joy; go there in order to be overwhelmed, and after a certain age, nine times out of ten nothing will happen to you."

Freshness and joy, finding renewal. Not easy matters at any age. How does a father communicate that to his kids? How do we get renewed ourselves? For you solitude and time in the world of nature lifts your spirit and reminds you of life's magic. The beaver in the pond outside your window is working near the edge of the shore as you write. You watch him and feel healed and renewed by his simple acts, by the endless cycles of time that live in his actions. Driving this morning past marshland near your house, you marveled at the ice-frost that last night's freeze created—the sun glistening through the crystals, the radiance alive within the yellow-brown fields of swamp grass gone—dead? hibernating?—for the winter. What a beautiful sight!

The miraculous surfaces, too, when we penetrate our normal human loneliness and find real connection between ourselves and those around us. The miraculous often lives in play and humor.

Last Halloween you came home from the office at 5:00 P.M. to meet your kids for trick-or-treating. When they came to the door they found you wearing your suit and tie with your daughter's court jester hat perched on your head. They shouted with laughter at the sight of a grown-up in a suit and tie wearing a silly hat. You loved to see the laughter in their eyes, and you hoped, too, that they could see the playfulness you felt. You don't want to overdo its significance, but for you this was a spiritual moment, a manifestation of your faith that adults need to play, too. You want your children to know that a wacky spirit can live within a suit and tie. You constantly have to remember that yourself. So many adults, yourself included, seem so serious all the time. *Do your homework! Take out the trash! Don't forget to practice your saxophone!* It's really important to get your work done, all your life, but that's not all there is to being human. Let's not forget play.

Being spiritual, finding renewal must also lie in our ability to laugh at our fate as human beings, to thumb our noses at the gods, and playful humor is a way to do that.

Which is fine for you, but what about your children's *moral education*, their sense of cooperation and fairness and respect for life, their awareness of history and tradition? When your kids were young you didn't have to think much about fostering basic values beyond what you and your family modeled every day, but now that your kids are older you wonder about what they're learning on MTV, from the advertising all around them, from their peer group.

As your kids close in on adolescence, you sometimes feel like circling the wagons before the materialistic values of our culture totally wipe out whatever deeper moral education you want to give your kids. "Moral education"? What does that mean exactly anyway? You really haven't thought much about that amid the daily crush of trying to raise your kids—get them to school on time, to camp on time, earning a living and keeping your marriage together. Who has time for "moral education"? Your wife hasn't forgotten—she keeps insisting, pushing, raising questions about what we really believe, what our moral values are. *After all, kids need structure and concrete symbols to believe in besides advertising slogans and TV commercials.* You agree, but you also feel inept, unsure. Fathers are supposed to have the answers to issues of faith and values and yet haven't you, a child of the 1960s, absented yourself from this part of your kids' life?

You went to Rosh Hashanah services in September with the kids, and to your surprise you felt a deep satisfaction at sitting next to your children with your tallis, the Jewish prayer shawl, draped around your shoulders, just as you did when you were a kid going to synagogue with your parents. The kids seemed reserved and tentative, as if being offered foreign food in some strange new restaurant. They liked missing school that day but were eager to get back home early enough that afternoon to see their friends. No one seemed eager for a return visit. This foray to a local temple didn't really resolve matters, for you or for them. The "religion question" was still on your mind three months later, in December.

So the phone call from a neighbor that came on a cold December morning the week before Hanukkah as you puttered in your kitchen felt almost providential. A mother in town was calling to invite you and your family to a Hanukkah party for families, "mostly interfaith ones," she pointed out. The public school in your small New Hampshire town was trying not to single out any particular religious holidays since some parents opposed bringing too much religion into the school, but others were angry that there was not enough "Christian celebration." So there was no Christmas party, no Hanukkah party, just a winter solstice party. Your son was pissed that there was no Christmas party; the "Winter Solstice" evidently didn't count for him.

The mother on the phone was almost apologetic for calling: "Your kids' teachers were reluctant to say that you were Jewish; they weren't sure if you wanted to be identified in that way." Has religious affiliation replaced sex as the taboo topic in our culture? She went on to say that her children were overjoyed to hear that there was another Jewish family in the school, and as you listened you impulsively wanted to blurt out, "Wait, we're not just Jewish, we're mixed." Part of you, resenting her call, didn't want to talk about the religion question.

You didn't say that though. In fact part of you was deeply pleased to think of the kids as Jewish, plain and simple. As your neighbor talked, friendly and direct, she mentioned something about her own interfaith experience: she's Jewish, but raised basically "nonpracticing," while her husband is a nonpracticing Catholic who clearly loves Judaism. Their son recently decided to be bar-mitzvahed: "He's told us he wants to think of himself as Jewish for now."

Talking with her you realized how lonely you've been struggling with this spiritual question. You and your wife talk a lot about belief and faith, you're fortunate that you're both interested in and skeptical of your own religious backgrounds and that you both respect and admire each other's traditions. You're aware of resisting becoming too involved in the Jewish part of your experience. *But it might be good for the kids to go to this party,* you thought.

Which is all well and good, but the weekend before Christmas your parents have just arrived for a short visit and you felt a familiar dread as you watched your elderly father, raised Orthodox, walk into the house to find a Christmas tree and Hanukkah menorah cohabiting. He's used to it already, he's seen it here before and he didn't comment. He's patient and understanding; by age seventy-nine he's seen it all.

You're aware, though, of having put the menorah out in the center of the room on a table with a book about Jewish holidays next to it. You make sure he sees them.

As the sun sets, it's time to light the Hanukkah candles. Your yarmulkes rest on the table next to the menorah. Dad puts on his, a regal white skullcap with the Jewish star sewn on it in purple, and you don yours, a knitted blue one with gold trim. The slight weight of the skullcap feels good on your head, a familiar feeling, a father's hand gently resting on your hair. You hand your son his yarmulke, light-blue felt material hand-painted with a city scene of old Jerusalem ... and he puts it down on the table.

He doesn't want to put on the yarmulke, he's reluctant and shy, and you find yourself suddenly furious. You want him to put it on even as he reminds you of yourself. As teenagers you and your brother snuck into the living room of your suburban home during a Hanukkah celebration and played Christmas carols on the record player as the candles were being lit in the dining room. The two of you had been possessed by a sudden desire to hear "Silent Night, Holy Night" just as your family was asserting

its Jewishness! You thought it would be funny and everyone would laugh. What rebellious planet were you living
on? Nobody got the joke; your father was furious.

Still, remembering your own struggles helps you with
your son's. Looking at his yarmulke on the table, you understand why a son or daughter would choose not to be a
part of a religion that seems so strange and unfamiliar, so
sparse and abstract, particularly here in this New England
town literally dominated by the white church on the
common.

How beautiful that church is, pure white and clean,
with long black shutters framing every window, the simple, elegant spire reaching toward the sky. Last year it was
renovated so that a basement could be built to house classrooms. While it was raised up on enormous jacks for several weeks, a jestful banner on the outside of the building
flapped exuberantly in the breeze proclaiming, "Nearer my
God to thee."

You wish you felt that freedom to be so public and confident about your religion. Driving past that bold banner,
you'd think about the fear of being different, how rarely
your children see the menorah and yarmulkes. No wonder
Judaism seems weird and different, particularly for a preadolescent boy trying to be in the in-group. He likely
doesn't want to wear a yarmulke because it looks stupid; at
age nine what's most important to him is how things look.
In this community he sees no one else putting on a yarmulke. Nor do you. There's a saying: It takes a village to
raise a child.

Finally, though, your wonderful boy looks at his dad and
his grandfather and he puts on the yarmulke. Your mother
and daughter say the prayers and light the candles and

open the presents for the first night of Hanukkah. Watching your seventy-year-old mother and her six-year-old granddaughter light the candles warms you, the sense of time and eternity and the flow of generations. Standing there you retrieve a memory long forgotten: As a boy your mother would light the Shabbat candles every Friday evening in the dining room and you'd all gather around the table in front of the big beveled mirror and she'd gather her hands around the candles in a traditional gesture of welcoming Shabbat into your home. You remember the grace of her hands those evenings. How could you have forgotten that?

As the children open their Hanukkah presents you wonder what you all will make of that Hanukkah party the next night. You mention it to your father, *Tomorrow night we're going to a Hanukkah party, Dad!* and he seems pleased. Oh, you do want so much to be a good boy for your father!

But come off it—that's not all there is here. Yes, you want to please your father and mother, and it's crucial to be aware of that wish so as not to sacrifice your children to your parents. Yet also *you* want to pass on some traditions, some sense of *belonging* to your son and daughter. How else do you connect the generations unless you pass on some of your beliefs and your heritage? This, if anything, is the parents' role, making faith and tradition real to their children.

You arrived at the party early the next evening, having come from a production of *A Christmas Carol* in town. Dad had sat quietly between his grandchildren through this celebration of Christmas past, present, and future and the restoration of faith in a man who had become so greedy and self-centered that he could not find joy any-where in the world. When Scrooge realized the depth of his loneliness and found joy in being alive you had tears in your eyes—you always cry at this point. And when he looked at the grave marker with his name on it, you couldn't help wondering what your father made of that—how do we face death as we age? You glanced across the seats at him in the darkened theater, but his face offered no clue.

After the play you dropped your tired parents off at their motel while they encouraged you to go to the party. Mom advised, "At least if you bring them up with the tra-ditions they'll have those traditions," and she looked at your daughter, concluding, "just in case she marries a Jew-ish man."

The party's at a home in a nearby village, small and quite wealthy. You pass a nativity scene on the common in the center of town along the way. As you walk up to the front door of the house, you're aware of not wanting it to seem *too Jewish* inside, whatever that means. Something about people wearing lots of jewelry, talking about the best schools and clubs.

Yet that's not the case at this house. You step inside the door and feel a wonderful sense of faith and tradition. There are bowls of sweet Hanukkah goodies—fruit, cakes, candy—and a beautiful blue and white ceramic menorah with the eight carefully sculpted candleholders rising from the base. All around the room are dreidels for playing Ha-nukkah games and bright decorations on the walls. About forty people, parents and children, are milling around. You're surprised to feel a comfortable sense of being among "your own people."

Like you and your wife, many of the couples at this party are of mixed backgrounds. A ten-year-old adopted daughter of one family is Asian. Your daughter walks right up to her and without hesitation asks, "Where are you from?" and without missing a beat the delightful girl replies, "I'm from Korea," and suddenly you realize that being among your own people means being among people who struggle with questions of faith and meaning. The chip on your shoulder about people who are "too Jewish" is really about people who think they know it all, have it all solved. In this sense you can be "too Christian" as well. In this gaily lit, festive living room this second night of Hanukkah, you feel welcomed by these people who have similar struggles. You're not an outcast, rejected by the temple, by the Church, by official dogma. Everyone here has his or her own idea of what to believe and how to raise a family. Here diversity as well as faith is welcome.

The centerpiece of this party is to be a kids' puppet show about Hanukkah, the Festival of the Lights that celebrates the victory of a ragtag Jewish guerrilla army led by the Maccabee family against the powerful Syrians, who were intent on destroying the Jewish faith and the temple in Jerusalem. In a corner of the living room stands a wooden stage with a purple curtain across it, waiting for the children's impromptu show.

The kids run upstairs to make their puppets. Curious, you trail after them. You find at the top of the stairs a large, well-lit attic with mattresses all over the floor to sit on. Colorful fabric, felt, cotton, velour pieces, glitter, paint, beads are strewn about. Your children look gleeful as they spot the materials. They sit right down and get to work, striking up conversations with the kids next to them on the mattresses. Older kids help younger ones. Some kids make the Syrian soldiers, other fashion the Maccabees. One child is working on Antiochus, the king of the Syrians. All these *Jewish* children, half-, part-, just-for-tonight Jewish.

While the kids work with the fabric and the paint, the parents make plaster heads and arms and feet, then sew the costumes onto the plaster appendages. Next the kids decorate their puppets with paint, glue, sashes, fabric. A Jewish star here, swords made out of aluminum foil.

Pressing a piece of blue felt onto your daughter's puppet to dry, you survey the scene: the kids talking about freedom fighters who lived thousands of years ago, about a tyrant trying to stamp out a people, about standing up for belief, about celebrating survival. The words of a friend come to mind: "Spirituality alone is not enough for kids, it seems. They need religion. They need the *concrete* stuff of spiritual life: stories, ritual, institutions, songs—and maybe parental behavior as well."

Your daughter runs up to show you a Jewish star she's made out of gold-foil paper, your son wants you to see the soldier he's constructed. It's true, isn't it? We can't just leave these matters to rabbis or to ministers or to whom it may concern—our kids need to see our active participation with them in reaffirming the values and beliefs we live by.

As everyone works on the puppets, you sit and talk, parents and children, on the mattresses. A sixteen-year-old girl tells you that her father is Episcopal, her mother Jewish. She says, "I haven't decided yet, it feels good not to have too much pressure and see what these different religions are like."

159

A friend of yours, a man who had been raised Unitarian by "closet Jewish parents" but took little interest in their spiritual background, once said sadly, "When you grow up in a home where all symbols are of equal value, you have none." Yet watching the interfaith passion of this young girl whose parents were exposing her to so much, you realize that the issue may not be whether there's one religion or several in the home, it's whether the parents are *vitally engaged with their children in the discovery of spirituality*. If you don't believe in the religion you are feeding to your children, if you keep your true faith and spirituality in the closet, out of sight, the children will feel empty.

How wonderful it is to see your boy hard at work on his superb puppet, working next to a kid wearing a yarmulke. One of the boys in the group is a pal from his summer camp, and later your boy exclaims: "Gee, Dad, I didn't know he was Jewish!" A mother once told you about sending her son, who had been partly raised Jewish, to a summer science camp. He came back and exclaimed: "I didn't realize there were so many Jews in the world!"

After a while you find yourself helping the hostess with the marionettes, stringing the figures onto the wooden controls. Most of the kids have gone downstairs to get the stage ready for the show. It's after 8:00 P.M., and the hostess says it's time to go downstairs and light the Hanukkah candles. "If I can remember the prayers," she adds.

You laugh, being unsure yourself. It begins, *Baruch attah adonai,* but you don't want to end with the prayers over the Passover wine instead of the Hanukkah candles. Suddenly you wish you had paid more attention in Hebrew school. You used to be able to read Hebrew, you were shaky, but could do it. Now it's gone entirely.

Do many fathers absent themselves from a vital religious dialogue with their children from the shame of not knowing, from being unsure about their own heritage? A rabbi once remarked to you that many fathers in interfaith marriages don't come to temple, even though they are raising their kids Jewish, because they can't admit that they— smart, successful, professional types—can't read Hebrew, don't remember their Jewish history. We suddenly become illiterate. The rabbi, a woman, observed wryly: "It's more appropriate for the mothers to come to temple or church and not know, that's been women's role in organized religion for generations."

It may be hard for a father to take a stand on faith within his family when he doesn't know how to meld, how to experiment, how to start a dialogue with his wife and children. So you get authoritarian (*Well, you are Jewish!*) or withdrawn (*Whatever you want, kids*). The father may need to start by admitting his uncertainty and vulnerability, admitting it to himself and his wife. Then he needs to reflect on what is truly important to him from the traditions of the past, and he needs to listen to his wife do the same.

Holding a collection of marionettes (the Syrians and Maccabees of olden times would hardly have recognized themselves), you and your hostess finally remember the prayers.

"Christmas, Hanukkah, these days I pray to any religious symbol I can find," you joke to your new friend.

"I sometimes just want to throw up I get so anxious

around the holidays," she confesses. December is the cruelest month for many of us, mixing the hope and light of the holidays with the tough struggle just to get through. There's such strain on marriages at these times. You want everything to be pure and good, and instead it's a dense tangle of expectations and disappointments.

But that night you don't feel like just getting through, you feel wonderful. There's the candle lighting and the kids all gathered around. Your daughter's the youngest so she gets to light the *shamus*, the first candle that lights all others, and you look at your son and daughter in a cluster of thirty to forty kids all looking up at the lights, the regeneration of hope, and you feel that this can't be done *just* in the family, that kids need to see other kids and to feel part of something, that we demonstrate our faith in the ways we connect to the larger community as well.

The play's about to start, but the kids have got the marionette strings all entangled. Sewing thread is all wound together, creating intricate knots. The parents have to sort them out. The kids are anxious to start, the evening is getting late. Your fingers get tied up with the marionettes' hands, feet. There *must* be a metaphor in all this tangle for your own life. *Is this a message from God?* you think frantically, unaccustomed to trying to decode such communiqués. You haven't thought about Him or Her in quite a while. *Sort out the tangle, my son.* Ach: Moses gets a burning bush, you get an enmeshed marionette!

It's possible for the puppets to work with some tangle, but you're determined to get it *all* straightened out. Finally another parent reaches over and says: "That's fine, really, it'll work now."

The play starts. All the kids get behind the stage, hidden from view. One girl, the one who's still deciding about religion, reads the story of Hanukkah, while the rest of the kids lower their puppets to act out the story. Has your son made a Hebrew soldier or a Syrian one? Which side is he on? You can't quite tell—perhaps he can't either. Your daughter has made a marionette daughter of the Maccabees.

It's wonderfully chaotic. The Syrian puppets march in, and there is Antiochus versus the Jews, and the puppets swing toward each other and knock into each other. The kids figure out they can do kick boxing with the puppets, so suddenly the Syrians and the Maccabees are kick-boxing karate fighters. *Très moderne.* One of the puppets has a Mohawk. Your son sits his puppet, knees crossed, on the false idol that Antiochus tries to force on the Jews. He flies through the air, guided by your son's unseen hands, and then perches on the tyrant's head. *Whose side is he on?* You hate to admit this, but you're searching for clues of allegiance in your nine-year-old boy's puppet.

Then in come the Maccabees and suddenly the narrator is reading about "Judy Maccabee" as several members of the audience suggest there should be female fighters and leaders as well, and you sit with your daughter, who has come from behind the stage to sit on your lap—feeling shy about doing the puppets—and you both shriek encouragement to the newly arrived female leaders and women warriors.

After the play the parents talk, while the kids bulk up on ice cream and cake and Hanukkah treats. In your group of chatty parents is a man who was raised Orthodox Jewish, yet hasn't been in a temple for twenty years.

Now he's married to a Catholic wife, and they have several children under ten years of age. He tells you about having felt so pushed around by his parents, forced into becoming devout, that "I didn't want to put my kids through what I struggled with, but now I want to give them something." His wife feels at home with the Jewish community so that they've decided to try and raise the kids Jewish. With a trace of sadness he says, "My father's dead, it's too bad that he'll not be able to see the kids' bar mitzvahs."

Another couple is unsure about the religious education of their children. The father's mother raised him to be "assimilationist," to fit in and not to have too much of a Jewish identity. Yet now this man is stunned to find his mother asking, "When will my grandchildren be barmitzvahed?" He is paralyzed by the question, and his wife is equally stuck since neither of them thought about their children's bar mitzvahs when they first married.

How many of us ignore questions about religion and morals when we first marry, and then, after we have children, things change and we need to begin a dialogue that may feel very strange and unfamiliar, whether in a single-faith or multifaith marriage? We feel a growing urge to make sure that our joint history is safe in the household. This is *our own past* we're dealing with, and no matter how alienated or unsure we may feel about how we were brought up, having kids makes us want to represent it well. Trying to ignore your faith is a bit like wishing your mother had never been born—you wipe yourself out in the process.

Also, let's face it: What does it *mean* in terms of your own personal history to marry outside your faith? Choosing someone different has many personal meanings, not the least of which is that you simply have met someone you love deeply and are grateful for it. It's not easy meeting *anyone* you want to share your life with these days. Yet marrying outside your faith and tradition is also an act of rebellion—it's not going along with the program, it's a rejection of at least part of what your parents stand for. Rebelling *from* doesn't answer what you're moving *toward*. A thoughtful fifty-year-old man once said to me: "I want to run from this discussion of faith and values, but where am I going to run to?"

So many of us who came of age in the 1960s are mavericks, going against the ways we were raised, trying to define ourselves for ourselves. Yet do we modern, hip fathers just skip out of town on the issue of what we really believe? You know there is supposed to be a religious revival going on in this country, but many, many of the fathers you know are strangely silent about faith and values. So of course it becomes the mothers who raise these issues: Many of us fathers know what we *don't* want, but not what we *do* want for our children and ourselves.

Talking that night with other parents you hear a new phrase—"internalized anti-Semitism": how we learn to turn on our own Jewishness, to feel ashamed of and devaluing of our own religious past. "I never wanted to identify with the Holocaust, with the Jews as victims," says one man there. You didn't either. Yet when you read in your local newspaper that a recent national poll indicated that 20 percent of Americans believe the Holocaust *never happened*, you begin to realize that maybe there is a lot worth remembering in your own heritage. *Easy for them to deny history—it wasn't their relatives who died.* The task of keeping alive generational memory, of passing on to your children the history of this part of themselves, becomes really important.

The kids are tired, it's gotten late, and so you leave the party, glad to have come. On the way home you contemplate the ways you *don't* want to look at your own past for fear of claiming it.

And so, one cold evening later that winter, you felt as skittish as a deer illuminated in a car's headlights when you walked up to your local synagogue for Friday night Shabbat services with the kids in tow. You and your wife had talked, and you decided to give the local synagogue a try in your explorations.

As you walked in you could see that the temple was lovely, different from the temple of your youth. The services were held in a large circular room constructed of bright oak wood, with windows all around. The pews were arranged not in straight rows, but in a semicircle around the Ark holding the Torah. At the top of the vaulted ceiling opened a stained-glass window, still bright with the last rays of the winter sun.

To your surprise, the service began with prayers of mystery and magic. A little girl in the congregation lit the Shabbat candles as the rabbi asked you all to read aloud: "To light candles in all the worlds—that is Shabbat./To light Shabbat candles/is a soul-leap pregnant with potential/into a splendid sea, in it the mystery/of the fire of sunset./Lighting the candles transforms/my room into a river of light, my heart sets in an emerald waterfall."

You had never heard such words before in a temple: *soul-leap, mystery, my heart sets in an emerald waterfall.*

Your heart opened as you sang songs in the service. Most of the evening was spent singing and dancing. You did a traditional folk dance with your daughter on your shoulders as you spun around the room. The rabbi's wife played the guitar for the congregation. You and your son and wife and daughter all held hands in the large circle, singing and dancing. You remembered that it was the fiftieth anniversary of the uprising of the Warsaw Ghetto—proud, defiant Jews rebelling against the Holocaust that was consuming them.

You began to realize: *Religion has changed a lot since I was young,* feeling a little like Mark Twain, who confessed astonishment at how stupid his dad was when he left for college and how much the old man had learned when he returned home. You listened to the rabbi talk about this form of Judaism called "Reconstructionism," which is dedicated to taking traditional Jewish ritual and belief and making it relevant to our current cultural context. For Reconstructionists Judaism is an evolving way in which we conduct our search for meaning in life.

The yarmulkes, the prayer shawls, the Ark of the Covenant holding the Torah, the Hebrew liturgy, so inscrutable and solemn, even the rabbi, all took on a different cast as you watched everyone dance around the temple, your children's warm hands in your own. Now these symbols no longer seemed like instruments of boredom designed to fill space, instead they felt part of the human community, a river of loving, working people of which you and your family were a part, a river flowing back in time and forward into the future.

While it's true that there is a difference between rituals and spirituality, rituals *can* carry spirituality if they are performed in the right spirit. Maybe that's the parent's task: to infuse concrete ritual with passion and joy for their children. As an adult your task is to breathe life into your faith for your children and perhaps for yourself.

A few weeks after this Friday night service, you're sitting over lunch with your son at Friendly's. It's your Saturday "special time" together, just the two of you, while Mom has gone out for her "special time" with your daughter. The two of you have been joking, even singing some songs together, fooling around. Then, just after the waitress brings your lunches, your son looks over at two burly young men in a nearby booth. You notice that their hair is close cropped in Marine fashion.

"Dad, are they skinheads?" whispers your son.

You explain that they don't look like skinheads, they seem to be simply guys who have cut their hair very short. You're mulling over your son's question, though, when he makes a statement: "Hitler was a very bad man, Dad."

Yes, you agree slowly, putting down your sandwich. It's the first time you can recall your son referring to the Holocaust.

"Where have you been learning about Hitler?" you wonder aloud.

"MTV had a show about skinheads," he replies.

You ruminate about the fact that he's learning about Hitler from the TV rather than from his family or from going to Hebrew school. *I should be doing this*, you feel, teaching him about prejudice and the Jews, the Holocaust, about pogroms and Dreyfus and what the Jews have been through. Yet then you also feel a protective rush of feeling toward your boy. You look at him quietly munching on his grilled cheese sandwich and you *don't want* him to know about hatred and destruction and the painful history of the Jewish people. You just want him to be able to eat his sandwich, have his ice cream, and grow up a simple American kid who won't have to struggle with prejudice and the horrors of history. Yet you also know he's going to have to deal with the reality of being part Jewish in our society. You feel caught in a cosmic joke: if you tell him about his heritage you open him up to pain and vulnerability and if you don't tell him you expose him to pain and vulnerability. Either way, you—and he—can't win.

Your son interrupts your rumination with a question, looking you directly in the eyes: "Dad . . . who did Hitler kill?"

For a moment you imagine you're hearing a thunderclap outside on the street, then you realize it's the sound of your karma knocking on your skull. *Hello? Anybody home?*

What do you say? How to answer this question? You wish he'd asked you about sex—that would be easier to talk about. For a moment you whine to yourself: *Why do these crucial moments happen when we're alone?* Then you realize: *Maybe that's why he's asking you now. Because it's only the two of you here.* And you realize what's called for: a simple, direct answer.

So you answer his question: "Hitler killed Jews, darling, lots of them, and Catholics." You want to go on: *and gypsies, and communists, and homosexuals, and whoever didn't fit into his mold of the straight and narrow.*

In the restaurant booth you're suddenly reminded of the decent, innocent people who have perished through the ages for what they happen to believe, for the honorable ways they live their lives. You think of a treasured lesson you've learned from being Jewish: *Be constantly vigilant about people's desire just to go along, to idealize leaders and lose themselves in mass movements, to be part of a cause that dehumanizes everyone who isn't a part of it.* You feel proud of your Jewish awareness of oppression, your cultural imagination about human suffering and being "the outsider."

You don't get to discuss all this with your son, though, because he interrupts you: "Well . . . how did he kill them? Did he really gas them?" So sitting there with your ice-cream sundaes now you tell your son as matter-of-factly as you can some details of the Holocaust. Between bites of ice cream you tell him a little about the poison gas at the concentration camps ("What do you mean *camps*, Dad? That's where kids go to play"), leaving out the part about the gas coming out of the showers where people thought they were going to wash up and begin their new lives, and then your thoughtful, inquisitive boy wonders, *Did he really burn the people?* and you tell him yes, he did, and then your boy wants to know if they were burned alive and you tell him that no, no, you believe that the Nazis disposed of the dead bodies by burning them. You wonder what more to say, when your son suddenly reprimands you: "Dad, stop, you're acting weird."

"How?" you ask, genuinely puzzled.

"Well, your voice got very low, and you have a strange look on your face."

You smile back at your boy, you love him so much, he's so finely tuned to what is going on around him, so smart and thoughtful. You realize how much faith you have in him and in your daughter. You really do believe that they will learn what they need to learn, that we will all be able to do this "values thing" together.

So you reach over and touch his hand playfully and tell him that maybe your voice got low because what we're talking about means a lot to you, it's important stuff and you want him to know more about it. And he says, *Okay, Dad, and now let's talk about what we're going to do after lunch*, and you know that it's enough for now.

Then you realize that you got it wrong moments ago when you felt caught in a cosmic joke: in fact, knowing more about this part of his history, his Jewish heritage, can be a source of strength and wisdom for your son, not just pain and vulnerability. To leave this part of his heritage blank is to make him more vulnerable and adrift in the world, not less. You want to start showing him what's important to you about Jewish history and faith, without force-feeding him.

This is all fine as an abstract goal. But as winter turned to spring you were still not sure how to link up faith, ritual, and meaning for your children. Spring brings both Passover and Easter, usually close together. You were determined to enter more deeply into the Passover celebration. Yet it still felt odd when Passover rolled around in April and you found yourself humming Sephardic tunes off the radio in your kitchen while you cleaned up and prepared for the first Seder ever in your house. A Passover Seder is a celebratory meal honoring the Exodus of the Jews from Egypt, the long march from slavery to freedom.

You haven't had great luck with Seders since your children were born. The year before, you had taken the kids to a fancy East Side temple in New York City, across town from where your parents lived. None of you had ever been there before, and it had been a disaster: a formal Seder in which the kids didn't know anyone, got bored, and you spent most of the evening trying to get them to stop hopping on stacked chairs in the vestibule. *Okay, kids, run up the stairs quietly*, while inside the congregation talked about freedom from slavery.

This year you're determined to shoulder the responsibility for Passover yourself. Yet not without dread: this was your first Seder without "the older generation" present. For years, beginning as a young child, your Seders had included your father, your cousin the rabbi, your second cousin a rabbi, all of whom *knew*, understood. They could read Hebrew and organize what had to be done so that everyone completed the Seder celebration at the dinner table before fainting from hunger. This year, through a combination of circumstances, you decide to do it at your home far from the others. You feel very lonely and unsure, *too young* to be taking responsibility for a Seder. *Too young? You're forty-eight years old—time to grow up!*

You've bought a modern Haggadah, the Passover story and prayer book, and invited your interfaith neighbors to the Seder. You feel both admonished and inspired by the Haggadah's opening paragraph: "According to tradition, it is our responsibility to tell the story of the Exodus to our children, making sure that it is understood. . . . For this story must become their story. They must understand its message so that they, too, will pass it on . . . from generation to generation."

All right, all right, you're trying.

It's about an hour before the kids come home from school the afternoon of the Seder, and your wife has asked you for the umpteenth time to make sure the house is clean since she'll be at work late. In particular the kitchen, she insisted, and at first you felt resentful and said, "Sure, sure," but then you noticed in the Haggadah that it is traditional to clean the house before Passover, a sort of spring cleaning, to do a *bedikat chametz*, a "farewell to chametz," a thorough search and sweep-up to clean the house of food containing leavening agents.

To your surprise you find yourself truly cleaning the kitchen. You don't go bananas like the penitent samurai warrior in *Shogun*, cleaning and purifying his home for his wife as an act of devotion, but it's close. You scrub the large kitchen table around which you'll all sit, wash the wooden backs of the bunk seats around the table, sweep and mop the kitchen floor.

There feels something wonderful in the cleaning, oddly feminine, as if you're doing a womanly thing, a task that goes back to the Spanish Jews and before, and all the while you're listening to the NPR Passover broadcast. You hear "Crossing the Red Sea," a vocal piece from Spain marking the Spanish Inquisition and the year 1492, when the Jews were expelled from Spain, and you're thinking about how the notion of an Exodus and a Passover recurs in Jewish history through the ages. Slavery and sacrifice and redemption.

But let's not get myopic here. This is also true of many peoples throughout the world—the Armenians experienced their own holocaust, and what about the Vietnamese, and the Cambodians, and the Bosnians, the list goes on and on and on, and why do we have to go back three thousand five hundred years to remember it, and why think only of the Jews? And then you realize that you're not only thinking of Jews, *This is for all people, it's for yourself and your chil-*

dren, it's to remember. An inner voice of encouragement: *You can do this religious-spiritual thing any way you want! Untangle the strings as you like!*

Then you think of the children and wonder, *What if you told them that the world was in flames all around them?* Nobody talks about the peace dividend anymore, now it's where are we going to send troops next? You could say that slavery and exploitation and sacrifice are all around us as we speak. In fact many people this very day are slaves and have nowhere to go, no place to Exodus to. But *that* felt overwhelming. How much nicer it is to place this in a drama hardly recognizable three thousand five hundred years ago. Yes, it's all around us still, but you don't have to drown your kids in that painful reality at age six and nine. Let them hear the old story and the familiar one, and maybe they'll learn about slavery and abuse and oppression in a way that will strengthen them to understand it in the world today.

Most of all as you cleaned joyfully, you thought about how decisions about faith and meaning are *not intellectual ones, they're gut ones.* One father you know struggles endlessly to verbalize "what my values are" with his wife, who wants to spend more time in the church. For him the question is very heady, but in truth these are really matters of the heart, and that kind of passion can be scary.

The school bus deposits the kids at home. They seem both intrigued and wary as they confront all the Passover food out on the counter, awaiting your attempts to cook. Jewish stars on familiar supermarket boxes of flour, what does "Kosher for Passover" mean?

Your daughter wants to set the Passover table and put out the flowers and make name tags. But your son is more unsure as he comes downstairs into the kitchen. You've set out all the ingredients for the *charoset*, a sweet mixture of apples, nuts, and raisins that signifies the mortar the Jews used to make the cities for the pharaoh. Your grandmother brought this thick pastelike mixture to the Seders when you were a child, and it reminds you of that lady. She was wonderful to you even though she was rather stern and old. Her *charoset* seemed to express her nature—thick and sweet. Over the phone your mother instructs you to add plenty of wine: "Don't make it too thick," as if she wants to distance herself from her own mother's *charoset*. Your goal is indeed a lighter version.

Your deeper goal is to have your son help you. You envision a father-son collaboration in the kitchen: Passover music playing, the two of you deeply engrossed in peeling apples, chopping nuts, and mixing in the raisins. "Drop the apples into the wine immediately after peeling them or else they'll turn brown," your mother advised, offering you a bit of old female family lore.

You put out the nuts, apples, raisins, and several knives, humming to the NPR Passover music—this one day of the year there's more Jewish music on the air than all the other 364 combined—a wonderful Passover cantata written by a Canadian Jewish rabbi using tunes remembered from his childhood Seders. *Dyanu, dy-dy-anu.*

Your son skips down the kitchen stairs, stops on the threshold, surveys the scene—strange, almost atonal music, unusual recipes, boxes with odd symbols on them. He asks what you're doing. For all he knows you're Merlin composing strange potions in your cave.

You tell him about the *charoset* and ask him to help and he says maybe and then goes over wordlessly and flips off the Passover music. That weird-sounding Jewish music! You walk over wordlessly and turn it back on, then he walks back and turns it off. You go on like this as if you're trying to listen to Radio Free Europe and he's the Thought Police, or perhaps *you're* trying to beam information across the Iron Curtain, until you give up and leave it off while your son peels some apples and enjoys using the food processor to mix everything up. Then both of you add the cinnamon, and after a little while he loses interest and asks if he can go play Nintendo. If there had been an *Exodus* video game you would have bought it. He takes a taste of the *charoset* and says, "Hmmm, good," and is off up the stairs while you turn to arranging the gefilte fish and horseradish.

Who's the pharaoh and who's the slave here? You want to order your children to attend to tonight's lesson about freedom! How hard it is to think about wooing children as a father rather than ordering them! This isn't an "authority issue" for you, it's a spiritual one: you really do believe that we need to approach the question of faith, with our children and for ourselves, as we do a lover, wooing her rather than ordaining obedience and love. But how to do that now with your own children, who are perched so precariously on the edge of their heritage?

At the Seder later that night you sit looking at the Haggadah and remembering how there was always the "leader," usually your father or another older relative, at your Seder, who would tell you what page of the prayer book to go to and ask individuals from around the table to read sections from the Haggadah. You plan on doing that, but as you start your wife says, "Oh, let's read the prayers over the wine," and someone else wants to do this and that. You read the prayers; only two of those present can really read the Hebrew—the neighbors' son, already bar mitzvahed, and their daughter, preparing for her bat mitzvah. The rest of you read the transliterated version.

As a kid you always went through the whole Haggadah before eating dinner. You want to be the leader, that's your image of the father's role. You suddenly feel defeated: *I'm supposed to lead and no one is letting me do that.* You all lurch through the Haggadah, sampling what seems interesting.

The kids are hungry, they're losing interest in the Seder, all the details about the meaning of the bitter herbs, about the plagues. The kids read the four questions, and then you all seem to run out of gas. "Let's have dinner," the kids protest. The adults hush them up. The Seder drags on, the kids feel the dragging feeling you used to feel, and a part of you comments silently: *Good, get to know that slightly bored feeling, it'll do you good in temple!*

The kids are hungry, but part of you empathizes with the pharaoh—just order them to do this meal, this service. The Seder threatens to become another struggle over freedom or slavery. The dad-pharaoh orders obedience. *Let's read a few more pages! Lift those heavy stones! Let's read about what happened to the Jews in 1854, let's remember the Russian Jews, let's build a big pyramid right here in this dining room!*

The kids, and the adults, look for a Moses to lead them to freedom, toward some deeper meaning, and maybe a meal.

Instead the dad-pharaoh wonders what to do, knowing that *you have to breathe real life into ritual, make it meaningful to your children.* Yeah, well, good luck!

Then the dad-pharaoh has a moment of inspiration. Remembering joy and fun and how great it can be to play, the dad-pharaoh recalls an idea he read about in this modern, updated Haggadah: "Say, kids, how about if before dinner we have a TV interview show about the Exodus from Israel?"

They look suspicious of the pharaoh but curious about the idea. The pharaoh turns to his own son: "Listen, you be the interviewer, and we can each be one of the participants in the drama."

"You mean like on MTV or CNN?"

"Exactly."

Your son, now totally engaged in this playful drama, climbs out of his seat, leaves the room for a few minutes, and returns with sunglasses, a broad-brimmed white Panama hat, and an adult overcoat reaching to the floor, all ready to face the "You Are There" cameras in the Egyptian desert.

The kids take turns being interviewed, while the adults watch. One of the kids is the pharaoh, another Moses, one of the girls is Miriam, Moses' sister, another wants to be a cat on the Exodus. In his interview the pharaoh talks about his pyramids and how come he wanted the Jews to build them: "I want to be remembered, I coulda been somebody," intones the marvelous teenager-pharaoh. Moses talks about standing up to authority and his conversations with God. The interviewer has a great question: "Listen, Moses, you actually talked with God, so I have to ask you—Is god male or female?" Everyone wants to become Moses to answer *that* question.

Finally: "Hey, Dad," commands your son, "come on up here, dude, and be interviewed."

"And who do we have here?" asks your son as you arrive in front of the cameras in the Egyptian desert.

"I'm a louse off the hair of pharaoh," you reply, laughing at yourself.

"Good, good, now tell us what you saw going on, Mr. Louse."

"Well, first let me say—boy, did that guy have dandruff!"

As you ramble on, looking at all the engaged children's faces, you hardly feel like a louse, instead you feel the joy of the moment. You are reminded again by your own religion that we constantly face a choice between slavery and freedom within ourselves every day, and you feel relieved that you had the wits this evening to refuse the role of pharaoh and find a way to play with tradition and meaning and hope with your children.

We go through this again and again with our kids. There's the joy, there's your father's passionate devotion, your mother's wonderful blessing of the Shabbat candles, the glistening pond outside the kitchen window, and now the daddy who jokingly becomes a flea from pharaoh's hair!

Here's your spirituality, your belief and your prayers about your children and their faith: to approach values and belief in a playful way in which there is true humanity, a recognition of your children as children, rather than making spirituality into an authoritarian demand about what you—and they—must believe. Before we ask our kids to connect to a religious tradition, to a particular community and tradition, the kids have to see us, their parents, open ourselves up to it. We have to start on their level, we have to be in this all together.

At bottom, we transform ritual and belief, we enliven it, we have the power to make it a gift from the older to the younger generation.

You know how ad hoc your spiritual solutions have been this year. You don't have it all worked out, but that feels all right. You're going to show your kids your struggle. Maybe you don't have to have it all worked out, to have all the answers, to do this religion thing perfectly. You have a lot of confidence in your children and their ability to make meaning in the world, to take from you what they need.

You have arrived at one answer in this year of spiritual experimentation: the importance of parents communicating some faith to their children, some wonder and belief in the world. It needn't be a traditional religion, it may be how we work or how we love, it may be a treasured hobby or how we live in a community. Whatever form it takes, kids need to know it's okay to believe; both parents and kids need to have a place where the heart can retreat for nourishment and renewal. We children, now parents, of rationality, we also need to show our children a reason to believe, to know hope and to be awed, to see the faith that gets us through the hard times.

Even as you write you can't forget last December, the year of an unusual convergence of Jewish and Christian holidays. Christmas Day itself was coming to an end, but as night fell it was still the seventh day of Hanukkah. Your in-laws were visiting, and you faced the question: Light the Hanukkah candles on Christmas Day? You felt very grateful to your wife for suggesting that you all light the candles together, all the cousins and in-laws together, your polyglot family. The nieces were excited, they were interested in knowing more about the yarmulkes and the Hanukkah *gelt*, the chocolate money. You didn't want to intrude on Christmas, this sacred day, but on the other hand you did want to carry out your own tradition. So after you finished your traditional Christmas dinner, after all the presents had been opened, with the tree lighting your living room, out came the menorah and candles, even some dreidels. Your brother-in-law sat there looking on. You wondered what he made of this transformation in the house's religious atmosphere. He contemplated the gold-foil-wrapped chocolate coins used in the dreidel games, picking one up and slowly turning it in his hand. He was thinking about something. Then he said, "*gelt* sounds like gold; is that the Yiddish word for gold?" You're not really sure, you never learned Yiddish, and again you felt that momentary panic: *What kind of Jew am I?* But you told him no, you thought it was Yiddish for "money," and talked with him about Hannukah. You treasured his interest and goodwill.

You put out the menorah and the Hanukkah candles, the kids all eager to get their presents. This day was a double goody for them all, Christmas presents followed by Hanukkah gifts! You're still amazed at children's appetites for surprises and gifts, they never lose interest. The kids had gotten the routine down. Your daughter got out the yarmulkes, your son got out the candles. He lit the *shamus*, and you noticed the yarmulke on his head, he put it on himself, no reluctance this evening, and the four of you said the prayers, as the rest of your family repeated after you.

You felt very grateful to your wife for her openness and for her urging you to practice so that you got the prayer right. You were proud to be saying the prayer for her family on Christmas Day. Looking into the candles—the mystery and wonder of the lights—you thought that none of us can really control our kids. In fact a rabbi you know just recently told you nervously that his son is going out with a Catholic girl. After all, rebellion against the past is part of the game, as is the search to honor our past. All you can do is show those you love what you believe and continue your own search for faith.

As you looked at the children's faces, the candles and lights of the festivals reflecting more brightly in their eyes, you realized that a part of them is and will always be Jewish, just as another part of them will always be Christian, and you can't tell yet which part is which, but you thanked God that you were all here together tonight. The joy of it all, the Christmas tree lights shining vividly, Bach's joyous music on the stereo, generosity and faith reaffirmed, and the menorah burning brightly, freedom and tradition reaffirmed, the Hanukkah candles sparkling as the Christmas tree lit the room.

You looked around that night of Christmas and Hanukkah joined and saw those blessed, bright-eyed children knowing the wonder of both faiths, and that felt wonderful.

Raise them one way, raise them both ways, invent your own religion if you want—the real challenge is to be there yourself, alive and vital. You thought of the thousands of years of the Jewish people, of the Christian people, of the search for faith by all of us. And you reveled in how we are constantly reborn, how your children have rekindled within you your own sense of wonder and awe.

CHAPTER 8

THE FATHER WHO TRAVELS FOR WORK

Bittersweet Pleasures

It's 5:30 P.M. Pacific Standard Time and I am hurrying back to my hotel room after a day of meetings at the conference I'm attending in California; it's an annual conference for psychologists, and often I teach seminars there as well as attend meetings.

At the moment I'm trying to get back to my room for my daily phone call home; that's not as easy as it sounds since "home" for me is under the reign of Eastern Standard Time. Calls home when I travel have to be planned: back on the East Coast, it's already 8:30 P.M. and the kids are almost ready for bed. I want to talk to them before they go to sleep, but there's only a small window of opportunity to accomplish that. I've snuck out of a meeting to get to the phone, and I walk down the corridor with the furtiveness of a high school kid out of class without a hall pass.

The hallway is crowded, students come up to me, colleagues have things to discuss, all are oblivious to my guilt. We're only together for a few days, so we're fueled by the manic energy of people hungry to "connect" and "network" with hardly time to do so. *Tell me, Dr. Osherson, about your seminar tomorrow on men and intimacy. Oh, Sam, are you giving an evening lecture this year on fathering in the 1990s?* Fathering! Intimacy! I just want to get to a phone and try to be a father to my kids, have some intimate moments with my wife. The window of opportunity is closing *(Gee, honey, you've called just as the kids are in bed—couldn't you call any earlier?)* and a colleague collars me with a really interesting idea—he's from Australia and invites me to come down there for a series of lectures and book promotions. He'll arrange it all and could I take a month so he can really set up a series of things and have I a minute to talk about that right now? To my astonishment, part of me thinks, *Oh, yes, let's talk, don't want to put this guy off, strike while the iron's hot, it'd be fun to go to Australia, I've never been there, a chance to travel, see the world, sell lots of books,* even while another desperate piece of me surges up wanting to exclaim: *Australia?! I can't even go to California without feeling agony! Get out of my way, I want to talk to my family!*

Instead I tell him I'd be delighted to talk with him later, after I make a pressing phone call, and I rush down the hall to get through that window of opportunity, reconnected with home, before it slams shut.

Many of us travel as part of our work these days. Worrying that our kids will suffer during our absences, we invent ways of connecting long-distance with our families. But these are half measures, and they only partially fill the gap in our lives. Many men today are discovering what working mothers have felt for years: the sense of never doing it right. Whether you're at work or home, you're guilty of not doing enough. It can be hard to juggle what you gain and what you lose from your travels—your pleasure at being away from it all competes with your hunger for your family. But it helps, when you travel a lot, to understand your own struggle to separate—to be clear inside yourself that you *can* derive pleasure from your work *and* from being really present in your family. There's a tension between the two, but it doesn't have to tear you apart.

Consider arriving in California for your annual conference there. Even after several years, you're still grateful for the chance to spend a week each year in sunny California. In fact this time you've finally done what you most want to do: rent a convertible at the airport instead of the nice "sensible" budget two-door sedan. You're ready to acknowledge the success you are, important enough to be invited to California to lecture and be paid for it. And so you drive up to the hotel entrance a legend in your own mind, the sunglasses on, the top down, you could be a real player here you're convinced, you even let yourself imagine what it would be like to be single now in Southern California: *What if you had moved out here after graduate school, taken the bold course instead of settling back east?* The very air seems lighter in California—free of the thick Puritan vapors of New England—so that you have an image of yourself as a new man. Your mind floats with reveries of beautiful, long-legged California girls who are *so* impressed with this older, successful man from the East. But as you stroll to the front desk your fantasies are interrupted by a visceral sense of loss. What is it about this hotel that has suddenly made you homesick? Then you notice the little girl playing by the fireplace, she's maybe five years old and is showing her little furry white toy bear the gas-lit "log fires" they use in California. For an instant, caught off guard, you think she is your own daughter— *She's here to be with you!*—and then you see her parents checking in at the front desk. Wrong girl. Then you recall how on the cross-country flight that afternoon, just after looking out at the Grand Canyon, still so stunning each time you cross it, the timeless Colorado River cutting through it, you saw a little boy in his seat, he looked a lot like your son, and you suddenly missed him, wished you could show him the Grand Canyon just as you saw it. So later on that flight when an older executive folded up his laptop, you weren't all that surprised when the couple next to him stood up to get their luggage ready to depart the plane, and he offered, almost asked, to hold their baby. They declined his offer with a smile, and he turned around with his arms out to get his suit coat. You had a new insight into father hunger then: how hungry fathers are for contact with kids. We overlook that in men. Especially when they travel, men are really excluded from enjoying kids. Indeed it's almost impossible for a man to make contact with kids who are strangers. Even as you look so longingly at the girl in the hotel lobby, you wonder if you look like a lecher rather than a lonely father. *Dear, you better go over to the fireplace and get little Darlene, that man with the sunglasses is staring at our daughter.*

So of course the memory of having just left your wife and children that very morning comes to mind. It was a cold, dark dawn back east and the cab was waiting in front of your house and your son came all the way downstairs in his jammies and out to the cab, as did your daughter, following you as you shepherded the suitcase up to the cab. There seemed something so sad in leaving, they were being brave, your daughter saying let's kiss good-bye like they do in France, touching you lightly on both cheeks, having learned this custom from her French aunt, and your son, older, quieter, puts his head on your shoulder for several moments and then becomes the man of the house, straightening up and shaking your hand good-bye. As you looked back through the cab window at them, you realized how much you loved them, your wife and kids, and then you were seized by the thought that *some men don't come back*, men leave, men run away from their families, they die traveling, in wars, and on business, and then you think, *What if I die on this trip? Then my son would be in charge, he really would be the man of the family, he'd have my wife all to himself.* You think: *I could be killed in a plane crash.* How poignant this moment of departure seems to you. You're aware part of you is morose as you pull away, even as you're tugged toward California, drawn along with the gleam of the headlights cutting through the darkness.

Maybe it feels too poignant. You wonder if your sadness is fueled by how good it feels to be leaving, something hard to admit. Maybe part of you looks at your son and thinks: *Let him be the man of the house, I'm outta here!* As the warm cab heads toward the airport and sunny California, you think about men's wish to leave the family—to get away from the burden of expectations and demands and worry. The gloomy thought of never returning may be a fear bloated by a wish: that you could really be free of it all, the worries about earning a living, the frustration of trying to get a kid to school on time, the impotence of the parent trying to get his kid ready for bed. Instead you could become an Odysseus who gets to wander the earth conquering and pillaging even as he misses his family. The great Greek warrior Odysseus, called to a ten-year war with Troy, regretfully left his wife, Penelope, and young son, Telemachus, behind. But then it took him another ten years to get home. Though he wept with longing for his wife and son, he still dallied for a year on an Aegean island with the nymph Calypso. Each time his crew suggested another place to pillage he went along. Only near the end of his adventures, when he was washed up alone, exhausted, on the island ruled by King Alcinous and the king asks the great hero what favor he can grant, only then did Odysseus say the words that touch you so much: *I would go home, would you take me home?* It's a parent's fate to be torn: I want to travel, have adventure, and I want to be home. It's a mother's fate as much as a father's, yet maybe we fathers are more easily able to slip away. *Sorry, dear, war calls!*

The cab stops at the red light and you hear the driver chuckle. A large, friendly man from Haiti, he looks familiar. You wonder if he's picked you up on some other trip.

"The children, they don't like to see their father go away," he observes sympathetically.

"The father doesn't much like it either," you confess.

As he turns the corner toward the highway he agrees: "You're so right. I drive this cab twelve to fifteen hours a day—some nights my daughters are asleep when I leave in the morning and back asleep when I return that night."

You're grateful for the directness of his reply, naming that loneliness of the parent away from his children, and it warms you as you drive toward the airport. You wonder, too, about the pleasure mixed in with the sadness of always seeing your kids asleep. *Not so bad!* a part of you observes—*he's off the hook of having to do the dirty work of parenting, all the stuff that happens when the kids are awake.*

Next day, still feeling sleepy from the jet lag and from your 6:00 A.M. walk on the beach, you're still preoccupied with your kids as you begin work.

The day starts with a meeting of all the faculty members teaching at this conference. You find a seat in the lovely meeting room of the elegant Spanish-style hotel, ancient by California standards, having been built in the 1920s by Charlie Chaplin. All the chairs in the room are arranged in a circle. You contemplate the spa on the patio just past the French doors that form one wall of the meeting room. People trickle in, people you haven't seen in months and years, and as the room begins to reek of propriety and business, you sit there with the familiar gloomy, empty feeling called homesickness. Everyone seems so cheery. *Hi! Great to see you!* A grumpy part of you wants to respond: *Great to see you, but it'd be better to see my kids right now.*

Since you're all psychologists, you start the meeting by spending about an hour going around the circle catching up with each other: *Let's everyone take a few minutes to tell the group what they've been up to the past year.* People talk about books they've published, kids married, kids off to college, grandchildren who've arrived, wives who've gone to work. People without children talk about their dogs, their vacations, their publications. You sit in your funk wondering what time it is back home and whether your kids are watching "X-Man" or "The Ghost Busters" on TV this Saturday morning. Several of the mothers say they miss their kids, but few of the fathers do. You keep wanting a father to say: *What the hell am I doing here—I want to be home with my kids,* but none do. You're sure not going to say that, you're not about to admit that the great Odysseus sits there preoccupied with his kids. The circle has almost gone around to you, you hear the woman on your right, both her kids in their thirties and working, telling the group how just this year she's had a new book published. And as everyone applauds you suddenly don't want to talk about kids, you want to talk about a book of yours, any book, you want to demonstrate your heroic ability to work, my sales are bigger than yours.

Yet when it's your turn, you look at the group and feel welcome. You remember that after all you *are* among friends, and you want to bring your kids in the room with these friends, knowing that if you can talk about them for a while you'll actually be able to get down to work. You feel very alone and very vulnerable, not knowing what to say, but then you find yourself telling the forty people in the circle about what had happened with your nine-year-old son the afternoon before you left: you found him filling out a form at the kitchen table, and he had all these questions as you cooked dinner and he wrote down your answers, first asking you about your zip code, then wanting the area code, but when he asked you to tell him his social security number, you were startled and asked him what he was doing. He replied that he was filling out a credit card application, the one included in the frequent flyer material he got after you registered him during a recent family trip to Florida. *Credit Card? Frequent flyer card?* Suddenly your child, who you can still remember doing a jig with the day he was born, holding him in your arms dancing a frantic dance of joy at his birth, your firstborn, now seems nine going on sixteen. How do you ever have enough time with them, how do you hold back time? Not even the great Odysseus could do that.

"Oh, they grow up so fast," remarks one of the older faculty members as you tell your story, and you're grateful to this man for the directness of his feeling. He has validated your feelings, cut through your suspiciousness, and quickly you feel less alone in this group and you recall how many of you at this conference truly *are* friends, even though you see each other only sporadically.

Something changes in the circle after your story. As the group continues to go around the circle, the other fathers talk, too, about what it's like to be away. Not in a deeply expansive way, but in the more telegraphic manner that we men have, showing our deep feelings quickly, then closing up again, as if we're worried about being wounded or rejected or humiliated if we open our hearts too fully. And what father—or working mother—doesn't wonder if he'll be perceived as less committed to his work, pay a penalty if he talks too much about his love of his family?

One man doesn't mention his kids at all, but when you look over he is drawing a picture on a piece of paper, a stick figure of man holding the hand of a child. He writes underneath "Daddy" and "Betsy" and puts it in an envelope to be mailed.

A father on your left says: "My daughter pushed over my suitcase yesterday morning when I told her I was leaving." Another man relates that he feels bad this morning about being away because "my son and I had a fight just before I left. I'm sorry we had a fight just at that point."

A savvy mother across the circle replies: "Maybe that's the point." Kids get angry when you leave them, they don't know of your work or your higher purpose or having to earn a living, they just feel left, and they may want to wound you on the way out the door.

You think about how you prepare your children before you leave on a trip so that your absence feels more manageable for them and has some structure—you've shown them on the map where you go, you have a ritual about the cookies you bring back from this special store in California that makes them as no one else does, you mark on the kitchen calendar when you're leaving and when you're returning. You worry sometimes that you do too much "ritualizing" of your travels—sometimes it feels as if the kids just want you to go and come back, not make the leave-taking into more than it is.

Once after a flurry of travel for book promotions, town after town and thousands of miles in two weeks, you called home eager to talk to the kids, yearning to be with them, but your kids didn't have all that much to say and you wondered aloud on the phone to your wife "if the kids are having a hard time with my being away" and she, after hearing your anxiety about this for the umpteenth time, informed you that "we deal with your being away by becoming numb to it. We're all doing fine, getting through, looking forward to your coming home. It's not like you're dead exactly." You're relieved to hear this while she goes on: "Your letters and postcards are hardly looked at. When you're away, you're away, and when you're home, you're home."

So you realize that what really matters for kids when you travel is your dependability and trustworthiness—that their world stays safe and understandable; that they know where you're going, why, when you're coming back, who's going to take care of them and for how long; that you miss them and will return. You don't have to bend yourself out of shape while you're away. How kids respond to our absences is really determined by how we are when we are with them. If they feel we really love them, that endures all kinds of separation. Being dependable doesn't mean always being there.

Sitting that night after your long day on talk shows in your West Podunk fancy hotel, beginning to realize after years of romanticizing travel that basically all fancy hotels are the same, you realize that your kids are going to be okay with your travel, and then you wonder how *you* do with your being away from them. You wonder how many fathers are really homebodies deep down who'd rather stay home than don their armor and go out into the world but who go out there and achieve only because they have to. You consider how many fights start just before you leave for a trip, fights with your kids or your wife. Somehow it clashes with your image of a man to realize that you want worldly success and regret it at the same time.

So as the circle winds down at your California conference, you're grateful to the other fathers for responding, even briefly and obliquely, for talking about their children. It helps you feel less alone at the conference, less of an oddball father. You realize that it's okay to miss your kids and be a man as well, in fact being able to talk about such matters feels part of morale building at work. You wonder how men cope when they are not allowed to express or acknowledge their homesickness at work; you think about all the drinking and partying men indulge in when they travel, how so many of us have to affirm our "manliness" and deny or repress our more vulnerable feelings because they are "unmanly" or because the powers that be feel they'll get in the way of the work. That's not been true for you: the circle discussion helps you get down to the conference "work" you needed to do, naming your homesickness helps you focus on course schedules, seminars, and teaching assignments.

Later that day, during a break, one of the female faculty says, "When I had young kids at home, I'd kill for one night away, much less several days—how come you can't just enjoy the time away?" You're reminded of how mothers who are friends of yours, warm and supportive women, often get a strange look in their eyes—as if they want to kill you—when you talk of not enjoying traveling. Maybe there's the rub: Mothers get enveloped so quickly by their family just by being "mom" that they may crave some relief. Yet how many fathers really feel like they are there as fully as they want to be? To enjoy being away, you have to know you're fully there. As fathers we're constantly exploring the boundary between distance and closeness, and we may never be sure if we really *are* there for our kids.

Finally, later that day after all those meetings, after your sneaky manic rush down the hotel hallway, you get to your room for the awaited phone call. You start to dial and look around the hotel room. Pretty nice. Through the windows you can see the beach. Several of the windows, flooded with sunlight, have panes of frosted glass embossed with a graceful silhouette of Charlie Chaplin, the Little Tramp. The view, the light, the elegance in this place seem miraculous.

In fact there's so much that *is* so good about traveling and being away from your family. You can admit it, the enjoyment needn't be so furtive. When you arrived at this room, the bellhop lugging your baggage, you threw open your suitcase and knew that you could really *spread out*— your clothes could go anywhere, you didn't need to worry about picking up after yourself, your wife wasn't there to remind you to keep ahead of the mess. The TV, so artfully concealed inside a teak armoire, was *yours*, you could watch any show or movie you wanted at the end of the day, R-rated movies, talk shows, sports—your kids weren't there to compete for ownership of the set, insisting that you turn off the latest Knicks-Bulls Basketball Armageddon so we could all watch "Inspector Gadget."

As the phone rings back east you think about how great it really is to be able to focus on your work without the distractions of family. You don't have your kids asking if you can go on a bike ride with them, you can really prepare for your seminars and spin out new ideas with colleagues without interruption. And you can find your notes and pens and pads without wondering if they have disappeared into the "office" one of your kids has constructed beneath your desk at home. Why, you can even flirt without having to apologize to your wife! Just last night you had dinner with a female colleague at an intimate California seafood restaurant on the coast. Your colleague is a lovely, smart, funny woman, and you both really enjoyed your time together. It was just a nice dinner, filled with jokes and gossip about other faculty and other people. Nothing inappropriate or secretive about it. Yet you knew that back home you'd feel a slight pang of guilt about choosing to have dinner with Liz when your wife and children were eating without you. Friendships with other women are sometimes hard to maintain when they seem to compete with your family. Here, away from all that, you can take the time to enjoy your friendships. Being away from your family can open you up to new sides of yourself, you can recharge. No wonder a colleague exclaimed to you that afternoon: "Being alone out here, without my wife, is good for me, it's good for *both of us!*"

Your reverie is interrupted as your son answers the phone.

"Hi, darling," you say eagerly.

"Hi, Dad . . . bye, Dad," he replies.

Silence. Then: "I'm playing Nintendo. Want to talk to Mom?"

"Wait, wait," you say, feeling oddly vulnerable, he's supposed to be waiting for your call, not vice versa.

"How was your day?" you blurt into the phone, seeking some engagement. A few years ago open-ended questions worked well to start a conversation. That was when your very young son probably thought you were *inside* the telephone. Now, a preadolescent, he's more taciturn; he knows how far away you are.

"Did you get my letters?" you ask encouragingly. You had spent hours before leaving preparing letters to your kids and addressing them, stamping them so that you'd remember to send a letter to each kid every day and not forget in the crush of all the work you had on the trip. Twenty prestuffed envelopes all ready to go were stashed in your suitcase on the way out the door. You had cut out your son's favorite comic strips from the daily newspaper and written funny comments on the pages, thinking maybe you'd laugh together about the adventures of Calvin and Hobbes when you called. For your daughter you put her favorite kind of stickers in the envelopes, and, pushing your lackluster drawing ability to the limit, drew pictures of yourself holding hands with each of them and ended each letter with a heart, with Xs and Os. You missed innumerable great Celtics basketball games on the tube, missed parts of Larry Bird's last games, all because *you wanted some response from them.*

One night in bed your wife watched you cutting up newspaper comics and stuffing envelopes and, amused, perplexed, observed: "You're afraid we'll all forget you while you're gone, aren't you? Don't worry," she reassured, "we won't forget you." *That* comment produced a flurry of denials from you, as you told her that no, no, your interest was in making sure the kids didn't feel you've forgotten them, but you know there's truth in her observation. It comes back to the odd way that men have of feeling easily overlooked, easily forgotten, as if their value doesn't amount to much beside paying the bills.

The wish to have a vital family life, the wish to be successful and off on your own. That's a tension none of us, men or women, are very good at tolerating. You imagine you have it easier than your wife: leaving kids with their mother means in some ways the family is still "intact." Is your absence felt as strongly as her absence? You know sometimes when she's gone for several days, at a conference or visiting friends, how cold and lonely the house can feel, the emptiness touching some deep childhood resonance about being away from Mom. The kids seem to feel that way, too, all of us wondering, "When's Mom coming back?" Yet deep down you know that when either parent is gone the family is not intact. Perhaps for fathers being away stokes the fear that we are fundamentally *inessential*, our mistaken belief that we *could* disappear and the family would roll on just fine, as long as Mom is there.

Your wife is crucial here to you in many ways: you appreciate her wisdom and her reassurance, and you are reminded again of your reliance on her, how when you travel she is the one who keeps your image alive within the family and who helps the kids understand your absence and its meaning. When a child says, "I miss Daddy," a wife may respond, "I'm sure he misses you, too," helping the child feel that his father remembers and cares about him; she can suggest the child draw Daddy a picture for when he returns, encouraging the child to act on his or her sense of connection to Daddy, or she can ignore the statement or even let her irritation at her husband spill out *(Yeah, he left me with all this work while he's having a ball in sunny California)* by replying, "He's never around when you need him." Children may feel further cut off from their father in the face of such behavior, instead of being reassured that it is okay to think about Father while he is gone and encouraged that they are cared about and beloved, held in their father's memory when he is away.

Trusting your wife keeps the family vital in your mind when you're away. You really don't believe they're all numb to you when you're gone, you feel loved enough to stay open to your love for them in times of absence.

What to say now to your laconic boy on the phone? There's silence on the line. Kids react to their father's travels so differently at different ages. For a two- or three-year-old who's so engaged with Mommy, Dad's travel may seem like no sweat. But an eight- or nine- or ten-year old boy may feel that the house is missing a vitally reassuring male presence when his father is away.

As you contemplate the silence, you remember the wise words of a working mother who travels a lot: "Be very direct and precise in what you ask about, and don't give up."

So you try it: "How did your teacher like the diorama of Marco Polo you made for your class book report today?"

He tells you it was okay, and then the conversation dribbles off.

It's easy at these moments to feel: *Why bother to talk?* The painful silences on the phone can drive you off or lead you to ask your child to put his mother on the line. Often the kids are just turning the tables on us. In Gail Godwin's novel *Father Melancholy's Daughter*, an estranged mother calls her young daughter while she is traveling far from her family and it's clear that the daughter misses her mother, doesn't know where she is, and so *resents her mother's caring questions*. It's as if the girl's mother should not be allowed to know about her daughter when her daughter knows so little about her mother's life and travels. After all, when we travel we have all the advantages: we know where our kids are, can picture them in the kitchen or the bedroom while we talk with them, yet our kids know so little about our whereabouts. They don't know of fancy hotel rooms and adult activities or obligations; their attempts to picture us working miles away only heightens the sense of separation. Only by keeping their activities and feelings secret, keeping us in the dark, do they have the power to do to us what we are doing to them:

creating vulnerability and uncertainty. No matter how well you "structure" and frame being away, no matter that all will be well, it still doesn't mean that your kids have to *like it*. Remember, it's a lot easier to leave than to be left.

Luckily, though, as you listen to the lonely hum of the telephone wires, you decide to act on the working mother's final piece of advice: *Don't give up*. So you just sit on the phone with your boy in silence, thinking about how silence in conversation can be one of the scariest experiences, but you just hang out on the phone, trying not to remember that you're calling long-distance and paying for the call. You don't want him to feel that you have nothing to say to him, but you also don't want to force him to hold on to a receiver that may feel like a hot poker in his hand. Basically you just want your son to know that you care and you miss him. But how to communicate this?

Suddenly your bighearted boy has an idea, making excellent use of the fact that you both have pushbutton phones.

"Say, Dad, let's pretend. If I hit the "1" it's a hug, and if I hit the "2" it's a kiss."

1–1–1–1–1–1–1, 2–2–2–2–2–2, 1–1–1–1–1, 2–2–2–2–2

This Morse code of the heart, back and forth, goes on between you for several minutes. Finally your son asks if you'd like to talk to your daughter and after you tell him that you love him and miss him, he hands the phone to your daughter and as you hear her voice you think that you could be playing with her right now if you weren't in this foolish place. Unexpectedly the sunlight outside your window feels kind of lonely and empty as does this fancy hotel room with the Charlie Chaplin frosted glass, and as you think about what it would be like to put your arm in

a familiar way around your son's shoulder as you sit together watching the Celtics game *(are they playing tonight
back home?)* or snuggling up with your daughter, or having
dinner alone with your wife that night after the kids are
asleep, you again realize that basic truth about life: *Things
don't replace people.* Okay, great, so now this sojourn in
paradise seems empty and you miss your family! Sometimes calls home can become an unwelcome emotional
roller coaster. And then your daughter advises you that
her envelope didn't arrive today and you reassure her you
sent it and that maybe two envelopes—filled with stickers
and confetti—will arrive tomorrow and then she becomes
direct:

"Daddy, I miss you," she says shyly. "How many days till
you're home?"

You and she count the days, and then you speak from
the heart: "Darling, I miss you, too."

Even as a part of you worries: *Am I creating a cult of
personality here, fostering my kids longing for me?* you also
know that a simple acknowledgment means as much as all
the cards and envelopes and frantic attempts not to be forgotten. You wonder how often you've wanted to hear such
direct expressions from those you love: "I miss you."

You think about how easy it can be for some fathers to
shy away from this basic human acknowledgment. They
may not have felt loved or cherished enough growing up,
and thus as adults they don't feel missed when they're
gone or are unable to understand that *they* miss their kids
or can't say it or can't admit that they need some direct response from their kids so that they feel remembered. Then
you think, too, of the trap for fathers who have *too much
need* to feel remembered and who therefore demand too

much response from their kids. You think of a man you know who comes home at irregular hours, misses dates with his kids, wreaks havoc with his family until his kids are in tears, and then he resolves to do better, saying tearfully, "I realize how much you all love me." He has to extort dramatic evidence that he matters to his family, so small is his own sense of self-worth, his confidence that he is indeed beloved.

As your daughter kisses you good night over the phone ("Hold the phone against your cheek so I can kiss you there"), you think about how it may be easier for a six-year-old girl than a nine-year-old boy to express directly affection and longing, how for the boy it may become necessary to disguise his feelings, how important it is for the father to hear both ways of communicating love. You wonder what it'll be like when they're adolescents. You hope you'll still remember then: *Don't give up*, that adolescents need to feel engaged by their fathers even as they are pushing them away. And you realize that it goes on throughout life. Even now, when your elderly parents, who have never given up their globe-trotting ways, go off on a trip, a piece of you—at age forty-eight—feels lonely, checks the calendar, and thinks about when they'll return, safe in their home.

Your own return home comes several days later. You feel both satisfaction and a familiar dread as the eastbound flight begins its descent into your hometown airport. The conference has gone well, and you sit in your window seat looking out at the beauty of the Massachusetts shoreline. From this elevation the water of Boston Harbor sparkles, blue and inviting, its pollution invisible. You're proud of your accomplishments at the conference—people saw you as competent, no, an expert, and you felt the rush of adrenaline that accompanies the conquests of work, so unlike the monotony of the daily grind of family that you are returning to: the familiar power struggles of home ("Can I have one more piece of candy?" "I don't want to go to bed! I'm not tired, why can't I stay up later and draw?") contrast so starkly with your expertise at work. But here you are, the returning conquering hero, back from California, your sunglasses still in your pocket, you might as well be returning at last from the Trojan Wars. As your plane banks over Boston the buildings become clearer, and you can see the cars and people milling around and you feel a sudden clutch of despair in your stomach. Why does returning home make us feel empty inside? Perhaps because we recognize at these moments that we are just ordinary people; returning to our families reveals that we are indeed fallible fathers and husbands, and somehow that realization deflates the high we felt on our travels as we played the part of the hot-shot professor, the savvy consultant, the ace businessman. Instead we return home and have to find a way back into our families, who have managed without us. Things have happened we have no idea about, and we may wonder, *Did they remember me? How bonded are my wife and children?*

You recall all the funny, poignant ways you've heard about men walking into their homes after being away, some suddenly giving orders to restore some sense of competence and purpose ("Hey, do we have enough fuel oil for the furnace? Who's been looking after things while I've been away?"), others getting silent and needing to go to their study to look at the mail or to the bedroom to unpack or to read the paper in the bathroom just to get "some space." Family life can swamp you after time away. You consider the debt you'll owe your wife, and your kids—you've been away, you've been free, you've had the salmon dinners with fine white wine in the hotel restaurant, and it hardly matters that you've been working, that in fact you're dog tired. You may feel as if you've been on stage performing all week, and part of you just wants to veg out in front of the TV eating nachos with your wife and kids next to you, but to the rest of the family it's as if you've been on vacation. You wonder if your wife is going to say, "Now you take over, you watch the kids while I go out, and by the way, Did you remember me?" and you resolve to find ways to reconnect with your wife, a kiss, some time together that night. The presents you've brought can't be enough, the connection needs to be real and not pro forma. You realize what she needs is not so huge—it's to know that you have not forgotten her, not fallen in love with some California beauty of your collective imagination, but that you still see her and love her.

And despite it all you can't wait to see your wife and kids. So as you exit the plane and walk down toward the gate where they're waiting, you look hungrily for them, and as you pass through security on your way out they spot you and the kids whoop with joy, "Daddy!" and your wife smiles her beautiful smile and you realize that you haven't been forgotten and they surge over you like the ocean surf in California and you're so glad to see them, and then one child grabs your hand exclaiming, "Daddy, come here, I want to show you where the planes are landing, you can see them!" and the other grabs your hand, pulling in the opposite direction advising, "No, wait, Dad, come here and see the science exhibit in the children's play area—it's great!" and suddenly you're pulled in two different directions, no three, as you realize you'd like to have a cappuccino with your wife. But she tries to calm the kids, telling them to give you a moment to catch your breath, and then you're no longer really the great Odysseus, you're a husband and father doing the best he can, and it doesn't feel so bad. With gratitude and resignation, you accept your fate.

CHAPTER **9**

REDISCOVERING OUR WIVES

Sex, Marital Intimacy, and Parenting

You're reading a bedtime story to your young kids while your wife putters in your bedroom down the hall. It's 9:00 P.M. and you're hungry for some time with your wife; the kids seem to go to bed later and later. It doesn't help that a friend recently advised: "Wait till they're teenagers. Our kids are up till midnight many nights, and they're so much fun to be around my wife and I have practically no time alone together."

Like a lot of parents these days, both you and your wife work, you both worry about how good a job you're doing raising the children, and you both feel that you don't make love often enough with each other. Both of you also know that too much stuff builds up between you when you don't have a chance to talk and spend time together; "marital sludge" is your term for the detritus of being parents that clogs up your marital relationship from time to time.

As a father it can feel as if you can never really get to your wife. There are always the kids to focus on. Your wife has admonished you recently to look more carefully at her, to really see her. "Really look at what I'm wearing, listen to what I'm saying," she asked. You wonder if she ever really sees *you*; in becoming a mother your wife has tapped into the deep, primal way that women focus on their children. Tonight you're going to spend some time reconnecting. You've decided to do so in the bedroom.

First, though, the kids have to be asleep. They look peaceful as you read to them. You've found a story that holds their interest: a novel about a young boy and girl who rescue another child with supernatural powers from government agents who want to spirit him away to a laboratory to find out what makes him tick. "Those bad men want to kidnap the boy from his mommy," observed your six-year-old daughter. *I wouldn't mind kidnapping your mother from you,* you think to yourself dryly. It's unsettling to think that you'd like to have your wife all to yourself. Every family is, after all, a stew of competing desires for attention and comfort.

"Dad, read!" admonishes your nine-year-old son, and you emerge from your reverie to complete the story. It ends well, good triumphs over evil. All the world is safe and in order. Even so, your six-year-old sits in her bed, jittery before going to sleep. It's not always simple to enter into the dark world of sleep. Your daughter needs to make sure that her familiar items are in order; lined up on the wall shelf above her bed are several troll dolls, pictures of her cousins, and various other treasures. So you help her check to make sure the trolls are comfortable and that all the treasures are safe on the shelf.

Then you sit with her and even agree to hold her hand while she goes to sleep.

"Hold as tight as you can; when I squeeze you, squeeze back hard." Feeling overcontrolled for the nine hundredth time, you spitefully contemplate squeezing that little hand too hard. Instead you grumble, "Please just go to sleep." You restrain yourself from pulling your hand away. Feeling your child's little hand in yours, you know you're protecting your little girl from her fears, from the darkness, from bad men wanting to steal kids away from their parents.

You sneak a glance at your wristwatch: *It's nine-fifteen and I have an early morning appointment tomorrow!* You feel a familiar resentment building as you wonder whether you and your wife will have any time together. You manage to keep your patience. You sit and hold your child's hand, and slowly she falls asleep.

Carefully you extract your daughter's hand from yours, waiting to see if she'll open her eyes as she did last night and scold you—*Daddy!*—for trying to leave the room. This evening she doesn't move; she breathes calmly, deeply asleep. Your son, too, you see, checking his bedroom, is fast asleep.

So you walk down the hall toward the bedroom where your wife waits. You're proud of your restraint this time, proud of the fact that this evening you got your kids to sleep without yelling at them. You have made the world safe for them. That's a present all parents must want to give to their children: a feeling that the world is safe, trustworthy, and orderly. At least until they're able to learn otherwise.

The corridor is dark, and the house is closed up for the evening. You step into the bedroom doorway, see your wife turn toward you, and feel both joy and hesitation at the same time.

How to combine marital passion with parenting? That may be the unanswered question of our age. Many of us are very good as parents, put a lot of energy into that relationship, yet we wonder how to enliven our relationship with our wives.

When you become a father, it's easy to stop seeing your spouse as a wife and see her simply as a mother. Keeping your marriage healthy means rediscovering your wife, recreating the sexuality and intimacy that often gets lost amidst the confusing thicket of parental roles. It's crucial to pay attention to the normal self-hatred that parenting and aging generates; when we project these unpleasant feelings onto our spouses, it leaves us alienated and cut off from them even as we want to rediscover them.

It's easy to say let's make time to be together, but it's another to walk into your bedroom at 9:30 P.M. and find your wife in bed waiting for you. Walking into your bedroom from the kids' rooms is like being whisked to a different planet. The air itself feels different. You've gone from being Father to Husband. Having just made the world safe for your kids, with all the restraint this has taken, now you have to open yourself up to your impulses, sexual and all. But you're having some trouble seeing this woman as your wife, rather than simply as a mother. After all, this is a mother you're looking at, and with all the accoutrements of a mother—she's cleaned up the dishes while you've put the kids to sleep and now, looking utterly composed, she sits in bed wearing her reading glasses, making lists of what needs to be done the next day to keep the household running. She seems, well, *formidable*, the way mothers do.

It's the kitchen work that gets you. You recall how your mother went back to work when you were a teenager and how you used to do the dishes late at night for her. Your mother seemed to be working so hard, and you worried that she was overworking. And now you're having some difficulty separating your mother and your wife, your desire to protect and your desire to find the sexual, potent part of yourself. Mothers, after all, are to protect, not to ravish.

Potent? Actually you don't feel too potent. You feel more drained, tired—you've taken care of business, come home and been a daddy, gotten your kids to finish their homework, weathered your son's anger and frustration at having so much work to finish. Underneath his sarcasm was the basic question whether he *could really do what's demanded of him*, a question you often ask yourself, so you knew it was really important not to get too angered by his provocations but to remain calming and contained, helping him to learn to soothe himself in trying moments. Maybe you got an inch farther tonight on that journey of one thousand miles. And then while your wife cleaned up the first floor, you got the kids into the upstairs, and then you and she got them settled, struggling all the way. The kids were tired through dinner and then at bedtime had a miraculous, Lazarus-like rebirth of energy, protesting that they *weren't tired and didn't need to go to sleep*, informing you that *you're a rotten daddy, and all the other kids get to stay up real late* and you didn't get upset, just talked the kids down to sleep and read them that book, and now you'd like some time for yourself.

Your wife smiles at you from the bed, and you smile back encouragingly, all the time wondering: *Do we really have anything to say to each other right now?*

It takes an act of will on your part really to look at her. You can glance at her, but something more is called for. You know you need to drink each other in with your eyes, but that's the last thing you want. Parenting some days can leave you so drained that the last thing you want is more human contact. The mere presence of your spouse can irritate you, the idea that someone else wants something from you feels intolerable. Sex itself can feel like a demand, having to get yourself in gear and up for it when you're running on empty emotionally.

Looking at your wife in her dressing gown, you want to be manly. *Any husband would have no hesitation.* You think of all your friends and you imagine they have little hesitation about sex, they take charge of the situation. Sometimes that's how things happen between you and your wife, one or the other "taking charge," yet in fact often sex seems to be a matter of waiting for who will make the first move. *How long has it been since we've made love?* is the anxious question that takes the temperature of the relationship, or so we imagine. If we make love "enough" we're okay, if not we're in trouble. But how much is enough?

As the husband, you feel as if you're supposed to know the answer to that question. You're supposed to want it anytime, constantly. You think about the wives who complain their husbands want too much from them sexually. You have a friend who cannot go to sleep at night without making love to his wife, and you wonder what that's like for both of them. Sometimes you do start things, but not tonight. Tonight you feel different, maybe it has to do with just having put the kids to sleep, with just having soothed them, and now they're in the next bedroom, and it's hard to feel like the Sexual Husband after having just been the Calming Daddy. You're reassured when you consider the thick wooden walls of your old house, the soundproofing offered by the sturdy walls separating the bedrooms. Yet it's not only about soundproofing, it's more, it's about crossing a boundary between one experience and another, about taking your wife sexually, asserting your sexual bond with her in the face of the kids' claim on her. A man you interviewed about fathering once said that sex with his wife is reserved for their weekends away: "I can handle intimacy serially, be a partner in parenting, then be a partner sexually, but I can't put the two together. Can't feel romantic when my son is around." Why? Is it too hard to show his possession of his wife? Do we feel that in being sexual we are kidnapping our wives, violating an old taboo about who has ownership of Mom—Dad or the kids?

Your wife meanwhile is looking fetchingly at you, and you love her. You look at her and realize that she is vulnerable, too: she's waiting for you to do something, she needs some sign of affection. You think about the fact that she's waiting for *you*.

For want of knowing what else to do, you go with routine: you start to change into your pajamas, wondering how appealing your body looks to your wife. You take your clothes off and walk toward the closet for your bathrobe. You think about how exposed you are to your wife, and she to you, how in marriage you really show each other everything, including the most minute parts of yourself. You think about your thinness and her body, the signs of aging in both.

A man blurted out to you once, "I'm scared of my wife's aging!" The gray hair, folds of skin, added pounds, the aging of his wife's breasts were all signs of physical decline and his own mortality. You're aware of not wanting to look too closely at her body and not wanting her to see your body. Yet you also want to be admired by her. You preen around in front of her, and as she watches you, you alternately want to cover up and puff your chest out, to look more muscular. Your kind father once said to you, "You have swimmers' muscles"—long and thin—but you've always felt that basically you just don't have enough muscles, a mesomorph trapped in an ectomorph body. Feeling tall and gawky, you find yourself surreptitiously tensing your arm muscles, trying to make the veins stand out in that manly way she likes. No reaction.

You're standing there in front of your closet, unsure what to do, holding your bathrobe and tensing your muscles like a stork in some mating ritual. You've hardly said two words to each other, it's as if you're circling around each other, returning from your travels of the day, two planes circling the airport, the pilots suddenly unsure of how to land, how to come to earth together, each waiting for a flight controller to talk them in.

Again, go to routine, try to act natural, don't show that you haven't a clue as to how you and your wife are going to land at the same airport this evening! You have, of course, a getting-ready-for-bed routine. Since your back has for years felt creaky, you do nightly sit-ups in a corner of the bedroom to strengthen it. It's nice to wake up in the morning without having to stoop over and slowly stand up like an old, old man. You want to do your back exercise, but you don't want to lose this window of opportunity with your wife. So you hurry through your sit-ups, trying not to exercise so quickly that you injure your back, but hoping not to take so long as to lose the moment.

Looking up from the floor, you notice that your patient wife has begun to read a Victoria's Secret catalogue, "catalogue therapy" you call this late night perusal of mail-order merchandise—L. L. Bean, J. Crew, Land's End. Neither of you orders very much, but slowly leafing through the catalogues relaxes you, cools you out from the tension of the day. Handsome, muscular men, lovely women, all smiling and having a grand old time in the sleek pages of the catalogues. Kids are in now, so the pages are graced with laughing children and adults in a variety of wonderful situations. The relentlessly happy, well-polished families that grace the advertising pages, husbands and wives and children—everybody so upbeat and obviously having a great time with this parenting, family thing—it only makes you feel lonelier.

As you lie there huffing and puffing doing your sit-ups you realize that this precious evening could slip away into "catalogue therapy." You have to say something, but what? You strive for conversation: "The kids were great going to sleep tonight." *Not the kids again! Can't we talk about anything besides the kids?*

"They must have been tired, they had a busy day at school," your wife agrees.

Then she looks right at you, lying there on the floor wrapped in your bathrobe, and she asks about your son: "Did you see the note from his teacher?"

"No . . ."

"He lost his music book again; I think we ought to tell him that if he's not going to practice, then he shouldn't be taking these lessons."

"What? The music lessons haven't been going well?" you blurt out before you can think. You're feeling the vulnerability of the spouse who is not home with the kids during the day. Your wife seems to know so much more about home life. She's the mom.

"Oh come on," she rebukes you, flipping the Victoria's Secret catalogue onto the bed in an impatient gesture. The catalogue falls open to a picture of a fetching model in a bathrobe, and you notice that you can see the outline of a breast, actually the "robe" she's wearing is open so that the front of the breast is covered but the rest is quite visible. The woman's breast is firm and smooth. You wonder what it would be like to put your hand on that breast. You realize that not one of these models looks like she's ever had children or nursed a baby—is it possible that none of these models is a mother? That can't be. You want to ask your wife, *Do you think it's possible that any of these beautiful women are mothers?* but that doesn't seem to be the tack to take in this discussion.

Your wife is still on the topic of your son's musical career: "You know that he hasn't been practicing for weeks, he just goes for the lessons, but we haven't signed his practice book once since last month," she says with an edge of irritation in her voice. "I wish you'd talk to him about practicing, too."

Well, now, you're an involved father, and you want to make that clear. So you tell your wife that just the other day he forgot his practice book and called from school, wanting you to drive over with it, and you remembered that you and your wife have decided to teach your son more responsibility and personal control by letting him take the consequences for his actions. You have vowed not to get him off some of the hooks he creates for himself, and so when he called you said what a shame it was that he forgot the book, but you couldn't bring it over because you were very busy right now and so he'd have to go to music class without it. He got pissed, ending the conversation with sarcasm, "Oh, fine, Dad!" but maybe he got the message. As you go on about this your wife interrupts you: *"Couldn't* or *wouldn't?"* You're not sure what she means, but can feel something unpleasant coming toward you. Your mind races to get where she's going ahead of her, but you fail: "You said you *couldn't* come, not that you *wouldn't* come. Don't make it sound like you can't. You want him to know it's his responsibility and you're not going to cover for him." She says this to you rather gently, but her very gentleness sparks your fury.

Oh, give it a break, you think. The fury you're feeling is the fury of exposure. Your wife has exposed your own difficulty in saying no to your kid. That call was really painful—you didn't want to let him down, didn't want him to get angry at you, so you fudged it and said, "I can't" when in fact, as your wife has just pointed out, what you had wanted to say was "I won't."

But you can't admit that to your wife. Who cares if she is right, you feel little and inept and exposed and so, like many people who feel shame, you want to start a fight, to strike back.

"Couldn't, wouldn't—oh, come on, so I didn't say it just right, give me a break," you grumble.

She says, "Well, there's a difference," but also, generous person that she is, she apologizes.

Yet there's still tension in the air.

Oh, give me a break, let it be! Get off the kid! You feel a familiar resentment. It's the schoolmarmish I-know-what-needs-to-be-done-here tone that you remember hearing from your own mother. You feel the pressure of mothers, mothers who seem to know everything or want to know everything. There's an ancient feeling tapped inside you, of wanting to get away from the insufferable caretaking of mothers, the way they never stop trying to get you to zip up your coat, to remember your lunch. Mothers need to "civilize" boys, and then, when those boys become fathers, do they ever forgive their mothers? Your mother took you for piano lessons in elementary school, dropping you off at the female piano teacher's house, and you remember hating the lessons, the rigidity of what was required to master an instrument. Your passionate desire to play an instrument was locked away undiscovered for years because you hated how she made you play those goddamn scales over and over—Why, you didn't practice either, you realize with a start!—and finally you made your teacher so mad that she kicked you out. When your mother arrived to pick you up from the lesson one day she found you waiting on the front step of the teacher's house, ashamed and defiant at being told never to return.

For a moment, lying there on the floor, you're confused: Are you the child or the adult here, a husband or a son?

"Okay, okay, fine, we'll finish this later," your wife suggests with a tone of retreat and dismay in her voice. There's silence between you. *It's now 10:00 P.M., is this worth it? I've got that early morning appointment, maybe it would be better to go to sleep.*

What are you going to do now? You remember a husband who said to you, "It's not just finding the time to connect with my wife, it's hard to start talking even when we're alone—so much has changed between us since we married that between the kids and our jobs there's so much going on I often don't know what to say, where to start." You're seized by a desire to read the paper, turn on the Celtics game, anything to distract you from this woman, your wife. It's actually your own clumsiness you want distraction from. You feel lost in an internal thicket of thorny, painful feelings. Angry at your mother, loving your mother. You think about all she did for you, how much you mattered to her, that she drove you all over the suburbs in search of piano lessons, orthodontists, dance lessons, how much she matters to you, how impossible a task it can feel to raise a boy. All of a sudden you're filled with regrets about the piano: *How come I didn't practice the piano, why was I so stubborn and rebellious, if only I had buckled down then I'd be able to play beautiful melodies now,* then you want to clamp down on your son, but, no, you realize that might only make him hate the very instrument you want him to love. You wish there was a piano right here in the bedroom, you'd play honky-tonk music to your wife, you'd play great jazz riffs, you'd woo her with Beethoven's Moonlight Sonata. Except there *is* no piano, and you couldn't play it even if there was 'cause you didn't practice when you were a kid! All you have is yourself, and you don't know what to do. But you have to plunge ahead, and so, like fathers through the ages trying to deal with their wives, to woo them, you say something because it's better than nothing.

"Okay, fine, let's just do some back rubs," you suggest haltingly.

"More work?" comes the response.

You glare at each other from opposite ends of the bed.

You know that now you're certainly not going to reveal that actually you're less interested in back rubs than in sex. Despite all, you really would like to make love this evening, but that possibility seems to be receding farther and farther into the distance. You want to put your hand seductively on her leg, but you don't want to be rejected. It feels as if those times when you've been pushed away in bed win first prize in the Most Shame Sweepstakes; it taps into some early concern about your sexual potency. You sit there frozen. You want to be assertive and manly for your wife and start something happening, but on the other hand you don't want to come on too strong and get rejected or act like a clumsy oaf. The hell with piano lessons: you wish foreplay was easy, something you had mastered, so that you could just raise your little finger and your wife would be magically sexually excited. *Foreplay, what's good foreplay?* you wonder, certain again that every other man has mastered this moment better than you have. You feel great shame that even after forty-eight years, even after fathering children and demonstrating your potency, you still don't know how to make love to a woman. What the hell is wrong with you?

You realize then that part of you just wants to fight with your wife, that you both just need to explode, to release the build-up of pressures and expectations from this impossible activity called marriage. It's the intolerable pressure of all the questions that have to be reanswered every day. *Bear down on your kids or not? Does my wife remember who I am? Why exactly are we together?*

The model from Victoria's Secret stares up at you from the bed, the catalogue lying open where your wife has tossed it. Looking at the model, early twenties, languorous body, you recall the early passion you had with your wife before marrying, before the kids were born, what sex was like in your twenties when you wanted to make love so badly and so often. A friend once confided to you his belief that "mistresses are the only way for us to keep our marriages together and passion in our lives." He said we expect too much from marriage these days, that it's impossible for us to be a parent, spouse, have careers, and also retain a feeling of spontaneity and passion with a wife. Better to separate passion and families: let your wife be the mother of your children, let her be your best friend, let her have a career, and then keep romance alive with a mistress across town or next door. You wonder what it would be like to know that model. You think how you've been interviewed on TV sets where many beautiful women were very available, you think how lovely many of the undergraduates you teach are, how much a hero you seem to these women, a professor, charming and humorous. You think about how often a man becomes more attractive as he ages, a distinguished father figure for women. A sulky part of you yearns to inform your wife: *I'm a hero, you know, to people who don't know me very well.*

Before you can point this out, she apologizes for her rebuff: "I just can't bear the thought of anyone wanting anything more from me right now. I'm exhausted. I feel wiped out."

Her openness softens you. You begin to talk about how depleted each of you sometimes feels after the kids are asleep, almost too raw to be touched, totally unable to tolerate another demand. In this mood, someone saying "Rub my back" becomes a fine excuse for a war since how dare they ask anything more of me!

Suddenly you realize that you need to sit and hold each other and talk, and maybe that will be foreplay, maybe not.

"I don't want to talk about the kids right now."

"Me either."

But you can't stop because your relationship with your wife is so entwined with them. She goes on: "I worry so much about whether I'm doing okay as a mother—how do all those other mothers get their kids to practice? It just looks so easy for them." *Like for other fathers,* you think. The silent oppression of parenthood begins to unite you, not divide you. *She and I are in this together,* you realize.

You get a picture of how lonely mothering is—that for all the romanticizing of how "interdependent" and "relational" women are supposed to be, they still compete with each other and still feel oppressed by performance expectations, by the relentless feeling of not doing well enough. Just like men.

Wanting to help your wife out of those awful feelings, you say gently, "It's okay about the music—look, he's *going* to the lessons, right? He's asked for them, and he's enjoying it. At age nine let's just let him get the feel of an instrument." You talk about your own experiences with music, and the two of you resolve to talk to the music teacher to find out more about what's going on in the lessons.

You realize that the tension between you has drained away. You feel a warmth and closeness with your wife. *We're getting through this!* you realize with joy. *We're doing this together!*

You look at your wife, sitting next to you in bed, and think how she has made her stand with you, that we are all so interdependent as parents, that our self-esteem is tied in so much with how well we're doing as parents. And you know she depends on you to keep herself sane, just as you depend on her. What a strange raft we are on in marriages, a sort of *African Queen* adventure, just Hepburn and Bogart trying to get through the jungles and keep the little boat from capsizing in enormous rapids. Of course we have allies and helpers—friends, counselors, rabbis, ministers—but when you come right down to it we depend so much on each other, husbands and wives. Courage is really needed to acknowledge our interdependence. You recall a quote you saw scribbled on a university building site once: "There is room for courage in the bedroom as elsewhere."

"Do you think I'm a good mother?" your wife asks shyly.

"Absolutely," you say, and then you can't stop talking: "Since we're fessing up, let me tell you about *would* and *could*. You're right, I was having trouble saying no to our boy. It felt so hurtful, there he was at school, what would it cost me to drive over there with it?"

"What would it have cost *him* if you had driven over there, if you can't say no and teach him limits and responsibility?"

"But I don't want him to see me as a judgmental, unforgiving father, you know, the Giant in 'Jack and the Beanstalk.' "

"Don't be silly. You're a very involved and present father. He needs you to be there for him, to be an authority who can set limits, that's different from being an ogre."

"Yes?"

"Really. You're a great father, you work hard and you're available. Letting your son take responsibility for his actions is *not* abusive! You men of your generation want so much to be available and supportive and different from your own fathers that you can't see that you also need to be strong and demanding—otherwise how will our children learn those things? Don't let your internal demons get you down."

As your wife talks you contemplate how husbands and wives rescue each other from their internal demons: the normal self-questioning and uncertainty that this impossible activity called parenting generates. You recall the other day how you and your wife and the kids were driving home and the kids wanted to stop for the umpteenth time, this time at a comic book store, just after you've bought two new bikes for them. You are thinking of the total cost of those bikes, and though you don't want to shame them by reminding them that you've just spent close to $450 on bicycles, still it makes a great deal of difference to *you* to save the twenty-five cents on the comic book so you say "no, no more stops" and the kids get angry and whiny and you continue to hold your ground, reassuring yourself desperately that actually this is a very important lesson you're teaching your kids in limit setting and not always having everything they want even as you drive along down the main street and note the calm that seems to inhabit other cars compared to the typhoon of feeling in your vehicle.

At such moments you yearn to be the kind of father who can "just say no" and feel fine about it. You wish the kids would say, "Okay, Dad, whatever you say." Sometimes they do that, but now all you can think about is how you can't even control your kids after buying them these fancy bikes, and what kind of failure are you? You plunge into your own internal chaos around authority and limits—am I being a hard-ass for no reason? Maybe I should just be a good guy and say yes? What's the big deal about a lousy quarter and a couple of comic books? But you said no, after all, so now you'd better stick to it or you'll show all the world that you suffer from the dreaded disease of Inconsistent Limits. You contemplate going to Parents Anonymous and blurting out, "I'm an Inconsistent Limiter."

Whereupon your wife turns to the kids and says, "Look, your father's right, now let's stop this." Her words help to restore your own sanity and self-worth. It hardly mattered that the kids didn't immediately come to attention and stop their requests; what did matter is that another adult joined you and you felt less alone, less adrift in your personal fears and fantasies of failure and imperfection. It's sometimes not so important what your wife says, it's just knowing that she's there with you. There's an affirmation in your wife's words—your limit makes sense, another adult has validated it.

You think of how a wife can rescue her husband in those tense situations or leave him hanging there, feeling like a lumbering, slow-moving ox of a father who can't make decisions and fails no matter which side of the issue he comes down on. She could just as easily have abandoned her allegiance to you and sided with the kids: "Oh, dear, that's ridiculous. Let the kids have a little pleasure, you're always rushing us so, you're just like your father—once you get behind the wheel of a car, you don't stop until you run out of gas." Ha ha.

You think about that intense, intimate connection between you and your wife and how it can distance the two of you even as it joins you. Your very dependence on each other can become a source of shame. Typically there are only two adults to witness what happens in your family— you and your wife—and there is great reliance and need in that.

Then you think about how you often abandon your wife, how at the end of a day after dinner has gone fine and you're getting the kids ready for bed, she comes up with yet another chore, as all mothers seem to, checking her internal sense of keeping ahead of the mess and reminding everyone that all the clutter and toys in the living room need to be cleaned up, and part of you feels that familiar *here-goes-mom* resentment and you roll your eyes and wander out of the room saying you'll find the sports section of the paper and put *that* away, and you're aware of how much fun it is to undercut mom but not so much fun for her. Now you see that it's normal and natural for parents to float on a sea of passion, sometimes united as mother and father, sometimes joined with the kids against our spouse. It takes a sense of humor to keep a marriage together.

You think about hidden battles for attention between spouses, about how fighting is a way of asking the painful question: *Am I still lovable?* Often it can be easier to fight with your spouse than to ask that question directly. A father who works as a newspaper reporter for a large metro daily paper got into fights with his wife about his helping his daughter get ready for school. His wife became furious one day at how he helped his six-year-old daughter put on her boots and then walked her to school as part of his morning ritual with his kids. There was a lot of yelling about whether he ought to help his daughter so much, until his wife said: "You don't even say good-bye to me when you leave in the morning" and then they realized the fighting had to do with the wife's wish for some attention from her husband. She wanted to feel as loved by her husband as her daughter was, particularly as she was getting ready to go to work. You know that it is normal and natural for both adults to want to feel cherished in the relationship. So much goes to the kids that the parents can end up feeling as if they live on separate icebergs. You wonder if often the parents are really angry at the kids for stealing their spouse away, but since we can't bear being pissed at the kids, the poor kids, so innocent and vulnerable, we get angry at our spouses instead. In all the talk about "family values," no one mentions the thicket of competing needs and wants that goes into a family.

You resolve to pay attention to a new family value: recognizing your wife's need for love and affirmation. You realize too that lovemaking and sexuality begins before you get into the bedroom, that foreplay starts when you wake up in the morning, in how you kindle your love through the day, not that you can be a constant romantic poet but that romance really has to do with complimenting your wife on how she dresses when she's ready for the office in the morning, with kissing her good morning when you come downstairs, with the touch on the arm, the arm around the shoulder during the day or the evening. It has to do with the kiss and embrace of your wife when the kids are present.

"Oohh-la-la," your children exclaimed the other day when you gave your wife a passionate kiss—it intrigued them and probably also scared them. This is not an insignificant moment in the family: it's Dad proclaiming that the mother in the family is also his wife. You *are* kidnapping their mother from them, albeit temporarily.

Your own parents come to mind: how they never really displayed physical affection in the home. Your father and mother are devoted to each other; they are an elegant couple together, and you admire the resilience and depth of their love for each other, but you can't recall seeing your father ever kissing your mother on the lips as a kid. You hardly have memories of him with his arm around her. You're willing to concede that this might be selective amnesia, that there is something scary about seeing your father's active sexuality because it points to his power in the family, the fact that he is bigger and stronger (at least for a while) than anyone else in the family. In turning away from our sexuality as fathers, we are also trying to keep the family a safe place for our kids. But maybe that's the point: for many of us as fathers the active flaunting of our passion may feel scary. Scary to us as well as to our kids. For a father it's no simple matter to keep the blue flame of sexuality burning, feeling potent and powerful, becoming the Giant in "Jack and the Beanstalk"—Woman! bring me my beer and bread and gold—melding together the very hungry, demanding passion that underlies sexuality with the wish to be paternal and protective.

You think about the fight you just had and how quickly you got through it. It's only 10:30 P.M. An hour of sparring, not too bad. That's something you've learned together: how to fight, not to be so scared of each other's anger. The fighting almost seems like something that you have to do, to blow off the steam of the day. You remember all the endless fights back in the beginning of the relationship, especially right after you were married, how you used to think that the fighting was about who was right and who was wrong. Once in the first year of your marriage, you fought for hours about whether you should have taken a cab to meet friends at a restaurant on a cold, rainy evening. It was a matter of five dollars, and you pounded at each other for hours after the meal, she saying, *Don't be such a tight-ass about money* and you saying, *That's five dollars when we could have easily walked through the rain, we can't afford such extravagances!* until you both got exhausted and fell asleep.

It used to seem that the fighting was a problem that had to be eliminated, that it kept you from intimacy, but now it feels more like fighting is a part of intimacy. Back then fighting protected you from each other, fighting expressed your mutual craziness about committing to each other, about merging your lives and becoming interdependent, it was a continuous series of temper tantrums about having your own way and not having to take the other person into account, until you realized that a part of marriage involved letting go, a giving up of control. Now fighting helps connect you, you need to get through the primitive, built-up passions and explosiveness of parenting, and you're proud of your ability to fight. The fighting cuts through the marital sludge, burns it away, so you can see each other. It feels like part of a passionate life together. Reading through the results of a survey about marital satisfaction, you were amused at the reply one man gave to the question about whether he and his wife ever think of divorce: "Murder yes, divorce never!" You think of friends of yours who can't get angry at each other and so never seem really to connect. So busy trying to "make nice," they don't dare get turned on to each other.

You're still scared by your wife's anger, the way it taps into ancient echoes of what would happen if Mother got *really* angry at you, childhood anxieties about Mother's power for good and evil, the fear of the "witch mother" who inhabits all our psyches. But you've learned to listen, to let your wife be angry without trying so hard to shut her up, while she has learned the same with you.

You sit and massage each other's feet, talking now at ten-thirty at night. Finally together, the kids asleep, you might as well be alone in the house. You're on a raft— around you flow all the worries and opportunities of your life: earning enough money, hoping the kids will learn what they need to in school, hoping they'll have the self-esteem it takes to have a joyous life, hoping they'll know how beloved they are, hoping you'll be able to separate from them and from your own parents' aging: *Ma and Dad, are you okay?* You think about how hard you both work to earn a living, how you could earn even more if you worked harder, but you spend so much time writing, your hourly wage certainly doesn't calculate out to what you'd have made if you were a high-powered lawyer. You think about your kids and your worries for them, how you leave your wife alone with her worries, then find her, and you think that any disappointment you have in her is matched by her disappointment in you. You know that she forgives you every day, and suddenly you feel enormous gratitude to your wife for being with you. You remember a dear friend who told you that at age forty-seven he is amazed that he is married, with a family, how back in college he wasn't sure if a woman would ever really love him, "warts and all," and you realize that this is the life you've created and she is your companion.

You recall with a rush your marital vows: "I welcome you into my life as the companion of my days." The wedding was in the woods on a friend's farm in the late 1970s, and you were so anxious about commitment that the night before at a party in the farmhouse you sat in an old New England rocking chair in front of the enormous stone fireplace and, staring at the fire, you thought: *What the hell am I getting myself into?* In the wedding ceremony, on a freezing Columbus Day weekend, after the welcome by the minister, you and she stood under the trees and you each made a statement to the assembled group of family and friends: Your wife talked about love and the future, and you did, too, but somehow you also segued into wanting "to remember those people around the world who aren't here, like the Nicaraguans fighting for their freedom from Somoza," and everyone listened to this statement with a straight face, this being the time of the *real* Nicaraguan revolution before the contras and all and so it seemed vitally important to you to remember the Nicaraguan freedom fighters, yet they likely had more pressing problems and so couldn't attend. In retrospect you wondered how you'd gotten onto *that* topic, but now it makes sense to you to see that you were so terrified of the commitment to a woman that of course you'd be thinking about fighting for freedom and so you wanted to remember that fight. It felt like the biggest decision you had ever made, whether to marry this woman or not, and now looking back you realize it *was* the biggest decision of your life, that your trust in each other made it possible to weather the weight of deciding to become a parent, to manage the difficulty of infertility before you became a parent, to bear the anxiety of all the choices that adult life requires. And gratefully you're aware of your wife's enormous trust in you and all that the two of you have accomplished in the world, made real; you're not thinking of material things, but of having been able to find each other and to marry and to have children and be parents and lovers together. You look at her and see her wonderful smile, this person who has been through it with you, really through it, and suddenly what you most treasure from the marriage are your vows: *the companion of my days.* You think of the man scared of his wife's aging and suddenly you feel the opposite: you look at the specks of gray, those few extra pounds she's always trying to lose, and you realize that these are the badges of your common life together, without them your life would not be real, and you love her all the more for being a real person, not a picture in a catalogue. You remember with a smile the comment of a friend of yours who *almost* had an affair, and when you asked what stopped him, he replied: "Well, I knew that anyone I really wanted to be involved with would basically be just like my wife."

Then you have insight into men's fears about their wives' aging, why it's so hard for us to *really look at our wives*— maybe it's about our terror of life's limits and the fact that our wives really know who we are. It's the death of fantasy. Our wives confront us with the "one and only life cycle" that Erik Erikson talks about. When you were younger, in graduate school, unmarried, wandering from one party to another, counting your loneliness as creativity and independence, you used to mock Erikson's notion that healthy adult aging involved the recognition of the singularity and meaning of your choices and decisions. In graduate school your life felt infinite, but now that you're a parent you see Erikson's point. Our wives are reminders of the reality of our choices; that we married *this* woman, worked at *this* job, had *these* children. No substitutes allowed.

And you begin to realize that this woman, your companion, will be your companion, you hope, long after your children have left. An older man once said to you, looking at his empty nest, "I got my wife back now that the kids are grown, but she's not the same woman I married." He meant that she had grown and changed and he hadn't noticed. You don't want that to happen to you. You don't want the two of you to grow so far apart while you're raising the kids that you can't recognize each other when they leave. You resolve to make the most of the "hit-and-run" intimacy of today's marriages, our generation of the massage oil, in which we're all trying to carve out enough time in our busy days really to see and notice each other, trying to find a few perfect moments before sleep, before the kids wake up, whenever. You recall how many men have told you that they can only connect with their wives when they go away for a weekend; there's that one weekend a year at the cape or on the island. "It can't be just twenty-four hours, it must be thirty-six hours at least," reported one man, and you know that's important, finding separate time to go away together, but as you look at your wife sitting across from you on your bed you know, too, that a lot can happen in a half hour if you give yourself over to it, and you resolve to try and remember that.

So as you sit and talk, all the time rubbing each other's bodies, you lean forward and put your arm around your wife and pull her toward you, remembering that there is indeed room for courage in the bedroom, and yes, you're so pleased that she doesn't push you away. Neither of you feels depleted any longer, but rather you feel very drawn to each other, both wanting to know again how wonderful your bodies feel. There's no question of aging when you get really close and you remember how wonderful making love with your wife is, and who cares about how early an appointment you have the next morning, why, you could make love all night. And then you realize after all that this conversation and back rubbing was indeed just foreplay.

CHAPTER **10**

REMAINING A FATHER THROUGH IT ALL

*A Cup of Coffee with a Father
Who Is Divorced*

One day not too long ago I met a friend of mine named Edward in Harvard Square in Cambridge for a cup of coffee. I hadn't thought of Edward as a close friend, and what brought us together, as it often does for men, was our work. Edward is in his mid-forties, the father of several young children, and divorced. He's a forceful type of man, compact and athletic. A business consultant, he and I are members of the same national professional organization. We are both on the same committee in the organization and since we had some minor committee business to take care of, we decided to do so over a coffee at a coffee shop not far from our offices.

I hadn't talked much with Edward in over a year, although since our children attend the same public school I've often seen him on the way in or out of school. I knew that he had been through a difficult separation, then divorce over the past two years, and we had made brief, glancing mention of the divorce in the doorway of the school after the kids had been settled in their classes.

"Ed! Sorry to hear about you and Betty!" "Oh, yeah, Sam, thanks, yeah, it's the pits, hey, got to run to my office, thanks for asking!" "Oh, sure, Ed, hey, let's get together for coffee sometime." "Yeah, let's make sure to do that." And so we'd each hurry to our cars, busy and off to work.

This snowy Cambridge afternoon was the first time Edward and I had sat down together in quite a while. We took care of the committee business rather quickly, perhaps helped along by the caffeine rush from the espressos. So we sat and looked out at the snow, as our talk turned to each other.

Edward said that it was hard for him to focus on this committee business because he felt so angry a lot of the time.

"Angry?" I wondered, puzzled, as I found myself hearing about his divorce, finalized just last year.

Yeah, Edward went on, he felt that the marriage had ended with a lot of bitterness between him and his wife. He had emerged as the bad guy in the eyes of everyone, cold and aloof and uncaring, and now he only saw his kids on two nights a week and on the weekends. Many of their friends seemed to think that Betty was the victim, when in truth it was much more complicated than that. I sat and listened with a mixture of curiosity and disdain, not wanting to get pulled into sorting out who was right and who was wrong. Often listening to someone talk about a divorce feels like passing a car wreck along the highway—you want to stare and to look away at the same time.

There was an intensity in Edward's voice, he clearly wanted me to know something: his words, like a freight train laboring uphill, seemed to be going toward a destination unseen.

"And *our* friends didn't really seem like *my* friends," he went on. "Actually, to tell you the truth these past two years have been a pretty lonely time." He looked directly at me as he talked, and I heard him say that he "felt abandoned by my friends, people I counted on to be there were not," and suddenly the atmosphere changed in the coffee shop as I realized we were dancing around something between us, that Edward wasn't just talking about some abstract "friends" out there in the snowy wastes of Cambridge, he was also talking about the friend sitting across the table from him. Or so I imagined.

I confronted then a familiar nervous feeling inside me as I wondered whether two men could deal with the disappointment and anger between them. *Forget it*, a cowardly inner voice counseled me, *he's talking in code, just ignore it, say something like "Geez, ain't that a shame" or "Life's a bitch." Skip over this stuff about 'abandonment' so you can talk about the Red Sox*, my inner counselor whispered. I'm seized by a desire to discuss the latest Red Sox off-season trade, renewing the time-honored Boston baseball fan's obsession with whether maybe this year the team will win a pennant. Underneath my fascination with the Red Sox at this moment lies an ancient dread: Can another man and I be direct about our anger or disappointment or envy of each other without things escalating into a fight? What would happen if we really put our cards on the table? We're two gamblers in the casino about to show our cards, will one of us also pull a gun? Too bad there's no place to check your weapons by the door of the coffee shop.

What to say? As I looked at my friend, he seemed suddenly forlorn and lonely. I plunged ahead. "Do you feel *I* abandoned you?" I asked, wondering inside, *Who, me?*

Edward looked relieved at my question and answered directly: "Yeah, Sam, I guess I do."

Edward and I stared at each other in silence, one of us married, one divorced, both fathers, looking out over the chasm of our difficult experiences.

We live in an age of divorce; it's become so commonplace that we have a new class of kids—children of divorce. Thinking about divorce and fathering, we all fancy we know what needs to be done: fathers need to be more in the postdivorce picture with their children, not lose contact with their kids, not abandon them. It's vitally important that divorced fathers and children find ways to hold on to each other past the divorce, regardless of the custody arrangements, or to reconnect even years later after the rupture of the divorce.

Yet we can't really understand the divorced father's struggle to hold on to his connections with his children unless we also understand the mixed feelings that arise between men who have never divorced and those who have. Shame, anger, hope, and love—these are not experiences just for divorced fathers. All parents struggle with them, but there are special pressures on divorced fathers that can split them off from their children. It's important not to sentimentalize or whitewash divorced fathers, but it's equally important to see them as real people, to acknowledge the sense of abandonment that many men experience after a divorce.

Which is all fine and dandy to affirm as a well-meaning socially conscious goal, but I'm sitting in a public place with another man, a guy larger than me, who has just taken the risk of telling me that he's pissed at me because I've let him down. I'm confused. "How?" I wonder, truly perplexed.

"Well, you never called, you didn't really try to get in touch with me, even after the separation when my wife and I decided she'd stay in our home with the kids and I was living in my little apartment near the campus." I picture that apartment, how forlorn that move had seemed when I heard through the grapevine that Edward had to leave his home of ten years, the house that he and his wife had renovated in better times, and move to the small rental place by himself where he was still living. *What is it like to leave your home, scurry away to a strange apartment, like going back to when you were a student, familiar and foreign at the same time?*

"Well, why didn't you call me?" I reply, remembering too that men don't really call each other for help, we speak in coded messages, a cryptic Morse code of the heart. I recall how about a year ago my wife had come home from dropping the kids off at school and casually mentioned how she had seen Edward at the school door and "He said he was thinking about you, hoped to see you soon," and I hadn't really picked up on it, probably in my rush to do something it had hardly registered, and I feel ashamed of myself for not listening better. Then I think, *He was delivering an SOS through my wife, the dumb jock, why didn't he just call me and ask?* and then I admit to myself: *If I felt like an outcast, if I were going through a failure of such magnitude as a divorce, how quick would I be to call my married friends?* I hope I'd be smart enough to remember to stay in touch, to go out of my way to collar my friends and not spiral into a pit of self-accusation and shame, but I'm not entirely sure I would be so smart. It's so easy for men to get isolated in difficult personal times. A man once said to me, "I'm a lone wolf, I like to return to my cave and lick my wounds in private," but I wonder now: *How about the wounds that don't heal, what do you do with wounds that just fester if you can't get out of that cave?*

Edward asks, "Do you know what it's like to see your married friends when you feel like you've just failed at the marriage and father thing? Not so easy."

Then I realize we're talking about shame here—that many men who go through divorce are first of all caught in a spiral of shame and failure. For a marriage to fail, after the romantic expectations, after the belief that this union would last forever—for we don't really enter into marriage thinking, *Well, remember, I might be divorced!* We marry with the expectation that this is permanent and forever, you're giving yourself over to your beloved—to get divorced after all these hopes and expectations, how can you *not* feel that you've just failed? You can't keep your wife attracted to you, you're unable to make a relationship work—how inadequate can you be?

I remember the words of one divorced father who looked back years after he had reconstituted his life, remarried now and with a decent relationship with his kids: "The most embarrassing moment of my life was walking out on my first wife, unable to make it work, and feeling that this could happen again."

Your statistical anonymity gets lost when you're divorced, it's like when you become gravely ill and lose the illusion of invulnerability about your body—*I've* got cancer, something went really wrong, what could happen next? One smart, savvy divorced father described why he became more and more socially isolated in the first few years after the divorce: "I couldn't be around my married friends, I felt like I had an illness that was catching." A committed father who wound up with an equitable custody arrangement with his wife, this observant, thoughtful man noted that his daughters seek out other divorced children at their school, it helps them deal with how different they feel from the children in intact families. But this man found that divorced dads make only superficial connections with each other. "We're men after all," he said sadly, "and we want everyone to know we're divorced, it's too large a wound or difference to just ignore, but we don't want to actually have to *talk* about it. So instead it'll be like 'You're divorced, too, oh, that's tough isn't it,' and 'Yeah,' and then it's on to shop talk, men-talk."

My friend sits across the table, stirring his coffee. He looks up at me tentatively, and I say: "I guess I hadn't really thought much about what you've been going through."

And we start to talk. He has all this energy, now he wants to tell me about what really happened in the marriage, he wants to set the record straight, it feels as if a dam is in danger of bursting, and I'm the one who'll be flooded. I sit and listen to him talk about how his wife is telling everyone that he was cold and unresponsive, she constantly complained that she could never read his feelings, he didn't talk enough, nothing he did was right to her, counseling didn't help, he could never really prove he loved her well enough, but in truth my friend says he felt as if he could never satisfy her, she became more and more critical and demanding. She was like a witch, he says, and as I listen I find myself drawing back from the table, almost wanting to leave, to stand up, to go find the bathroom, make a phone call.

It feels impossible to sort out. I sit and listen to my friend, the husband, talk, and I feel a lot of sympathy for him—*Gee, that must have been hard*—and I mean it. Part of me feels, *That rotten ex-wife of yours, how impossible she was!* Yet I know that if I sat and listened to his wife, as I've done in other divorce situations with friends, I'd hear her side of the story about how he did this and that and I'd feel *Why, that horrid man, how could he do that to you?* As he vents his anger and dismay and confusion I'm having a rubber-band experience, feeling pulled in many different directions, stretched and twisted, wondering who's right and who's wrong. Where is the truth? It's awful to feel as if you have to side with one person when you want to side with both. I feel as if I'm watching *Rashomon*, except I *want* to side with someone, I want the truth, to find out what really happened, I can't tolerate the uncertainty.

Why? Because, I realize, as I listen to my friend's pain, that *there but for the grace of God go I*. I think about my own marriage—how I can't even imagine divorce, my commitment to my wife and family seems unshakable, and yet it doesn't help when my friend replies with a knowing smile, "I felt that, too, before we ran into our troubles and couldn't solve them and got divorced."

What would drive me so far as divorce? I remember a recent fight in my marriage about where to live. My wife is so happy in the country, she could live there forever she says. While I'm enjoying our year away, I favor moving back to the city eventually, the city feels like home, I'm closer to my work and old friends. My wife, who's found interesting work up here, would like to buy a farm just down the road. As we both struggled with whose wishes and needs and work commitments had priority I suddenly thought, *Jesus, what if we're really different? What if we have irreconcilable differences in values, and tastes, and desires?*

A friend of mine, happily married many years, once remarked, "There are so many times in the marriage when I think 'Is this really worth it?' but of course you go on." I had gotten ahold of myself that night of the argument and said to my wife, "We have to approach this decision about where to live assuming that we can both get enough of our needs met," and the argument felt healing. As we talked it became clear that my wife and I were less polarized than I thought. But what if we really, really were different or couldn't find a way to arrive at a pleasing compromise? I think about how easy it is sometimes to withdraw from my wife, how quickly I sulk when we reach a hard place in the marriage, and I wonder about the games I play. What if she had said she'd had enough of that? And I—such a marvel of self-control, or so I think, my ability to stay focused and get the job done is a source of humor between my wife and myself—what if for a moment I were not so self-controlled, what if I were traveling at a lonely or difficult time in the marriage and the normal flirtations that occur away from home turned inexplicably into a real affair?

What if I came home hiding a secret and it was one that my wife and I could not get past? Or what if some conflict in my personal history just reared its head, what if my wife or I got really depressed after a loss, what if some ancient sorrow or inability to forgive surfaced one day in the way that the past can roar up, as if from the ocean deep, to savage our soft psychic underbelly?

I wonder how I'd cope with *that* and don't want to think about it. I don't want to think about divorce. Okay, my friend abandoned me in his shame, he didn't call, but did I abandon him in my fear, in the frightening questions about my own life any divorce raises?

Even as my friend goes on, he's on a roll now, talking about seeing his kids for two days every week and every other weekend, I don't want to think about it. He lives only ten city blocks away from them, but he picks them up on Tuesday night and brings them home Thursday night, and then he has them on alternate weekends. *Giving up my kids all the time! Having to pick them up and drop them off at a different home!* Losing your kids feels like the hardest part of all.

It's odd to speak of "losing" them since they're not really lost, but there is a loss, it's the loss of the intact family. For me family is like bedrock, and I've noticed as I've gotten older that I don't like to be away from my family for more than a few nights at a time. There is something so soothing about returning home to my family. I can't help wondering whether the fragmenting of the family touches on some primitive sense of loss inside each of us. It's like the child coming home from school, bursting in the door, exclaiming: "Mom? Dad? Are you here?" At some deep level we all want to know everyone's home.

What does it feel like to be so apart from your children? Loss can shape the very experience of fatherhood for a man who is divorced. "For me and a lot of divorced fathers, the kids are not just down the road," reported one father. "The biggest loss wasn't not seeing them every night, it was thinking of them so far away." After the divorce his ex-wife moved with his seven- and nine-year-old son and daughter from New York City to Europe and then to California before settling in the Pacific Northwest. He was telling me about the divorce fifteen years after it happened, but he still remembered vividly "struggling with depression almost all the time." Sitting in the living room of his New York City apartment with his second wife of ten years, he told me how his longing for his kids was *visceral.* "A part of me felt ripped out, it was a physical feeling after they moved, loss and emptiness like in an echo chamber." With some gentle prompting from his wife, he described how he used to listen for echoes of his children, how he would wander around the house looking for them before and after their twice-a-year visits. "I'd be trying to remember things about them. Voices and conversations we had when they were getting ready to go to bed, things they left behind, how lovely my daughter's bedroom looked, *yet she wasn't there.* I'd just sit in the room and try to absorb the relationship that was now gone."

For this man reestablishing relationships with his now grown children over a period of years is the major accomplishment of his middle age: "It's not been easy, we're all trying to learn how to play together as adults, that's something I missed with the kids when they were younger."

Playing with your kids postdivorce can be a trying experience, underlining your own incompetence and reminding you of the mother who is no longer your wife. For some fathers who are divorced the first "visiting day" is also the first time ever that they've been alone with their kids. While this is an opportunity to learn how to be close to your kids, it is also a moment of painful emptiness and loss: you're trying to reconstruct your family life without a mother there to "facilitate" things. One wise father who over the years has slowly made things work with his kids reported that at first, "I'd pick up my kids and try to find things for us to do when they were with me, but it was empty and felt pointless." He concluded with a poignant image of loss and vulnerability: "We were like baby sparrows stumbling around on the ground. The time is a jangle of sharp memories over a long, dull ache."

Another man told me about having his kids move after the divorce to a different part of the country, to a home without a phone: "I desperately wanted to stay in touch with them, so we had an arrangement that they would wait by the pay phone at the convenience store down the road every Sunday morning at 10:00 A.M., and no matter what, I would call." For months at a time that would be this man's only connection with his children, two thousand miles away. He talked about how much he missed as a father the overt symbols, what he called "the soft side" of fatherhood—their report cards, visits to their schools on Parent's Day, hanging out with them during Little League or Brownies. "Finally, when we would visit with each other it'd be all catch-up." With a tone of regret he revealed that "the kids' high school years for me are a complete blank." Yet with pride he concluded: "but I never missed one of those Sunday morning phone calls."

Phone calls and letter writing figure prominently in conversations with fathers who are divorced. These are moments of connection and loss combined. A fifty-five-year-old father of teenagers says, "I have made a point of calling every midweek without fail for ten years, along with being there as promised every other weekend except one (big storm) in all that time. I do feel good about that. But I also feel like I miss a lot, I'm just not always there in their life, and so I also need constant reassurance that that's okay." With a trace of irony he adds, "And mostly even 'constant' isn't enough."

One father remarked on the different ways his teenage son and daughter make contact: "I've had about five hundred long-distance phone calls with my kids now, literally. My daughter has usually been easier because she seems to have an agenda ready and generally brings some item to the phone to discuss. When she was younger, it was a story she had read or a film seen; she would regale me at enormous length with every detail. Later it was tales of her writing or dramas with friends. With my son it was different. He often has less to say, but interestingly, no less need to hang out on the phone. True, there have been a few times when the call interrupted a TV show or computer game, but I've found that with my boy I have to hang in there even in silence. He figures out things to do with the phone, including putting it inside the toilet bowl as he flushes it. 'Can you hear that, Dad? Isn't that awesome?' " The father tells me that the bottom line is his willingness to tolerate being left hanging, even long-distance, for the sake of their relationship. "In the long run, I feel it's crucial in keeping open the capacity to talk—about anything, just talk. We do know, they and I, how to do that."

Hanging your heart in a toilet bowl, listening to it flush,

you and your child. Other men pour their hearts into letters to their children, trying to maintain the connection, often with great creativity. One father, a minister, wrote a letter every week to his young son, addressing it directly to the boy; the son was a "junior," and the father hoped their shared first name on the envelope would reaffirm the continued bond between them, "claiming and naming him as my son, unique to me as a boy in all the world." The son's letters would typically end with a huge "Love, Bob."

All the efforts to fill up the void, to do well enough, to remember what is constantly lost. I wonder about the father's wish just to get away from the evidence of that loss and failure, to numb it out, deny it. How easy it must be for some men just to wipe out that constant tenuousness, to distance themselves from the pain of coming and going. An older divorced father who *has* stayed in touch revealed, "I can understand when a man says he just can't do it. In fact there were times when I couldn't do it. For a number of years seeing kids my children's age was just too painful. I engaged in a lot of avoidant behavior—being with intact families reminded me too much of what I didn't have."

After all, as a married father I know it's tough enough to stay truly grounded in an intact family, and I'm a guy who gives a fair amount of conscious thought to the importance of "being there." The other day I arrived back home in time for dinner after several days away on business travel and I realized that my son's Cub Scout big-deal annual Pinewood Derby Car Race had taken place two nights before. He and I had worked on that car together, and I wanted to be there for the actual race, which all the parents and the entire Cub pack attend, but my business commitments had taken me across the country that night. I knew he had wanted me to be there and I wasn't, and, with a start, sitting at the dinner table, I realized that I had forgotten to ask how it had gone. So I asked him now, and he replied with that child's mixture of wariness and flippancy disguising his deep, deep wish for me to know about it, "Oh, okay." It turned out that the car didn't win anything, it placed first in one heat, but then got eliminated, and I pulled these facts out of him, but I wanted to energize the whole event for him, I wanted him to know how proud I was of him (and myself) for designing that racer and carving it and sanding it and shellacking it and painting it. He had painted it a dark black with a neat yellow racing stripe on it, and I had encouraged him through it all. He didn't want to follow through at times, but he stuck with it and got the whole thing done, even though I cheated a little while he was at school and smoothed some of the saw cuts and sanded it down more and even put another coat of paint on it one night after he had gone to bed, because I wanted him to do well on this day of the race. And I knew some part of my own fatherly performance was at stake. *Fathers help their kids with their Pinewood Derby racers*, I felt. This was one of those marker events, a father-son rite of passage. So when I couldn't be there for the race I felt bad: my wife went, but I know that it's just not the same as having both parents there. The words of a child of a divorce rang in my ears, a sixty-year-old man who remembered the junior high school Father's Nights events after he began living with his mother: "I remember wrestling with the question of why my father was not the person who took me. My mother was sensitive to this and would periodically say, 'I'll be both father and mother to you,' and

I love her for that, but still, standing there in the school gymnasium without my father, I felt ashamed of myself."

I know, though, that even if I were absent from the derby race, my interest and attention can make up for it, even days later. So that night at the dinner table as I'm trying to get my son to talk, with limited success, I want him to know that it doesn't matter to me if he won or not, I love what he's done, and I want him to see my enthusiasm and pride in what he's accomplished. And then, as I talk about how much I wish I could have seen the race, my wife puts down her fork and says, "Well, I videotaped the race for you," and my son exclaims, "Mom, you did!" and she smiles and we start talking about the videotape at the table before I've even seen it. My wife reminds our son about the other cars and tells me about the heat he won and the funny thing that happened with the tubes of graphite lubricant when someone pressed too hard on one and the slippery stuff went all over the track so the cars went out of control, and we're all laughing about the event and it's as if I had been there, I feel a part of it again, no longer *a father who was not there*.

But *what if my wife hadn't made a videotape for me*? As my friend Edward sips his coffee he tells me about how his kids hardly talk when his ex-wife drops them off or when he picks them up. I think about my gratitude to my wife, how much I depend on her to help me feel a part of things and how she depends on me for the same, and I wonder: *What would it be like to have missed the race and have no one helping you be a part of things*? How easy it would be to become invisible, to miss these small moments with your kids.

I think about the work that has to go on between a divorced husband and wife, how you "divorce the wife but not the kids," as one father told me. Yet in some ways you don't divorce the wife either. For the children to manage the rupture the parents have to work together, have to stay in touch, and they need to keep their own anger, shame, and grief out of the relationship with the kids. I think about the mental work and restraint that's demanded of divorced parents, the carefulness that needs be involved.

The kids need to hear that they're still loved by *both* their parents, that it's okay for them to love *both* their parents even if both parents may not love each other anymore. The kids need to be able to be angry at and disappointed in the end of the marriage yet also feel seen and heard and loved. This is not all that different from what must happen in any family: the kids need to know that they can be angry at and still love their father and mother.

A divorced father, a forty-five-year-old engineer looking back eight years after the divorce, told me that the divorce became a very healing event for him and his children: "We found, the kids and I, that we could speak honestly to each other." His words echo those of another man who realized, "I didn't really become a father until after the divorce. It was a *wake-up call* that I really hadn't been there for my children, really hadn't been alive in my life, and that I had better start doing something or I would lose my children emotionally. It felt to me that here was a whole part of life I wanted more of."

The engineer told me that he realized he had to make clear to his daughters and son that the divorce was not their fault and that both he and his ex-wife still loved them as much as always.

"How'd you do that?" I wondered aloud to this engaging, wry man.

"Many times!" he replied with a somber smile. "You have

to go over it and over it." He told me about his thirteen-year-old daughter at one point during a long summer visit wanting to go home to her mother, suddenly missing her mother, and his sitting on her bedside as she cried, telling her that it's okay to be homesick and sad, that he understood. Even if she needed to go back home to her mother, that would be okay with him. He told me about his son going off to college and becoming very angry and unsure of himself. The boy was constantly testing his father, and as the time to leave for college approached he got more and more angry and finally, the father explained to me, "I somehow found the grace to tell my son, 'It needn't be this hard between you and me, you can leave with my blessing, that's okay, you can go when you're ready and return when you're ready.' "

The engineer talked about constantly trying to be aware of the anger and disappointment between him and his wife and how hard it was to resist the urge to turn the kids into instruments of revenge: "Both my ex and I were very careful not to disparage each other in front of the kids. You never fully succeed in keeping everything clean, but you can be aware of when you're getting the kids in the middle." He told me about delaying the phone calls with his ex-wife during the difficult period of making final divorce decisions, waiting until after the kids were asleep so they didn't have to hear it.

Now, in the coffee shop, I look at my friend Edward and wonder if he has some skill that I lack, the courage to go on after a big defeat, to find new inner resources, to play well the hand life deals you. I realize that I have plenty to learn from divorced fathers and mothers about not giving in to despair, about the noble daily fight against chucking it all and giving up. At a basic level the task is the same for divorced fathers and married ones: *to be there for our kids, not turn our backs on them in our fury or shame or adult preoccupations.*

And what if there is a replacement for you? What if you had to vie constantly for your kids' affection not only with your ex-wife but also with another man, a stepfather?

I remember a father talking about the moment of rage he felt at his son and daughter when their stepfather came to pick them up. He said that the stepfather and he had an okay relationship. It was a Sunday night and the kids were with him over the weekend and it was time for them to go. The kids had been playing in his backyard, and when they came in to gather their things they had mud all over their boots, which they proceeded to track all over his carpet. He flew into a fury at the mud, yelling at them to think a little more, to put on clean shoes or wipe off the mud. He was livid as they left. Why? He wondered—that certainly wasn't typical of him, and he felt awful that the parting between him and his kids had been so hard. Yet then he began to realize what it felt like to have this other man come into his house. He wasn't a bad guy, he was kind of nice, in fact, *but he was their stepfather,* and thus spent more time with the kids than their own father did because of the custody arrangements. That felt intolerable, the leaving felt intolerable. What kind of part-time father was he? And here was this other guy who hadn't even fathered them; was he doing a better job than he, their biological father, was? This father had recently made the effort of going to his son's baseball game in the neighboring town where the kids lived with their mother and stepfather, and when he got there his boy seemed unsure how to introduce him to his teammates and coach. Of course, the boy said he was his father, but to his kids' friends he was a stranger and Dave over there was *really* the father they knew, so what did that make *him*? So at that moment in his own house with the mud on their boots, as he was saying good-bye to his beloved children for the umpteenth routine time, all this built up as he and Dave stood there. His own shame and his anger and his disappointment in himself and in his kids (*why wouldn't they stand up and say proudly 'He's my father!'*)—it all came boiling to the surface, and it felt to him as if this divorce was mud that would never come off, a stain that he had to live with. Every time he saw his kids his joy was undercut by the gnawing question: *Had he really done his best, had he done well enough?*

When his kids came over the next week he apologized for the yelling and told them he had been upset about saying good-bye and it was not their fault, they had done nothing wrong (except please wipe your feet before coming in the house), and the kids said, that's okay, Dad, we love you. As I listened to the story I also thought about how healing kids can be for their fathers, divorced fathers as well as nondivorced ones, how important it is for any father to know that he is still loved as he carries with him his heavy internal atmosphere of rules, expectations, failures, successes, hope, and love. Sons and daughters pay a terrible price for a broken connection with fathers. But what about the price fathers pay for losing touch with their kids? They don't get the chance to find out that the kids are okay, that the family can deal with this rupture, that he is not a devil or monster, a failure, a leper of his own imagining.

So when my friend Edward puts down his coffee cup

with a sigh, saying, "Sometimes I feel like I'm just a wallet, you know, help pay the bills but not good for much else with the kids," I realize how easy it is for fathers of divorce to get discouraged, to give up. That's true for all fathers, but the sporadic contact that divorced fathers have with their kids may make it harder for them to achieve the sustained renewal with children that all fathers need.

Are divorced fathers just wallets? Are they doomed to be financial providers, without emotional connection to their children? I think about the mutual "hunger" between divorced fathers and their children. I recall what happened recently at a workshop I led on "Men, Women and Their Fathers: Unfinished Business." This was a weekend-long retreat at a rural conference center in the mountains. Sixty people, all of them grown sons and daughters, some of the men fathers as well, had come to work on their relationships with the first man in their lives. I've done these workshops for over ten years, but this weekend a new thought occurred to me: I've never made any special time for divorced fathers and children to talk together about their experiences. This time I want to try that because I feel more aware of divorced fathers. Maybe it was the letter I received a few weeks before the workshop from a group of divorced fathers who meet regularly, asking me to come and talk about fathering with them. The author of the letter—a local doctor—reassured me, "If you can come and talk with us I think you'll find that we're not a bunch of angry, deadbeat, divorced dads, but rather we too have a story to tell." This shy, apologetic line moved me deeply. Do we as a society have trouble seeing divorced dads as real people? How much stigma do they confront? And in talking with the men, I found that most of them were indeed thoughtful, caring people, often trying to do the best they could in difficult circumstances.

So at the retreat I offered to use a part of the afternoon "free time" to meet for any hour as a group with any divorced fathers and/or children of divorce who might be interested.

As I announced this to the assembled mass of sixty people sitting in front of me in the conference room, I was tentative. After all, I'm not divorced myself and I imagined the group rising up, accusing me: *You're not divorced yourself, why do you want to meet with us?* But that's not the reaction I got; instead about twenty hands shot up from the group, each indicating, *yes, I'd like to meet.* The men and women seemed grateful for the opportunity, if also anxious about what might happen.

Later that afternoon I sat with twenty people intimately acquainted with divorce, men and women, mostly white, several Hispanic folk. Among the group was a father, about sixty, and his son, about thirty. The father was the owner of a construction company, his son was a minister. It turned out that the father had left the house when the son was eight years old. Both parents had a drinking problem, they couldn't keep the marriage together, and ultimately the father left amidst great acrimony to live apart from his ex-wife and son. Now after twenty years father and son were here at this retreat trying to work things out. The father tried to explain that the hardest thing was not leaving his wife, but leaving his son, but the son interrupted and said, *No one said anything to me when you left—you just walked out, it was like a secret.* The son hardly raised his voice, but his anger sounded like a polished stone: "You left and I lived with mother. She would bad-mouth you, and I'd never really know what was going on!"

Now it turned out that after all these years the father was remarrying. The son felt torn: Did he even want to go to the wedding ceremony?

The people in the room shift uncomfortably, expressing the anxiety that comes when two men start arguing. Would this escalate into a fight? Would someone die? There are few things more frightening than father-son anger.

The father tried to explain, but the son cuts him off: "You won't listen to my anger!"

The two sat there in silence, shaking their heads.

Then another father, also divorced, older, said, "Listening to the conversation I think how lousy a job I've done—I handled things for me, not the kids. It's so easy to get caught in self-pity and a martyr complex when you divorce." He reminisced at age seventy-two about how he wanted just to get away from the marriage that wasn't working. He sold their house soon after the divorce; the kids hardly had time to salvage their things before their home was gone and they had to move elsewhere with their mother. As he described this devastation, I thought again of a divorced father's rage and shame, his wish to destroy and get away. How much the separated father lives at the mercy of his anger. "I just wanted to get rid of the evidence of the marriage," this father said. "I just wanted the world to know that I was no longer legally married." He paused: "Only now that the kids are grown up am I working on the relationship with my sons and daughter."

The room seemed to calm, listening to a father acknowledge his sadness and wish to make restitution. It's as if everyone had been waiting for a father of divorce simply to say: *I'm sorry.*

We went around the room and heard how far men and

women from divorced families would go to seek out and try to reconcile with their fathers. Sons and daughters spoke of searching out fathers who've drifted away, of taking real psychological risks to try and open things up with their fathers. A quiet man, a cab driver, spoke in that familiar diffident tone of the divorced father, prefacing his remarks by wondering "If I have anything really to add here," as if he were not a *real father* because he was divorced. But then he told the group that years after the divorce he and his teenage daughter started to see each other again and he felt at first that he had to bring her big gifts because of how guilty he felt about the breakup of the marriage. "I couldn't even provide my girl an intact home," he said, so he brought presents instead. But after a while he realized that what his daughter really wanted was his time and attention, that's all: "I realized that she would rather have a pine cone that we pick up on a walk through the woods than a fancy dress that I bought for her when I was by myself."

As I listened to these survivors of divorce, I thought again of the importance of the father-child bond, how even after all these years, all this disappointment, these children still wanted to find their fathers.

Our bond to our parents has an emotional gravity that pulls us toward them, that transcends our will. Your father is your father no matter what. I think about my own father, how I grew up in a family in which the word divorce was never uttered, I wager it never entered anyone's mind (or so I imagine). At times I'm still disappointed in my father, I wish I had gotten more, but always he is my father, and even now I truly want to curl up in his arms. I think about the rolls of carpet I used to play among in his floor-covering store forty years ago, how much time he spent in that store, time I wished he had been with me. It's too much to say that he divorced me for the store, but there is a kind of divorce that many fathers and children experience when work becomes a jealous mistress that steals our fathers away from us. I think how children are always, always at some level eager to forgive their fathers. The memory of the rolls of carpet lined up in my father's store is warming to me, running amidst them, playing hide-and-seek, lying down on the warm, fuzzy carpet to rest or to read on, sometimes my father would sit with me, the soft tufts, the colors, and smell of the fabric, they're like pieces of my father—I didn't get everything I wanted from my father, work took a lot of him away from me. But I got enough.

We need to be cautious here, remembering the cost of a grown child's attempts to forgive his father. It is painful to have a father who cannot respond, and some children continue to try to change or heal their fathers even after the cost to their self-esteem or ability to get on with their lives has become far too great. On the other hand, as I sat at the workshop and looked around the room of open-hearted men and women who had been through divorce from both sides I realized that it's never over, that there is always the possibility of redemption and blessing between parent and child.

Bob, a divorced father at the afternoon session, a physician about thirty-five years old, spoke of his most treasured moment as a father with his son. The doctor was a child of divorce himself, there was a lot of anger, secretiveness, and recrimination in his household when he was growing up. So he didn't have a lot to go on when he became a father himself; he was distrustful, often on the verge of exploding at his wife or child. And then he wound up divorced as well, like his own father. Yet he had worked very hard to be there for his child, and so he treasured a moment that occurred recently when his seven-year-old son said to him, on the occasion of a weekly stay at his father's house: "I love being with you, Dad, always." Bob, crying, says this was so important to him because "it meant that I can transcend this horrible cycle of abandonment across the generations, that I didn't have to repeat my father's mistakes—that, yes, I had divorced, but I hadn't completely failed my children."

Healing and redemption, children to father. It works both ways—the father may also heal or wound his grown child who is going through a divorce. A divorced father relates how he became "a pariah in my family, at least to my father." After his divorce, the first ever in his family, this man, embarrassed and vulnerable, came home for a holiday stay. He felt nervous about visiting his parents, but his mother was open and said all the right things: "Sorry this happened," "I know it must be difficult for you," "Hope you can live without bitterness through it all," and, most important, "We love you still, no matter what." But his father, "who doesn't like bad news," revealed nothing as his wife and son spoke of the divorce, instead turning away and saying in a tense tone, "Let's get dinner going."

These matters of shame can resonate through the generations: How many of our fathers see *our* failures as *their* failures, like the father who told his son, "If I had raised you better, this never would have happened."

I sit and ponder the importance of a father in the child's life, throughout both their lives. A friend of mine is getting divorced and he, too, is making that holiday trip back home after the end of the marriage; he's nervous about showing up without his wife, and even though his parents know, he hasn't spent any time with them since the divorce. I think about how hard these holidays and social events must be for divorced folks, everyone going about familiar routines but *You are different, someone is missing.* My friend is facing that void of loneliness, failure, and confusion, and he, too, worried and worried about what his father would say, until he sat down with him soon after his arrival and the father said, "I suspected something was wrong, I'm sorry to hear about the divorce, my boy, but you know I love you. It must be hard on both of you." With his father's gentle help, the son could acknowledge his sadness, not just his anger.

So as the afternoon workshop divorce session wound down, a man across the room said something to the angry father and son, the construction company owner and the minister, both locked in their silence. He told about the remarriage of his own father after the divorce and how he attended it feeling that he was invisible, as if his father was going on to a new life without seeing him at all. It was only years later when he told his father how angry he was at him that they began really to talk together. So the man said to the son, while the father listened, "You know you can say that you're angry at your father, that you don't want to have any part of this remarriage, that you don't want to have to be a good boy for your father."

The son replied: "I am angry. I'm angry about what happened. I'm angry about the remarriage—as if you expect me just to be a nice son and attend and act like the divorce never happened."

"I know you're angry at me," answered the father.

"*Do you!*" replied the son. "I need to know that I can be angry at you and you won't abandon me again. That you won't walk out if I say something you don't like."

I hoped the father was really listening, that he could see how important it was for a child of divorce to be able to talk straight to his father without the father again turning away. Perhaps he *was* listening. Later that weekend the father and son had their arms around each other, walking to breakfast at the dining hall.

There's the task for fathers, divorced or not: to be *dependable* in the face of our children's feelings, to be able to face their anger at us, their disappointment in us, their love for us. To let our children have their feelings and not walk out on them. Sometimes we walk out on our kids without leaving the house. My daughter comes to mind, how she and I got into an angry fight just a few nights ago, the night before I left for a two-day trip to do this retreat. She often gets volatile just before I leave, she's angry and disappointed in me for going. She's only six years old and doesn't understand how come I have to go away "to teach." Sometimes that worries me. The other night I said I was going "to teach a neighbor" how to use his new computer in a few days and my sweet daughter started to protest and I realized that "teach" had become a code word in her mind for "going away." This night it was near bedtime and I wanted her to get in her jammies, in fact I was so tired that I had gotten into *my* jammies, hoping to inspire her, but my daughter wanted me to get her something downstairs for the umpteenth time and I said no and she had a fit and started accusing me of being the world's worst father and I was tempted to walk out or to nuke her back in response, to roar at her to BE QUIET as I sometimes do. But this night I didn't do that. Instead I found the inner reserve just to sit calmly in my pj's while she was angrily getting into hers and I didn't get very upset. Somehow I had the wits about me this time just to stay calm in the face of her fury, and after a while she stopped yelling and I put out my arms and she came over and cuddled with me and said, "Daddy, I love you," and I told her that I loved her. And I hope I will always be smart enough to remember not to overreact to my kids.

And smart enough not to *underreact*. I've watched my friends stand around looking cool and in control while their kids become frantic to get a response out of them. One friend, a divorced father, a nice guy, dropped off his seven-year-old daughter at his ex-wife's house after a weekend visit, and the little girl was having trouble gathering her things up out of the car to go into "mommy's house." As the child got more and more tired and hysterical searching around the backseat for some little item, obviously unable to let go of her father, probably wanting to put *him* in her little handbag to take home, my friend stood there holding the car door open and telling her to "act reasonable." Why didn't he get down on her level, help her, pick her up, hug her, and tell her how much he loved her and looked forward to seeing her again soon? Sometimes a little overreaction does a body good.

Anger and restitution, sadness and love. We really are all in this together, divorced parents and married parents.

So, this snowy afternoon in the Cambridge coffee shop, I want to say something to Edward who wonders if he's just a wallet; I think how lonely parenting is when you're married, how much more lonely it must be when you're divorced. What to say?

"You look like a real father to me."

He smiles and I know I've said the right thing. He looks directly at me and thanks me.

We talk some more, and soon it's time to go. My friend gives me a warm handshake when we part, and it feels as if we have penetrated some of that masculine loneliness that surrounds us through fathering. I resolve that divorced fathers and mothers will no longer be so invisible to me as I walk into my kids' school each morning.

Edward returns to his office. It's late in the afternoon: what to do now? I start off for the university library to prepare some material for a class I'm teaching. At the library entrance, I spot a pay phone. Suddenly, I know what I *really* want to do—to call my wife and kids, to tell them I'll be home a little early today. I tell them I want to see them, spend some time together before dinner. They're delighted, especially my wife, who realizes that getting dinner ready will be much easier with me home. And I walk to my car, to begin the trip home through the snow, deeply grateful for their presence in my life.

CHAPTER **11**

LEVELS
OF THE GAME

Vital Relationships with Our Children

It's a beautiful late spring day. The ice has finally broken up on the pond outside our house in the country. When the pond first began to freeze back in November it took days and the contraction and expansion of the ice made enormous WHOMPING noises. For days if you listened carefully you'd hear the sounds of the pond becoming more and more glacial—WHOOMP, BOOM, WHAP—sounding as if baby whales were being born, until finally a silent thick sheet of white ice capped the pond, protecting the fish through the winter, keeping the water underneath it warm enough for the trout, bass, and pike swimming below, waiting for the rebirth of spring.

As the ice thawed over the past few weeks, it was silent, no noise. You might have missed this event if you hadn't really looked. The thick, silent mass of ice first broke up into little icebergs on the small pond, with thin sheets of ice just skimming the water and gradually shrinking until one warm sunny day the kids ran into my study upstairs on the third floor exclaiming, "Dad, Dad, the ice is gone, all gone—can we go swimming?"

As much as I love seeing the water again, I'm also sorry to see the ice go. The pond has been a companion through this year of exploring fatherhood; I've watched and observed and tested myself on the ice over the past months. It's been a long, cold, snowy winter, a wonderful winter to be in the country. The kids have learned to ski and finally so have I. And on this pond I really learned to ice skate. Not the confined skating on a half-inch-thick city puddle, but rather the joy and thrill of going out a quarter mile alone or with family or friends, gliding along on a frozen, silent, mysterious four-foot-thick sheet of ice. When I was growing up in the suburbs, falling through the ice was never a problem—there wasn't enough ice to fall through. The skating was fun, I loved it, but I was bounded by the narrowness of the public rinks or perhaps my parents' scrutiny on the log-bordered rinks plowed near shore on the town reservoir. Up here, partly at my wife's prodding, I've learned what it's like to strap on skates and go as far out as I want on the lonely, untouched, magnificent ice, a diamond glistening just for me. I was scared at first, scared of being alone out there, scared of falling through, of some disaster happening to me, but I learned to pay attention to the ice, to look at the fault lines running through it, refracting the dark water below, to see the crystals trapped within, the beauty of the bubbles of air frozen into the ice. I came to know how thick the ice was, how it really could support my weight, I learned how the air temperature affected the ice surface, when I could go out, how far, and when I could not. I entered into a relationship with the ice, came to know it and came to know myself as I learned to master my fear, my impatience, and my desire. I played a game with myself on the ice this winter, a game with several levels.

Now as I sit in my study and look out at the pond, I realize that my games on it have helped me learn more about what it means to be a father in my own family. Fatherhood is also a kind of game with our children, and it, too, has several levels. On the surface level we're struggling with getting the job done, being a father, dealing with "power struggles" with our kids, providing for them, setting limits—all the normal, everyday stuff of parenthood. But on a deeper level the real game that we play with our children is "the relationship game."

Fatherhood is a relationship, not a role, I wrote back at the start, and that seems the key. How to have a vital, dynamic, authentic relationship with our children instead of fading into an abstract image of "Father" that leaves us and them feeling cold and empty. We're so important for our kids, and they're so important for us—can we really be there for each other?

Playing the relationship game as a father means you have to know your kids, know yourself, communicate authentic regard for them, and come to terms with your own childhood, with the great transformation from being a son to being a father and also a son at the same time.

The kids are downstairs as I work in my study upstairs on this late weekday afternoon. My wife is working in town, so today it's my turn to be home when the kids return from school. The soothing sounds of happy play in the living room float up the stairs. My daughter has turned seven this past May, my son just turned ten this March.

"I'm the teacher and running the classroom," says my daughter. "No, no," says her brother, "I'll be the older brother and you be the little daughter, let's pretend." He has offered to stop reading and play a game with her.

As I listen to them playing, I think about how vital it has been to me to really see and know who my kids are, what makes them special and individual, even as they go through their "typical developmental stuff." I think about my son, the firstborn in the family, and his struggles to be big and powerful and gentle, to get what is rightly his as the firstborn son, to feel beloved in the family, how sometimes I put pressure on him to be mature and strong beyond his years. I think of my daughter's need to prove herself, the youngest in the family, her powerful drive to get what's hers and to feel beloved in the family.

My thoughts linger on how I've needed to take the time to come to see and know my kids. How impossible, even frightening, a task fathering can be if you don't really know your kids, if you are out of the house all day obsessed with your job or if your wife is your major link to your children so that you don't know that your eldest kid loves to wear your sweatshirt and if he is really upset he can be calmed down if you offer it to him. If you're gone all day, you don't know that your son has been talking all afternoon to a friend on the phone so that your younger child's sudden desire to make a phone call after dinner when you're trying to get her ready for bed is not a power play or a personal assault on your authority but part of her desire to show that she, too, can do this "big boy" stuff—call friends and invite them over.

"God is in the details," Flaubert supposedly once remarked, and maybe so, too, is fathering. Knowing who your kid is, taking the time, helps you know more when you need to set a limit, when your authority is called for, and also when your caring and support are called for, when to think about teaching competence to your child and when to allow him or her to regress. It's never entirely clear how to respond as a parent, you're often guesstimating, but knowing our kids intimately and minutely allows us to be more creative in how we respond to them, so we don't just get authoritarian, angry, or remote.

The more you come to understand your kids the more marvelous they seem and the less scary parenthood will seem to you. The more you are able to see your kids as people the less they feel like insoluble puzzles put on earth to demonstrate constantly how ineffectual you are.

Think how important it is to know yourself, to sort out your own feelings, so as to see your children and yourself more clearly. Out on the pond the wind whips up the waves, today is such a sunny, warm day, how different from the cold, bleak aspect of the pond during the winter. We have an *internal weather* as parents as well, our own feelings and how we react to our kids, what they provoke in us. The irrational anger that kids can stir up in us, like when we find ourselves throwing bathroom toys at the wall when we're trying to give our five-year-old a bath and she won't cooperate. We wonder, "Where did that come from?" The dreadful fear of not being a good-enough parent, the shame that comes when we realize we've failed our children, and the deep joy that arises when we truly feel our great love for them and theirs for us. Just trying to bridge the distance between our love for and resentment of these beings we care so much about can be daunting. Parenting at some deep level touches our very soul, so of course our children loosen our primitive passions. Often the anger, shame, fear of parenting has more to do with us than it does with our children. Becoming aware of our internal storms can help us manage them, even if sometimes we feel swept away by their power.

As I listen to my kids' play turn to bickering downstairs, I'm aware of a deeper tension within myself: the residual memory of being the older brother in my family. I find myself wanting to go downstairs and overprotect my daughter, to side with her in whatever the argument's about, perhaps from a childish memory of the older sibling's power and fury; then I overidentify with my son, wanting to tell my daughter to *be quiet and leave your brother alone*, perhaps in some unfinished resentment at my younger brother's "unfair" demands on me forty years ago. I hope they can sort out this argument and remember that often they do just fine when I let them work things out.

Knowing more about your own struggles doesn't make you an ineffectual parent who can't set limits for your kids; rather it means that you tend less to personalize everything and misinterpret it out of your own struggles. And it helps you empathize more with what your kids are going through.

Most of all, think about the importance of being *authentic* with your kids when you are with them. It's a question of *really* relating to them rather than being in one of the typical father modes—Disciplinarian or Answer Man or Nice, Engaged, New Age Father. Our kids want *us*, not a role, and ultimately that's what many fathers want. To be seen and to be present for our kids.

I'm still learning. The other afternoon I was sitting in the living room next to my boy, who was playing Legos, and I didn't want to be there, I was preoccupied with some work I had to do and it would have been better if I had set a clear limit and said to him, "No, I can't play with you," rather than *again* trying to do two things at once. The problem wasn't that I tried to work while my kid played, sometimes that works fine; it was that I was annoyed at not being able to concentrate on a complicated report I was trying to write while I sat with him trying to act like the Good Daddy. Every time he asked me, his supposed space explorer partner, to find a four-unit red piece, my mind was grinding over how long it would take to complete this report for the dean. So when I answered him, I had a pissed-off tone in my voice. And so then, at the end of the afternoon when my son said, "Dad, do you like me?" I was stunned. My heart sank as I thought: *How could he even have wondered? How could either child wonder if I like them, yikes, do they wonder if I love them, too? How's that possible—they are my heartbeats!*

Then I realized: *How could they know that unless I show it?* Kids are very concrete and run around in their own bubbles of preoccupation and misinterpretation and we can't assume they know how much we love and cherish them unless we show it.

That afternoon I replied to my son: "Yes, I like you! I like you and I love you," and I picked up my wonderful, observant, thoughtful boy, who doesn't miss a trick, I picked him up in the way he loves and spun him around and told him that in fact he is the hottest, greatest boy in the world. We even talked some about being distracted, how work can preoccupy your mind. And I realized how I no longer felt embarrassed about really, truly telling my children every day how much I love them.

Love is crucial, but I've learned that it's not enough, that I can't just love my children in some bubble of "feel-good, everything is okay."

I'm also aware of how hard it has been for me as a father to learn how to say no to my kids. I didn't struggle with my own father about boundaries and authority and so I'm constantly learning about that now, making it up as I go along. I was warmed by the words of one father who told me, "The most central struggle I feel as a father is my difficulty in saying 'no.' I come by it honestly, of course. My father said 'no' on a regular basis, but it felt mostly arbitrary. I swore that I would never do that to my son or daughter. Now my wife is constantly on me to be able to set limits with my kids, and I've begun to succeed. But seeing that I can say no and still love my kids has been my biggest struggle as a father."

There's that cold edge of fathering I've been working on. One day I was out on the pond, learning to skate, wanting to go out there right to the middle of the pond, to feel confident; the sun was shining, the pine trees surrounded the pond like a green frame, and I was halfway there—alone— when I heard scary sounds like ice cracking and had to stop and look around and calm myself, reminding myself, *It's cold enough, you've just been outside skating yesterday, you aren't going to fall through, what you heard was ice* contracting under your weight, *not* cracking.

There are similar moments as fathers when we're put there trying something new and we run up against our fear. For me it's saying no, it's establishing my authority; for other fathers it may be spending time alone with their kids or it may be saying yes to them. For all of us there come moments when we bump up against our deepest fears and have to stare them down or talk ourselves past them.

Hmm, maybe saying yes isn't that easy for me either. Learning, for example, that I can apologize to my kids has left me at times feeling as if I am ice skating across the pond naked. Every father has times when he blows it, loses his cool. Not too long ago after dinner I was getting the kids ready for bed and my daughter was jittery and got more and more hyped up as I tried to calm her down, running around the bathroom, refusing to brush her teeth, and my son kept pestering me to explain some word in his Cub Scout manual and *he* was hardly focused on brushing his teeth, but actually that night he was being the more cooperative, not really having a meltdown like his sister, he had just become fixated on getting a merit badge and wanted an explanation of something that confused him and so he wasn't brushing his teeth, but his almost cooperativeness really made it worse. Who knows, maybe I thought he could take my anger better than she could because when he interrupted me as I chased her around, waving the toothbrush in my hand, I reached the limit. I yelled at him loudly to be quiet and brush his teeth and just to be quiet about merit badges. He did that, but he got very quiet, in that way when I know I've rattled him, and I realized I was off base. So later that night I went into his room and apologized, said that I had overreacted, that I had wanted him to get his teeth brushed, but I didn't need to yell. But as I walked into his room, I was aware of an internal resistance, as if I were trying to skate out to the middle of a pond and felt on very thin ice. I wanted to hug the safe shore of being the paterfamilias: *How dare you question my authority*. Part of me felt that fathers shouldn't have to apologize to their kids. And I just didn't want to get into this position with my son. Even as I sat on his bed while he stared into his Cub Scout manual, trying to wall me off, I was thinking, *Why go through this with your kids, are you overdoing this*? But then when I apologized and explained quietly to my son how come I yelled and that I regretted it, I realized from the way he looked at me that I had done the right thing. It wasn't the words exactly, it was that he felt respected and heard. The boy needed to know that I understood that what he was asking about was also important and not forgotten. He needed to feel my respect and my love for him. What I said was less important than the fact that I went to him. And as I sat on my son's bed and talked about losing my temper and about how come I expected more from him because he's older and, most important, talked to him about how he could get the merit badge he so dearly wanted, I felt good that I was showing my child that grown men can apologize. Watching how my son responded to my efforts to repair matters, his deep willingness to meet me there, I realized that *it's never over as a father*, that relationships can be stretched and strained far more than I have ever done with my children and still the bond between father and child can be resuscitated.

Out on the pond I often had to talk myself through my panic; I had to decide whether I was going to master the experience, really sail out there on that beautiful ice and do it, or whether I was going to give in to the hopelessness roiling around within me. I often feel that same choice when I'm with my kids. One day I'm in some battle with my child, who is really upset and storms out of the room and I'm not really sure who's right, me or my daughter. I realize that I could just blast her or let her work it out by herself, she has to learn limits, and besides she's wrong, and I know that's all true, but I also think that *she's the child, she's doing what children do*. I have a choice here—I can be the child or the parent. Often I do act like the child, I have a tantrum just like the kid, but I also find that sometimes I am capable of doing the hard work of being the parent—of seeing that there is a kid here who is out of control and needs help and containment and soothing. I remember fondly the advice that a friend of mine gave his teenagers: "Your job is to be a teenager and test limits, and my job is to be the parent and make sure you get out of adolescence alive and still a member of our family."

As I look out at that inviting pond this sunny afternoon I think of how much warmth and caring lives beneath the surface of fathers. I've come to see fathers differently. The other day I was on an errand in my car and saw a father out with his son for a drive in the truck, his son sitting next to him, not across the seat but right next to him, and I knew that something important was being negotiated just in their being together, the two of them sitting side by side as father and sons have done for generations. And the other night I was at Little League and watched a big, beefy father, the first base coach, with his little nine-year-old daughter. "Good hit!" he exclaimed. *Good hit, my beloved daughter.* How very important for a father to applaud his daughter's competencies. I'm beginning to see that fathering is defined by these little moments, not by some imaginary grand Defining Moment of Fatherhood, but rather by the little details.

We put such performance expectations on ourselves as fathers, as if good fathering means spending endless amounts of time with our kids or having all the right answers or knowing just what to say. We live in an age of *technique*, we all search for just the right thing to say or do to be A Good Dad. Yet there's really no magic trick to fathering. Sometimes it's simply a matter of a pat on the shoulder, an encouraging word, taking the time to really see or hear our children.

One evening I dropped off the teenage baby-sitter at her home. She's gangly and developing and unsure of herself, a big girl going through that female adolescent transformation in which she wants to be attractive to boys but also powerful. She's lovely and smart but clearly unsure what to do with her height, with her power really. That night I was so touched as I stood in her living room about to go when her father came in with a friend who looked at her and exclaimed, "Gosh, Sally, you're so tall!" whereupon she seemed to shrink a little until her tall, strapping father came over, put his arm around her shoulder, and said, "Yup, she's my girl, big and strong and beautiful, she's tall enough to be my daughter!" And she seemed to stand taller after her father affirmed her that way.

For many fathers affirmation of their children doesn't come with lots of words, it comes from the simple gesture, the brief moment, what is not said as much as what is said.

It's easy to miss these unspoken moments since, as men, we often count our success by what we do and provide and how good we are, how well we live up to rules. As fathers we can focus on the external task and miss the relationship game with our children, miss seeing and hearing our children altogether. One day in my office I watched this happen to a father with his son.

The family had gone through a divorce, and the father was living apart from the son, who was eight years old. The boy had been doing poorly in school and clearly missed his father. He was also angry at his dad, but at bottom he felt thrown away. The father, an executive in a large business, was taking several hours out of a busy schedule and making a real effort to be there for his kid. He reminded me of how naked and unsure of ourselves we can feel as fathers—on one hand he could manage so many people, yet coming into my office one day alone with his boy he looked as if he were about to confront a tiger. It's easy to underestimate the simple courage it can take for a father to make time to be with a child.

The father and son looked for something to do around the office. "Want to play a game, Johnny?" the father asked and the son suggested checkers, and they started to play and it got hot and heavy and the son jumped the father's pieces and the father went to get some kings and the son threw new rules like "corner jumping" at the father, who struggled to keep up ("Hey, we never played that way as kids!"). I thought of the kid's need to assert himself over his father, to keep his father off balance just as his father had done to him throughout the divorce ("I know a few things you don't know") while also needing his father to be able *to take it*, not to get too wounded by his desire to be on top this one time. The father meanwhile got some kings himself and taught his son a few tricks. They were engaged in combat but also having fun; the father obviously enjoying his ability to teach his son how *to play the game of life and win.*

Watching the father and son at play, I thought about how much connection and love are often expressed within the quiet daily activities of fathers and children—fathers taking their kids to the dump on Saturdays, playing catch with their children, sitting around watching TV or listening to the radio together.

After several sessions of combative checker games, things changed. The son played more slowly, became more thoughtful, and started to talk. He told his father about grade school, what was happening and all, and I was watching, thinking how great it was that everything was happening just as it was supposed to, father and son were *talking.* And then all of a sudden I heard the father say, "Wait, wait, Johnny, stop telling me about school and make your move." He looked at the clock. "We have to finish this game before the end of the hour when the doctor has to stop."

Then I realized that the father only got one level of the game—because checkers was only part of it, the aggression was only part of it, the deeper game was the way father and child connected within this safe place called "a checkers game."

Seeing the father watch the clock and the kid close down that day, I thought about the challenge for the father truly to look at his kid, truly to let him or her be. We're often not in control of our own feelings, we aren't sure if we're doing a good enough job, so we shut them down. The father may have been worried that his kid might blame him for the divorce or show too many feelings, start to cry or get angry: *Dad, how could you leave me? Why are you and Mommy getting divorced?* The father may have wondered if he'd know what to do or say, and deep down he may have struggled with every parent's secret nightmare: *What if my child tells me I'm doing a lousy job as a parent on top of everything else I'm struggling with right now in my life?* A father once said, "I'm not sure I can fix the things that my kids are going through, so often I don't want to hear them." I realized as I listened to him that our task as fathers is often not to fix things for our kids, but just to listen, to affirm our kids, to witness their lives. And I wondered if we fathers sometimes fear our own children because we don't know how to play the relational game with them.

And yet isn't a piece of me just like that father? Even as I work upstairs today while my children play downstairs, on the edge of a quarrel, I don't want them to interrupt me. I just want to get this work done up in my study. I measure myself so much by rules and how much I accomplish that at times I miss out on the beauty and majesty of my children. One thing I've learned from this year is *to take the time to be with my kids.*

There are times my son or daughter will invite me to do something with them—"Hey, Dad, let's shoot baskets" or "Daddy, come draw with me"—and though I'm often drawn to something else I realize that these are the moments not to be missed. Being with one's children is one of the marvels of life, a quiet moment, often private, no one else knows about it, we get no rewards for it, we don't get a promotion or salary increase for it (indeed often the opposite is true). Watching my daughter take a brown crayon and make a house, with a tree next to it, and then a red crayon to draw hearts rising up above the house, then draw slowly, carefully, sucking slowly on her lower lip while she concentrates, four figures with smiles on their faces in front of the house, and then say, "That's us, this is our place by the pond," I feel part of this little creation of hers and think what a miracle life is. And when my son comes to me and says, "Dad, how do you get good at basketball?" while dressing that morning for school and I start thinking about practicing and jump shots and layups and foul shots and I'm rushing to explain this because it's time to get dressed and I have visions of doing this right and really practicing in the afternoons, and then my fourth-grader replies, "No, no, I mean today, I'm on a team with Michael, and we're playing two sixth-graders at school" and I realize that I'm talking to a ten-year-old here, a boy who's concrete and here and now, and I'm tempted to say, "Later, we'll talk about this later when you come home from school, we'll shoot some hoops," but instead I take an extra few minutes and say to him, "Well, there's this play, it's called a 'pick and roll,'" and I show him how one guy inbounds the ball to the other, then cuts to the basket and how to pass it so that he can do a layup, and I demonstrate for a few moments with a wadded-up paper and a wastebasket. I just don't want to miss these invitations, even if it means taking a few extra minutes in getting to school.

And yet let's be real here: You can never really get it "just right"—you want to work and you want to parent and often there are terrific conflicts between them. You know that being a parent can feel like living right above the San Andreas Fault—you never know when there is going to be an earthquake of feeling that can shake the house. Sometimes you're the earthquake. Yet like good Californians, you go right on living, making it through the tremors, always hoping that there won't ever be the Big One, the doomsday earthquake.

I think about how I *do* miss many invitations, how not doing it right is part of parenthood, that all parents fail constantly because we can never give our kids as much attention and love and protection as they want, but we also succeed constantly because we can give our kids the love and protection and attention they need. What a joke! I'm part of a generation that thought it would be perfect parents, so much better than our own parents, but this is just one more adolescent conceit or part of our youthful rebellion. And yet in truth now I seem more like my own father than different from him, and, you know, that feels okay. I'm part of a long tradition of men and women struggling to raise the young. I do believe that many fathers today *are* doing a better job than their fathers, that the time and effort that characterizes many men's commitment to their families does make for better fathering. Even so, there's been a shift in my whole way of thinking about myself and the world—I'm no longer the young, wise guy Mr. Potential, but now have much more understanding and sympathy for "older" people. I realize that being a parent has given me much more tolerance for the imperfections of life; I have less contempt for evil, having struggled as a parent with all my mixed passions and those of my children. I often smile remembering the words of one father who told me how hard it was for him to work with childless business associates. People without kids often struck him as smug in their attitude toward authority because "they have never had to deal with the tyranny of children."

And yet balanced against that tyranny is the primal pleasure we may take in our children. I think back to the raw, untamed pond, the primitive pleasure that exploring the pond gives me. The broad expanse of water, so constantly responsive and shifting, the mix of pine trees, white birch, oak, the wind caressing me, the constant variation and deep resonance I feel when I am at play on that pond—it all reconnects me with a world I often lose in my suit-and-tie life of being a busy grown-up, father and professional. Our children also connect us with a primitive world that we may yearn to reenter: Their deep feelings of sadness, love, anger, hope, their ability to play and explore, their wish to enchant us and bring us into their world rekindle those parts of us.

Ah, the parent's dilemma: our desire to participate in the child's world and our need to hold ourselves apart from it at the same time. Because of course we can't entirely become children along with our children, we also have to earn the living, keep the home safe, keep our passions more under control, and remember to get them to school on time. There's the great sacrifice of parenthood, having to be the adult at the same time that you may want to be the child.

That day of the checkers game in my office I took the father aside and said that maybe it'd be better not to worry about finishing the game but to listen to what his kid had to say, to talk to him. The father seemed grateful for the suggestion even as he looked puzzled. I suggested he might say, "That's interesting," or "I want to hear about that," or "Wow, that's great" to his son's exploits or "Gee, that must hurt" to his difficulties. The point was to offer whatever encouragement he could and to be sure to say, "Gee, I love being with you," in whatever way he was comfortable saying it.

The father replied, "You mean just talk?" and I said, "that's right, just spend some time together talking." He tried that, then stopped playing checkers, and eventually his son said, "Gee, it's nice to talk, Dad, but can we also play checkers?" And so I realized that often kids, maybe especially boys, need *both* the activity and the connection. The activity to *do* together—a playful game, a Saturday trip to the hardware store, a shared hobby—as a setting for the relationship and the relationship itself, the authentic response from father that means the child also feels seen and heard, *valued* by Dad.

Dads are encouraged to be more involved with their children these days, but are some of us in danger of becoming overinvolved? So many fathers I meet tend to mix themselves up with their kids. I think how I'm unsure myself how much to say to my kids about my own pain, how sometimes I want to turn the kids into my own confessors, I want them to absolve me. I want them to be more masterful and grown up than they really are because *I want them to be more of a hero than I myself am.* You need to be aware constantly of not making your kids into more heroic versions of yourself. You need to let them be who they are.

We're all still learning how to play this "father-child game"—how to communicate and affirm our love for each other, how to see our kids truly and let them see us. Sometimes really seeing them means enforcing a limit, being able to discipline them; sometimes it means giving way, getting into the one-down position; at other times it means to look beyond the surface issue to the deeper upset, to acknowledge the wish for a pat on the back, a hug, to be reaffirmed and soothed by a father or mother.

As I ruminate about these matters I'm suddenly aware that the noise from downstairs has changed. There's a loud dispute, punctuated by shrieks and accusations. It feels as if the weather has suddenly changed, gone from sunny to stormy, and I feel irritated and interrupted. And embarrassed: it didn't work to let them work it out themselves. So I run down the stairs.

The kids' fight is over who can do what with the footstool in front of my reading chair. My daughter wants it because she's the teacher who can give my son orders, but, no, my son claims it because he was reading his *Nintendo Power* in the chair and he's not taking orders from his younger sister. I find myself having to mediate yet again between warring siblings. Paper goes flying, angry children shriek. I separate them, the three of us pack up the mess.

"Dork," says my son, with the insouciance of the ten-year-old.

"Idiot!" screams my daughter, with the wounded desire of a seven-year-old.

The disputed footstool sits between them, each child gripping one end and pulling.

I stand there wishing I had the wisdom of Solomon. I could suggest splitting the footstool in half, as Solomon did with the disputed baby. I'm seized by a yearning to take out a chainsaw and hack it in two. One piece to my son, the other for my daughter. They'd probably find that fun. So would I: the noise of the chainsaw would drown them out, the relentless force would overwhelm their anger. The chainsaw massacre of the chair, my fevered brain imagines. That would restore my control of this impossible situation. Better hack up the footstool than the kids. Did Solomon speak in frustration or wisdom when he offered to split the kid?

Yet suddenly I realize I'm not Solomon, I'm just a dad,

doing the best he can in an impossible situation. The kids are going to fight over my stuff as long as they are siblings, which I hope will be forever. They're kids, and I'm the adult—I think about that for a moment, about how what's required here is for *me* to supply some greater perspective, for *me* to tolerate and resolve these feelings in a way they can't. I think about the task of being a grown-up, that we really do sacrifice ourselves for the young, one of the sacrifices being the chance to give in to tantrums. I feel both great joy and sadness in that realization: in being a parent I've had to give up the wish for some bigger and better "father" or "mother" out there to solve all the problems so that I can remain the little kid, but there's also tremendous freedom and opportunity in recognizing that I am now the father, that this is my life to live, fully or not.

Right at this moment, though, I'm not sure. There's a frantic negotiation going on in my head among my most trusted internal advisers. A large, impatient counselor hisses: *Nuke them, they've interrupted you. You should be able to finish your book!* Then a more temperate voice: *Wait a minute, wait a minute, they're kids, this is sandlot play. They're fighting over part of you, they want a piece of you, your footstool. They're allowed to be kids. It's just part of childhood.* Followed by another hothead internal counselor: *Yeah, yeah, Mr. Thoughtful, and what was that about your younger brother, always on your case, that was so unfair, and who does this little girl think she is, why, your poor son, always being intruded on by that overreaching sibling, never having anything of his own that she won't want to grab! Punish her!* Interrupted by another urgent voice: *Whoa, wait a minute! You almost demolished that younger brother of yours! Remember that time as a kid, the two of you were playing a game about boxing and you said you'd show him how to punch someone and not to worry and just stand still and you aimed a punch at his mouth just to demonstrate, really, really intending to miss, and instead you walloped him in the kisser! Older brothers never quit, they don't let younger sibs survive—be careful, don't let your older son demolish his sister, protect her! Clamp down on that evil boy!*

As these inner counselors whirl around my brain, I'm not sure what to do. What's the perfect answer? And then I realize, *There is no perfect answer!* Trying to be perfect is part of the problem. *Will I always feel torn and divided in life?* Yes, probably, I realize with a sigh—that's what life is all about. Rilke said, "Take your well-disciplined strengths/ and stretch them between two/opposing poles. Because inside human beings/is where God learns."

Maybe fathers learn there, too. For then I have an insight: what I'm feeling, so scattered and unsure of myself, is probably what *they're* feeling. Don't ask the kids to be older than they are. Don't expect them to be more mature than *you* are. I realize that really being there for your kids means listening to your heart *and* your head. But how to do that?

"Okay, stop," I warn them, striving for a foreboding tone of voice. I *do* try to divide the footstool, to impose order. "Your feet here on this half, you work here on the other half."

Fine. Except the footstool lurches as my son rotates it skillfully with his feet, messing up my daughter's drawing. Then she spins her brother's feet off it. I grab for the spinning footstool as they both yell at each other, ignoring me. I slip, fall to the floor, bounce back up trying to look like

I'm in perfect control, checking mentally to make sure I didn't wrench my creaky back. *Solomon would never let himself be spun around like this*, I imagine ruefully.

The kids do a great job of double-teaming me even as they seem to be fighting each other. "Stop it!" I yell, grabbing onto the last refuge of the impotent parent: a loud voice. They're not impressed, and together they run around to the other side of the footstool. So now my son and daughter are on one side of the footstool while I'm on the other. I'm mad because I can't have my way; I want to *get this solved* so I can go back upstairs to my peaceful meditations on fatherhood. But they're not upset at all. Suddenly I realize they're on the edge of enjoying this. I can see the amusement in their eyes, a smile quivering on their lips.

Slowing down, I turn the stool playfully toward first one, then the other. My son looks darkly at me, then giggles with pleasure. When I spin it toward my daughter, she laughs and runs around next to her brother, her erstwhile enemy, now her ally.

I'm in the middle of a game, I realize, and then: *Maybe that was the point of this whole thing—get Dad to play with us!*

"Hey, Dad, let's pretend you're a sea monster and we're on this island," my son says, pointing to the footstool. My daughter and he hop onto it. That's me: Solomon the Sea Monster.

But what about the book! part of me protests.

Yet as I look at my big darling boy and my wonderful graceful girl poised on that footstool, balancing as it moves ever so slightly under their weight, their eyes eager with excitement, waiting to play with their father, I realize: *The book is done, it's time to go play with my children.*

I'm filled with wonder at it all—how much my children have given to me, how the love in their eyes kindles the love in my own, how constantly learning and relearning to be there with them reminds me of what's important in life, how grateful I am to have a wife who encourages, even demands, that I explore this world. For a moment I think about my wondrous year away, the search for renewal it represents, my testing myself out on that ice this winter. I think about renewal in men's lives, how often we attempt to find renewal outside our families—with new cars, new projects, new plans, moving this, changing that. Now I see that my family had itself been a constant source of renewal for me as well, and I feel blessed for that, blessed by my wife now on her way home from work and my children, perched there on the footstool waiting for me.

So, with deep gratitude and delight, Solomon the Sea Monster, trying to look scary but unable to suppress a smile, crawls toward his children, who giggle with pleasure, their eyes merry with anticipation at being pounced on and rolling around the floor with their father over and over again.

NOTES AND REFERENCES

CHAPTER 3

P. 63: Judy Collins and Jane Dyer, *My Father* (Boston: Little, Brown, 1989).

P. 70: Seamus Heaney, "A Hazel Stick for Catherine Anne" and "A Kite for Michael and Christopher," from *Station Island* (New York: Farrar, Straus, & Giroux, 1985). pp. 42–44.

P. 75: Muriel Rukeyser, "Waiting for Icarus," In *The Muriel Rukeyser Reader* (New York: Norton, 1994).

CHAPTER 4

P. 81: Bill Geist, "Hardball," *The New York Times Sunday Magazine*, March 29, 1992.

CHAPTER 5

P. 104: James B. Nelson, *The Intimate Connection: Male Sexuality, Masculine Spirituality* (Philadelphia: Westminster Press, 1988). p. 34.

CHAPTER 6

P. 135: Leo Rosten, *Captain Newman, M.D.* (New York: Harper's, 1956). p. 328.

P. 138: Alvaro Cardona-Hine, "Hearing My Son Play," in Perlman, J. (ed.) *Brother Songs: A Male Anthology of Poetry* (Minneapolis: Holy Cow! Press, 1979). pp. 47–48.

P. 138: William Kloefkorn, "Out-and-Down Pattern," in Perlman, J. (ed.) *Brother Songs* (Minneapolis: Holy Cow! Press, 1979). p. 50.

CHAPTER 7

P. 150: C. S. Lewis, *The Four Loves*, quoted in A. N. Wilson, *C. S. Lewis: A Biography* (New York: Fawcett, 1992). p. 275.

CHAPTER 10

P. 246: Robert A. Raines, *Going Home: A Personal Story of Self-Discovery, A Journey from Despair to Hope* (San Francisco: Harper and Row, 1979). p. 35.

CHAPTER 11

P. 284: Rainer Maria Rilke, "Just as the Winged Energy of Delight," *Selected Poems of Rainer Maria Rilke* (Trans. Robert Bly) (New York: Harper and Row, 1981). p. 175.

ABOUT THE AUTHOR

SAMUEL OSHERSON, PH.D., is a practicing psychotherapist and a research psychologist at the Harvard University Health Services, where he specializes in mens' adult development. He is also on the faculty of the Fielding Institute and lectures extensively around the country to professional and public audiences. Dr. Osherson is the author of *Finding Our Fathers* and *Wrestling with Love* and has contributed articles to many newspapers and magazines.